Sport and Social Identities

Sport and Social Identities

Edited by

John Harris

and

Andrew Parker

palgrave
macmillan

First published 2009 by
PALGRAVE MACMILLAN

Palgrave Macmillan in the UK is an imprint of Macmillan Publishers Limited, registered in England, company number 785998, of Houndmills, Basingstoke, Hampshire RG21 6XS.

Palgrave Macmillan in the US is a division of St Martin's Press LLC, 175 Fifth Avenue, New York, NY 10010.

Palgrave Macmillan is the global academic imprint of the above companies and has companies and representatives throughout the world.

Palgrave® and Macmillan® are registered trademarks in the United States, the United Kingdom, Europe and other countries

ISBN-13: 978–0–230–53527–5   hardback
ISBN-10: 0–230–53527–5   hardback
ISBN-13: 978–0–230–53528–2   paperback
ISBN-10: 0–230–53528–3   paperback

This book is printed on paper suitable for recycling and made from fully managed and sustained forest sources. Logging, pulping and manufacturing processes are expected to conform to the environmental regulations of the country of origin.

A catalogue record for this book is available from the British Library.

A catalog record for this book is available from the Library of Congress.

10   9   8   7   6   5   4   3   2   1
18 17 16 15 14 13 12 11 10 09

Printed in China

Dedication

In loving memory of my Nan and Gramp
Thomas John Jones
Winifred May Jones
JH

For Beckie
AP

Contents

Acknowledgements

Doing sociological research (and disseminating it) is always a collective venture, and we wish to record our grateful thanks to those who have helped us to produce this book.

We are especially indebted to our contributors on several counts: for agreeing to be involved in the first place, for their attention to detail on editorial queries, and, indeed, for their patience concerning final publication.

We are also grateful to friends and colleagues who have offered encouragement and support along the way and who have endured our endless questions and discussions on this topic. We are also extremely thankful to Emily Salz and Anna Reeve at Palgrave who have given generously of their time, and to the two anonymous reviewers who provided insightful comment on an earlier draft.

Last, but by no means least, we would like to thank our partners Danielle and Beckie for their love, patience and support, and for taking care of all the things that we should have been doing while we were working on this project. Needless to say, the inadequacies and inconsistencies found herein are, of course, entirely our own.

Notes on Contributors

Ben Clayton is Senior Lecturer in the Socio-cultural Aspects of Sport in the School of Sport, Leisure and Travel at Buckinghamshire New University. He has published widely in the areas of sport masculinities and the sports media and is currently engaged in research concerned with student learning experiences in higher education and with university sport initiation ceremonies.

Samaya Farooq is a Ph.D. student in the Department of Sociology at the University of Warwick. Her research interests centre on sport, physical education and Muslim identities. Her current work focuses on aspects of self-identification in relation to the sporting experiences of young, British-born, Muslim women.

John Harris is an Associate Professor in Sport Administration within the School of Exercise, Leisure and Sport at Kent State University. His research interests include sport and national identity in Wales and the cultural politics of sporting celebrity.

P. David Howe is Lecturer in the Sociology of Sport in the School of Sport and Exercise Science at Loughborough University. A four-time Paralympian, his publications include *The Cultural Politics of the Paralympic Movement* (2008) and *Sport, Professionalism and Pain* (2004).

Grant Jarvie is Deputy Principal (Learning and Teaching) and Chair of Sports Studies at the University of Stirling. He is an Honorary Professor with the Academy of Physical Education and Sport at the University of Warsaw, Poland and has held senior positions at the Universities of Warwick in England and Heriot-Watt in Scotland. His social and historical research has covered aspects of sport and health in China, Denmark, France, Kenya, Poland, Scotland and South Africa, his most recent books being *Sport, Culture and Society* (2006) and *Sport, Revolution and the Beijing Olympic Games* (2008). Grant comes from an international sporting family and has served on both the 1996 and 2008 Research Assessment Exercise Panels for Sport.

Andrew Parker is Professor of Sport and Christian Outreach in the Faculty of Sport, Health and Social Care at the University of Gloucestershire.

His research interests include sport and the media, sport and religion, and physical activity and schooling. Andrew also has an interest in law.

Nancy Theberge is Professor at the University of Waterloo, where she is appointed to the Departments of Kinesiology and Sociology. She holds a Ph.D. in sociology from the University of Massachusetts at Amherst. She has published widely in the sociology of sport and the sociology of the body, and is the author of *Higher Goals: Women's Ice Hockey and the Politics of Gender* (2000), winner of the North American Society for the Sociology of Sport Outstanding Book Award in 2001. She served as the Editor of the *Sociology of Sport Journal* from 2002 to 2004 and in 2005 received the Distinguished Service Award from the North American Society for the Sociology of Sport. Her current research is on the medicalisation of the sporting body and the system of sport medicine professions in Canada.

Theresa Walton serves as an Assistant Professor in the School of Exercise, Leisure and Sport at Kent State University. Her research focuses on investigations of power relationships and the ways in which they are both resisted and maintained within mediated sport narratives. She has published work in periodicals such as the *Sociology of Sport Journal* and *Women in Sport and Physical Activity Journal*.

Introduction: Sport and Social Identities

Andrew Parker and John Harris

Social identity is a concept which has come to be much talked about within the orbits of social science and yet which has proved notoriously difficult to explain. Widely adopted across a range of contexts, it is a term which is used to denote a variety of ideas, primarily regarding the relationship between individuals and the societies in which they live, and the processes of identification which take place via everyday interaction. Academic scholars have articulated the shifting and contested nature of identity in various ways. Jenkins (2008, p. 18), for example, suggests that, 'identity is our understanding of who we are and who other people are, and, reciprocally other people's understanding of themselves and of others (which includes us).' One of the things that is common to explanations of what social identity is, and how it takes shape, is that it is neither fixed nor static but, instead, fluid and ever-changing, as Maguire *et al.* (2002, pp. 143–144, original emphasis) point out in relation to the context of sport:

> The term *identity* should not be seen as a rigid one: one that absolutely categorizes people into one group or the other. It is used to identify common attributes or beliefs that mark out a group of people as having something quite significant in common with one another, and equally, as being different from others … Identity in sport can symbolize common ground or become a manifestation of difference. … Sport demonstrates how people see themselves as well as how others view them. It is a potential environment for the construction and display of identity.

Like the parent discipline of mainstream sociology, the sociology of sport has traditionally played host to a variety of theoretical, conceptual and empirical ideas, each offering insight into the everyday social worlds

1

that we inhabit. These ideas are the tools of the trade that social scientists use to further investigate, analyse and explain social events and circumstances, including those which emerge in and through sports settings. In this sense, sport is not treated as something that exists within a social vacuum. On the contrary, one of the things that sociologists of sport set out to do is to examine how broader cultural forces, patterns and trends permeate sporting life, be they in relation to participants, spectators or media coverage. The collection of chapters presented in this book demonstrates the way in which the respective authors have carried out such investigations in relation to specific sporting spheres, providing a series of accounts which seek to illustrate the way in which sport both facilitates and promotes the individual and collective identities of those who frequent its locales. Thus, of central interest to these writers and others like them is the extent to which modern-day sports represent key sites for the formation of identities.

Research within the sociology of sport has uncovered a plethora of data about how and why social identities are constructed and maintained in and through sporting activities. Such accounts offer insight into the detailed nuances of identity construction, yet often lack any in-depth discussion of what the term 'social identity' (or 'social identities')[1] actually means or how it specifically relates to sporting milieux. In order to provide some kind of corrective in this respect, and to contextualize further the way in which this body of literature has taken shape, it is to a brief definitional overview that we initially turn.

Social identity as a concept

Much of the early work on social identity was carried out from a (social) psychological perspective. Since then 'social identity theory', as developed by scholars such as Tajfel and Turner, has achieved a certain prominence across a range of disciplinary areas (see Tajfel, 1972, 1978, 1981; Turner, 1996).[2] But what, we might ask, is the study of social identities all about? Identity is something which is common to us all: everyone identifies as or with someone or something and, perhaps just as importantly, we all exhibit a variety of identities to different audiences. We are, as Jenkins (2008, p. 3) notes, 'different things to different people ... in different circumstances' and because of this our identities should always be seen as provisional, contingent and unfixed. The way that we identify ourselves often distinguishes us from others. At the same time, we have things in common with other people, sharing an identity with them.

At its simplest, social identity and the process of identification is about the similarities and differences that individuals and groups display. As Jenkins (2008, p. 18) argues, it can be defined as

> the ways in which individuals and collectives are distinguished in their social relations with other individuals and collectives. . . . [and as] the systematic establishment and signification, between individuals, between collectives, and between individuals and collectives, of relationships of similarity and difference.

While for Jenkins (2008) notions of similarity and difference are fundamental to any discussion of identity construction, two other issues are equally important: first, that of affiliation or attachment; that is, how and why people identify themselves in relation to others; secondly, the notion of the 'social' – that identity is not solely about the 'self' but about how we construct ourselves in accordance with broader *social* processes through interaction, communication and negotiation. Together, these elements comprise the basis of identity formation.

Of course, discussions of identity are part and parcel of everyday life. It is relatively commonplace, for example, for us to talk about the ways in which people are similar and different in terms of what they do, what they stand for and who they are. Individual and collective identities are constructed around a broad range of issues and circumstances, i.e. nationality, social class, 'race'/ethnicity, gender, sexuality, religion, spirituality, each of which, in themselves, demonstrate diverse sets of values and beliefs that raise questions concerning similarity, difference and affiliation. Though by no means a novel concept, in recent years social identity has come to represent a mechanism by which groups of people (collectives) have identified themselves as a political force, challenging aspects of social inequality and injustice, hence the emergence of terms such as 'identity politics' and/or the 'politics of identity'.

How then does identity construction actually take place? It is largely accepted that individual identities are formed early in life via processes of socialization. Using the work of Mead (1934) and Cooley (1962, 1964), Jenkins (2008) derives an understanding of the construction of individual identity as a two-way process between what we think of ourselves (i.e. who we think we are) and what others think about us (i.e. who and what other people perceive us to be). In this sense, Jenkins (2008, p. 40) argues that the formation of one's identity is: 'an ongoing and, in practice simultaneous, synthesis of (internal) self-definition and the (external) definitions of oneself offered by others'. Thus, identity is generated both internally (within ourselves) and externally (through our social involvement with other people). For Jenkins, this process (which he calls the 'internal–external dialectic of identification'), forms the basis of all identities, both individual and collective, providing, as it does, the means by which we identify ourselves (self-image), by which we identify others, and by which we are, in turn, identified by others (public image). Hence, an individual's identity is based upon self-image and public image, and the interrelationship between the two.

As a final point of reference before we move on, it is worth noting that investigations into collective and individual identities have traditionally varied as a consequence of their respective emphases: the former have tended to focus on issues of similarity, the latter on notions of difference. To this end, Jenkins (2008, p. 102, original emphasis) states that similarity and difference should not be seen as mutually exclusive; instead, each must be viewed as emerging out of the interplay between the two:

> Collective identification ... evokes powerful imagery of people who are in some respect(s) apparently similar to each other. People must have something intersubjectively significant in common – no matter how vague, apparently unimportant or apparently illusory – before we can talk about their membership of a collectivity. However, this similarity cannot be recognised without simultaneously evoking differentiation. Logically, *in*clusion entails *ex*clusion, if only by default. To define the criteria for membership of any set of objects is, at the same time, also to create a boundary, everything beyond which does not belong.

The central aim of this book is to uncover how individuals and groups seek to identify themselves in and through sport, and, in so doing, how they negotiate these very boundaries. Rather than espousing the opposing characteristics of identity formation (i.e. a 'them' versus 'us' scenario), it is our intention to focus on the interconnections and interrelationships *within and between* various identities in order that we might better understand the dynamics which serve continually to (re)shape them.[3] This reflects a wider shift in the sociology of sport whereby in recent years researchers have come to be more concerned with the experiences of individuals within particular cultural contexts, than the rehearsal and (re)creation of theories and grand narratives detailing particular ideological positions. This does not mean to say that we seek to undermine the theoretical ideas that have formed the historical bedrock of sociological thought (and the sociology of sport). As will be evident

during the course of each of the following chapters, individual contributors have drawn upon a range of what might be termed 'classical'
sociological perspectives in order to locate their work within a broader
disciplinary context. Indeed, when foregrounding any discussion of the
role of sport in the formation of social identity, it is important to consider the wider literature concerning sport and sociological thought and
it is to this task that we now turn.

The sociology of sport and social theory

No single sociological theory or set of ideas is used as the basis for this
text. During its development we asked all of our contributors to construct
their analyses in line with the sociological concepts, themes and/or per-
spective(s) which they felt best suited their own research findings. As a
field of academic study the sociology of sport has developed markedly
in recent years and there now exist a number of general texts which provide informative overviews of the relationship between sport and social
theory. In the USA, for example, Coakley's (2007) *Sport in Society* is one
of the most popular books of its kind, clearly outlining how particular
theories have assumed significance over time. In the UK, Cashmore's
(2005) *Making Sense of Sport* also includes useful discussion on how different theoretical ideas might help us better understand the structure
and function of sport and its role in society. Horne, Tomlinson and
Whannel's (1999) *Understanding Sport* and Jarvie's (2006) *Sport, Culture
and Society: An Introduction* both offer informative analyses of sport in
modern Britain. For postgraduate students undertaking work in this area,
Jarvie and Maguire's (1994) *Sport and Leisure in Social Thought* provides
a detailed mapping of the various concepts and theories that shape the
subdisciplinary terrain. More recently, Giulianotti's (2004, 2005) work
has also engaged with the major schools of sociological thought, detailing the way(s) in which the ideas of various social theorists might be
applied to sports-related research.[4] While it is beyond the scope of this
particular work to comment in detail upon each and every one of these
texts, what their existence proves is that the subject area is buoyant and
that its theoretical underpinnings are well-grounded.

   Accompanying the proponents of established theoretical ideas are
those (both within the sociology of sport and elsewhere) who believe
that society is now so diverse that it is virtually impossible to develop any
single theoretical perspective that offers an over-arching explanation of
how it works.[5] In this sense, it has been argued that traditional sociological ideas can be somewhat restrictive, as opposed to facilitating notions

of empowerment and emancipation. It has also been argued that restrictions of this nature run the risk of marginalizing or distorting the voices of respondent groups and overlooking the finite detail of everyday life. Of course, such arguments are nothing new, nor are they unique to the sociology of sport. Half a century ago Mills (1959) suggested that social scientists should move away from a reliance on 'grand narratives' and should instead focus their energies on forms of empirical investigation attuned to the complexities of social life. With these thoughts in mind, and against this broader theoretical backdrop, we turn our attentions now to the way in which sociologists of sport have more recently begun to utilize the concept of social identity as a way in which to explain and analyse contemporary social phenomena.

The sociology of sport and social identity

If, as Maguire *et al.* (2002, p. 143) suggest, sport represents 'a potential environment for the construction and display of identity', how, we might ask, do identities take shape within this context? One of the first writers to try to define the term 'social identity' in relation to sports settings was the social anthropologist Jeremy MacClancy. His edited collection, *Sport, Identity and Ethnicity* (1996), provides an introductory chapter which highlights the various ways in which we might begin to think about identity in terms of sport-related activities. In outlining the role of sport in the identity-making process, MacClancy makes a series of insightful observations, all of which go to the heart of why sporting activities are so conducive to both individual and collective conceptions of identity. Through particular forms of expression, sports, MacClancy (1996, p. 2) argues, 'help to define moral and political community. They are vehicles of identity, providing people with a sense of difference and a way of classifying themselves and others'. In turn, he goes on to suggest that 'sport may not just be a marker of one's already established social identity but a means by which to create a new social identity for oneself' (p. 3). While emphasizing the potential for individuals to develop multi-faceted identities in and through sport (i.e. as participant, spectator, consumer, etc.), MacClancy is also keen to highlight how particular sporting activities should not be viewed as inherently limited in terms of their expression of values and meanings; rather, they should be seen as 'embodied practices' through which new meanings can be generated 'and whose representation and interpretation are open to negotiation and contest' (p. 4). As we have seen, sporting identities may be constructed in relation to a number of social variables, i.e. social class, gender, sexuality, etc., but what MacClancy seeks to emphasize is that their formation is always underpinned by power relations. In this reading, sports act as social settings where certain values and meanings are on display, and in accordance with which individuals and collectives seek to construct their identities. Moreover, as well as portraying a sense of difference (i.e. individuals or groups being different to others), sports also constitute social spaces to which people might gravitate as a consequence of their sameness (i.e. similar values) (see also Maguire *et al.*, 2002).

Another author who has offered useful insight into the relationship between sport and social identities is Jennifer Hargreaves (2000). In her book entitled: *Heroines of Sport: The Politics of Difference and Identity*, Hargreaves specifically addresses the ways in which gendered identities are constructed in and through sport, foregrounding this with discussion on the conceptualization of identity itself.[6] Utilizing the work of Zaretsky (1995) and Hall (1996), Hargreaves lays bare the origins of 'identity politics' (i.e. the 'politics of difference'), mapping the underlying principles upon which this particular concept is based and, perhaps more importantly, uncovering the relationship between notions of 'difference' and 'identity'. Significantly, what this discussion provides is an explanation of how we might apply these two terms to our own understanding of the social world and, more specifically, to our investigations of sport. To this end, 'difference' is presented as a concept, which emphasizes the need to avoid the aggregation of groups of people into broad categories (for example, to refrain from referring to the working classes as a homogenous group), while 'identity' relatedly emphasizes the need to refer to the nuances of particular identities within such groups. In turn, Hargreaves (2000) goes on to pose the kinds of questions that might arise when notions of identity are placed at the centre of sociological investigation into sport: how are identities produced and performed? How do people understand themselves and construct personal and group identities in and through sport? How and why are identities constructed between individuals and between communities of people? Like MacClancy (1996), Hargreaves is especially keen to map out the historical and cultural contexts within which identities are formed and, in so doing, highlights also the necessity of considering power relations and social divisions in any such analysis.

MacClancy and Hargreaves certainly provide helpful examples of how identities are both constructed and shaped in and around sports settings. Jarvie (2006), however, takes things one step further, suggesting that while sport can clearly be seen to be a site of identity construction and one of political force, it must not be viewed as a context where the notion of identity is simply used as a kind of 'catch-all' concept, devoid of theoretical grounding.[7] Like Hargreaves (2000), Jarvie examines the rise of 'identity politics' in sport and seeks to provide an overview of how notions of identity have been thought through within this context. Significantly, Jarvie critically evaluates the way in which identity has been used in discussions of sport, and puts forward reasons why the identity politics model should, in his view, be replaced by what he terms a 'politics of recognition and status'.

The central problem for Jarvie (2006) here is one of theoretical and conceptual clarity, the fact that at times identity is used too loosely as 'a signature phrase or rationale in itself for talking or writing about a wide range of topics such as sport and nationalism, sport and religion and sport and ethnicity' (p. 284), and that, because of this, there is a danger that it might be conflated and 'confused with the struggle for recognition that is ongoing through sport' (p. 285). Like Hargreaves (2000), Jarvie notes the underlying principles of identity politics as those which seek to counter a sense of anonymity and marginalization; a way in which individuals and groups may assert their social existence and the meanings and values which they represent. A further problem, however, is that such assertions run the risk of replacing, in a somewhat fragmented way, any idea of community in sport. What is needed, Jarvie goes on, is 'the formulation of a political framework that can take on corporate power and control and empower local organisation in sport while at the same time valuing human diversity and recognition' (p. 286). As Jarvie accurately points out, the conventional approach to identity politics in sport tends to emphasize notions of recognition which, in turn, has a tendency 'to reify identity in sport as an end in itself' (p. 289). Utilizing the work of Fraser (2000) and Woodward (2002), what Jarvie puts forward is an alternative framework which avoids a pre-occupation with the promotion of 'essential fundamentalism' (i.e. the importance of identity *per se* – which has the potential to promote separatism and inequality) and instead accommodates a 'status model of identity politics' which incorporates interaction across interest groups and promotes a sense of social justice by assisting in the egalitarian redistribution of power and wealth. When applied empirically, Jarvie argues, such a model replaces a preoccupation with recognition with a more theoretically and politically balanced approach to identity politics in sport.

Such discussion is useful insofar as it provides a basis upon which we might consider the theoretical and conceptual groundings of identity formation within sporting contexts. But where, we might ask, does all of this leave us in terms of empirical research? One of the things that all of these writers promote is a sense that one must be rigorous in one's practical application of the notion of identity and careful in one's interpretation of how sport serves to shape the contours of individual and collective lives. The study of the relationship between sport and social identity is not simply about the investigation of how people with similar attributes, values and beliefs gravitate towards each other, or indeed towards particular sporting contexts. It is the study of how people might adopt multiple identities in and through sport, how sports as embodied practices might generate a sense of political significance and leverage, and how sporting identities are negotiated and contested within particular cultural contexts. To this end, the chapters in this book aim to demonstrate how the concept of social identity can be applied as an investigative tool within sports settings. In turn, they detail the way in which social identities are not only constructed, shaped and maintained in and through sporting activity, but how specific identities are challenged, contested and reworked across particular sporting terrains. As editors of this collection, we have not imposed particular theoretical ideas or frameworks upon our contributors. Far be it from us to dictate how scholars conceive of the notion of identity either theoretically or conceptually. Instead, what we have encouraged is a mapping of the identity issues which each contributor sees as most pertinent to the settings to which their accounts relate. It is left to the reader to interpret the findings of these investigations as they see fit.

Chapter structure and outline

We have already alluded to the fact that those writing within the sociology of sport have drawn upon a range of theoretical, conceptual and empirical ideas in order to analyse and examine the relationship between sport and social identities. The following chapters bear testament to this sense of diversity, demonstrating, as they do, the multifarious ways in which identities might be created, defined and maintained in and through sports practice.

Of course, where discussion and debate of theoretical or conceptual ideas takes place, issues of definition are crucial. For this reason we begin in Chapter 1 with an examination of the way in which the notion of social identity has been traditionally conceptualized and how this might be re-evaluated in an ever-changing world. We have previously made reference to Grant Jarvie's work in this area where he has persuasively argued for a move away from the 'politics of identity' towards a more in-depth consideration of the 'politics of recognition and redistribution'. In his contribution to this collection, Jarvie develops these ideas, focusing specifically on the relationship between sporting identities and the body. He concludes that the body is a key site around which a politics of recognition might take place within the context of the global sporting arena, and that this should be acknowledged by those in the field as a way forward in terms of both theoretical and conceptual discussion and of empirical investigation.

That the body should be considered a central element of debate surrounding sporting identities is a theme highlighted by the majority of our contributors, and Chapter 2 is no exception in this respect. Here P. David Howe extends his earlier work in the field of Paralympic sport by exploring the problematic nature of the current system of classifying athletes with disability. Utilizing the theoretical offerings of writers such as Pierre Bourdieu and Michel Foucault, Howe presents a critique of the historical development of the process of athlete classification in Paralympic sport, demonstrating the ways in which existing practice has the potential to discriminate against certain athletes on account of the disabilities which they exhibit, and, in turn, how this might lead to particular (sporting) bodies being regarded as somehow more 'acceptable' than others.

Highlighting the potential for individuals to both define and redefine institutionally circumscribed identities, in Chapter 3 Nancy Theberge addresses the notion of professional identity, with specific reference to the factors that shape professional practice in sports medicine. Drawing upon her own recent research with physicians and physiologists in Canadian elite-level sport, Theberge investigates how issues of accountability and autonomy play out between these two groups and how their roles, relationships and identities are subsequently constructed.

Of course, identity boundaries are not always flexible, particularly where specific social practices, assumptions and values have become established over time. Chapter 4 provides evidence of how certain sports can act as much as a barrier to identity formation as they can be facilitators of it. Here John Harris presents a qualitative analysis of a women's collegiate football team in England, portraying respondent interpretations of their own enactment of the game within the context of the highly masculinized aura surrounding football at the national level. What transpires is that, for these women at least, the heavily gendered assumptions and beliefs which are attached to both amateur and professional football in the UK serve to influence their everyday perceptions of themselves and, therefore, their identities as people and as players.

Organizations and institutions are often highly influential in shaping the contours of sporting identities, but there is perhaps nothing more powerful, in this respect, than the nation-state. In Chapter 5, Theresa Walton considers the case of the black athlete Sydney Maree, whose sporting identity was caught betwixt and between the racial barriers of apartheid South Africa and the nationalistic expectations of the place where he chose to ply his sporting trade, the USA. Walton's account provides evidence of the ways in which sport might exacerbate notions of social exclusion not only at the level of the state but also at that of the national psyche. Her chapter shows how sport has the potential to promote commonsense assumptions, beliefs and expectations. At the same time, Walton's account highlights the importance of media reportage in the tracing and recounting of the construction and reconstruction of sporting identities.

The relationship between identity formation and the media is a theme which is taken up further in Chapter 6. Exploring the interface between formalized religion, sport and schooling, Samaya Farooq and Andrew Parker look at how more recent world events have led to the emergence of a deep scepticism towards young Muslim males and how this has impacted both the public perception of Islam and the lives of those who adhere to (or are associated with) its precepts and practices. Presenting the findings of a qualitative study of one British Islamic independent school, the chapter discusses the specific role of Islam in allowing pupils to counter negative media portrayals of their faith and how physical education served as an avenue via which they could both embrace and embody their religiously informed identities.

The role played by the media in identity formation has long since been accepted both within and outside of the sociology of sport, as has the fact that advancements in technology in more recent years have generated an intensification of the sport/media relationship. All of this has affected the way that sporting identities have come to be constructed in and through modern-day media accounts. In Chapter 7 Ben Clayton and John Harris address this issue, considering the place of gender/sexuality in the media coverage of sport and, more specifically, the interplay between popular cultural narratives of masculinity and the changing nature of masculine values inside sport. Taking the contemporary notion of metrosexuality as their focus, Clayton and Harris discuss the way in which print media portrayals of sport often proffer a criterion-based assessment of the behaviours of elite performers in an attempt to categorize them in masculine terms. Clayton and Harris argue that the extent to which such assessments are valid, or indeed in any way accurate, is one of contention.

While the cultural kudos and financial rewards of sporting notoriety are often considerable, popular cultural recognition can generate a series of tensions around the public and private lives of modern-day sports stars. What this means in a commercial sense is that where once image rights were the preserve of the Hollywood greats, nowadays sporting celebrities themselves must continually consider the marketing, promotion and, ultimately, the ownership of their identities. Charting the legal problems and dilemmas facing contemporary sports stars in their quest for identity-ownership in Chapter 8, Andrew Parker assesses the extent to which current English law protects the image rights of star performers, suggesting that existing legal provision in England is somewhat lacking in this area and in need of amendment.

In our closing Afterword we summarize the key themes raised by our contributors and suggest ways in which the ideas put forward might inform future research in this area. To this end, *Sport and Social Identities* aims not only to reflect on the ways in which sports participation and practice might challenge the constraining and repressive features of broader social life, but also to add to the momentum of research findings which disseminate the numerous means by which these challenges take place both at an individual and a collective level.

Notes

1. Whereas numerous writers, both in mainstream sociology and in the sociology of sport, have used the singular term 'identity' as a conceptual vehicle through which to express their ideas, we also utilize the plural 'identities' as a reminder that we, as individuals, are both singular and plural, each possessing a number of different identities at any given point in time.
2. For a more detailed discussion of the development of social identity theory see Huddy (2001).
3. Binary oppositions of this nature are unhelpful insofar as they are often undercut by differences within groups and overlaps between them, thereby negating the heterogeneity present amongst groups of people who may identify in broadly similar ways.
4. See also Tomlinson (2007) for an excellent collection of seminal readings on sport.
5. We are aligning ourselves here with neither one theoretical position nor another, mindful of the fact that to downplay the value of traditional social theory would be, at the very least, rather naïve.

6. For more on the historical and sociological aspects of gender identity and sport see Hargreaves (1994).
7. See also Jarvie (Chapter 1) in this volume.

References

Cashmore, E. (2005) *Making Sense of Sports* (4th edn). London: Routledge.
Coakley, J. (2007) *Sports in Society*. (9th edn) St Louis, MO: Mosby.
Cooley, C. (1962) *Social Organization: A Study of the Larger Mind*. New York: Schocken.
Cooley, C. (1964) *Human Nature and the Social Order*. New York: Schocken.
Fraser, N. (2000) 'Re-thinking recognition?', *New Left Review*, 3, May/June, 107–120.
Giulianotti, R. (2004) (ed.) *Sport and Modern Social Theorists*. Basingstoke: Palgrave.
Giulianotti, R. (2005) *Sport: A Critical Sociology*. Cambridge: Polity.
Hall, S. (1990) 'Cultural identity and diaspora', in J. Rutherford (ed.) *Identity, Community Culture, Difference*. London: Lawrence and Wishart.
Hall, S. (1992) 'The question of cultural identity', in S. Hall, D. Held & T. McGrew (eds) *Modernity and its Futures*. Cambridge: Open University Press/Polity.
Hall, S. (1996) 'Introduction: Who Needs 'Identity?'', in S. Hall & P du Gay (eds) *Questions of Cultural Identity*. London, Sage.
Hargreaves, J. (1994) *Sporting Females: Critical Issues in the History and Sociology of Women's Sports*. London: Routledge.
Hargreaves, J. (2000) *Heroines of Sport: The Politics of Difference and Identity*. London: Routledge.
Horne, J., Tomlinson, A. & Whannel, G. (1999) *Understanding Sport*. London: Spon.
Huddy, L. (2001) 'From social to political identity: A critical examination of social identity theory', *Political Psychology*, 22 (1), 127–156.
Jarvie, G. (2006) *Sport, Culture and Society: An Introduction*. London: Routledge.
Jarvie, G. & Maguire, J. (1994) *Sport and Leisure in Social Thought*. London: Routledge.
Jenkins, R. (2008) *Social Identity* (3rd edn). London: Routledge.
MacClancy, J. (1996) (ed.) *Sport, Identity and Ethnicity*. London: Berg.
Maguire, J., Jarvie, G., Mansfield, L. & Bradley, J. (2002) *Sport Worlds: A Sociological Perspective*. Champaign, IL: Human Kinetics.
Mead, G. H. (1934) *Mind, Self and Society from the Standpoint of a Social Behaviourist*. Chicago: University of Chicago Press.
Mills, C. W. (1959) *The Sociological Imagination*. New York: Oxford University Press.
Tajfel, H. (1972) 'Experiments in a vacuum', in J. Israel & H. Tajfel (eds) *The Context of Social Psychology: A Critical Assessment*. London: Academic Press.
Tajfel, H. (1978) (ed.) *Differentiation Between Social Groups, Studies in the Social Psychology of Intergroup Relations*. London: Academic Press.
Tajfel, H. (1981) *Human Groups and Social Categories*. Cambridge: Cambridge University Press.
Tomlinson, A. (2007) (ed.) *The Sport Studies Reader*. London: Routledge.

Turner, J. (1996) 'Henri Tajfel: An introduction', in W. Robinson (ed.) *Social Groups and Identities: Developing the Legacy of Henri Tajfel*. Oxford: Butterworth-Heinemann.

Whannel, G. (2002) *Media Sport Stars: Masculinities and Moralities*. London: Routledge.

Woodward, K. (2002) *Identity and Difference*. London: Sage.

Zaretsky, E. (1995) 'The birth of identity politics in the 1960s: Psychoanalysis and the public/private division', in M Featherstone, S. Lash & R. Robertson (eds) *Global Modernities*. London: Sage.

1
Identity, Recognition or Redistribution through Sport?

Grant Jarvie

The concept of identity has had a long history in relation to sport. For-mulaic constructions of identity have become a symptomatic feature of much of the present body of knowledge that informs our thinking about sport in society. Yet it is perhaps time to move on or at least think differently about a concept that has grown out of all proportion, is vaguely misrepresented and, at times, appears to be a signature phrase, or rationale in itself, for talking or writing about a wide range of top-ics. Subjects such as sport and nationalism, sport and religion, and sport and ethnicity, are but three areas where the term 'identity' is loosely used. While tending to assert a common essence to which special mean-ings are attached, the term identity is, in itself, weaker than terms such as 'recognition'. Is it not recognition in and through sport that so-called collective identities are seeking to establish, challenge and consolidate rather than just identity in itself?

There are numerous shades of the same basic argument about sport, namely that sport can provide the technical means for creating political and/or social identities and that these are thereby reflected or embedded within national and local cultural identities. This is often reinforced by suggesting that such political identities in sport can help to challenge a certain world order and allegedly prepare the way for democratiza-tion: cricket and the break from colonialism in the Caribbean during the 1960s; table tennis diplomacy in China in the early 1970s; rugby union and soccer in apartheid South Africa up until the early 1990s, and the significance of athletics and, in particular, middle-distance running in Kenya and Ethiopia today, are all illustrative of this line of thought that sport has helped to pave the way for forms of democratization or liberal-ism. The term 'identity through sport' is often evoked to depict a strong national identity but in reality it often obscures a wide range of questions (e.g. scientific, political and sometimes religious). It is tempting to suggest that the concept of identity as it is used in writings about sport seems particularly well suited to function as an ostensive screen, camouflaging vagueness of content in a blaze of expression. If identity is a signifier that carries with it histories of sport or people or nation, then it is important not to conflate or camouflage the complexity of sport through the use of stereotypes or plastic words such as 'identity'. It certainly must not be confused with the struggle for recognition that is ongoing through sport.

Contemporary struggles for recognition in and through sport frequently take on the guise of particular forms of social identity. This is often aimed at championing the cause for a particular social difference or form of representation from disenfranchised or less powerful sections of sport. Such approaches to sport and identity might be viewed in the first instance to be misconceived on at least three accounts: (i) the failure to foster authentic collective identities across differences has tended to enforce separatism, conformism and intolerance; (ii) the struggle for identity in and through sport has tended to replace struggles for economic justice and the redistribution of wealth which often condemns different sporting groups to some grave injustices, and (iii) the failure to realize that, while levels of social inequality between and within certain groups maybe decreasing, levels of poverty in certain places remain on the increase. Is not the primary motivation for many Kenyan and Ethiopian runners to run not for the sake of identity but rather to gain recognition and, in many cases, capitalize upon the opportunity to escape poverty? The notion of identity through sport for identity's sake is not enough on its own and alternative forms of social thinking about the relationship between sport and identity, therefore, are urgently required.

Sport in the age of identity politics

The rise of identity politics and identity history in sport forms a certain kind of logic that has been attractive to writers who have sought to comment upon changes in sport, culture and society in the post-1980s period, yet few writers have offered an analysis of sport during what Balakrishnan (2002) critically labels the age of identity, and what Woodward (2002) refers to as the crisis of identity. The march towards global sport has meant that the processes associated with globalization have placed questions of identity centre stage in terms of explaining the importance of sport to those countries. The break-up of the former USSR and other European countries such as the former Yugoslavia have highlighted the importance of identity in and through sport. Many nationalist movements during the later part of the twentieth century fought to develop and sustain forms of identity, and sport has become one of the very visible forums for the expression of such imagined communities, whether they be nationalist in orientation or not.

The rise of identity politics in sport is a mode of logic, a badge of belonging, and a claim to insurgency. It operates across states but also through the personal in the sense that the calls for identity have come from a myriad of traditionally marginalized groups. Identity politics presents itself as a way of escaping anonymity in an individualized, impersonal world in that groups, countries and individuals are searching for answers to a cluster of questions such as: Who am I? Who is like me? Whom can I trust and where do I belong? Identity politics in sport slides toward an uncritical acceptance of the premise that social groups have essential identities which, if enforced, have the potential to forge divisions, separation, and fragmentation. In essence all identity politics involves a search for community, a quest for belonging and recognition. The problem with this, and the point I wish to emphasize, is that the thickening of identity politics through sport is inseparable from the fragmentation of sport as different groups assert their identity. In large measure the hypothetical challenge to sport is that while being the focus for a myriad of identities, personal politics as well as national identities, something at the centre needs to hold sport together. The idea of commonality or social sport and the quest for community runs the risk of being replaced by separate assertions of fundamental identities that can only lead to fragmentation.

Very rarely does one find carefully crafted accounts of identity politics in sport which empirically substantiate different forms of identity construction while, at the same time, confirming what Naomi Klein (2001) has called 'reclaiming the commons'. What this means is the formulation of a political framework that can take on corporate power and control and empower local organization in sport while continuing to value human diversity and recognition. There are concerns about all kinds of prosaic issues in sport in the twenty-first century to the extent that sport at times is taken out of its own hands and into the law courts or the boardrooms of the major global companies. There is little space here for local decisions or concerns about human diversity. The women's marathon at the 2004 Olympic Games in Athens was run at a time to suit American television, not the athletes or the local organizers of the games. The goal for sport should not be better far-away rules or forms of governance by faceless rulers, but close-up democracy on the ground.

One of the few carefully crafted studies of human diversity and identities in sport which respects the common ground is Jennifer Hargreaves's (2000) account of the politics of difference and identity among sporting heroines. This text does not lose sight of the common ground of social relations, different social divisions and women's sporting experiences across the globe. At the same time, the stories of sport that are told illuminate exclusion, difference and identity in sport as experienced by black women in South Africa, Muslim women in the Middle East, Aboriginal women in Australia and Canada, and lesbian and disabled women. All of these accounts of heroines in sport have contributed to knowing more about the lives of ordinary women (many of whom are on the margins of mainstream sport) and how their own personal and group identities tell us something about who they are and those to whom they belong and whom they trust. Hargreaves's account is all the more powerful because it avoids the danger of presenting a fragmented list of identity politics in sport which are unconnected and separated from the common ground of social relations, power and human diversity in sport. It is very much a social account of sport that champions the cause of the public intellectual making a difference, struggling for a new world order, and recognizing that identities in sport are not fixed but are subject to continuous interpretation and reinterpretation. This account of the identities of sporting heroines avoids the temptation of so many 1970s and 1980s feminist accounts of sport which proclaimed and promoted the alter ego of white middle-class women.

The usual contemporary approach to identity politics in sport tends to start from the idea that identity is constructed dialogically (Fraser, 2000). The proposition is that identity is forged by virtue of the fact that one becomes an individual subject only by recognizing, and being recognized by, another subject or group. Recognition is seen as being essential to developing a sense of self, and being misrecognized involves suffering a sense of distortion of one's relation to one's self and consequently feeling an injured sense of identity. This logic is transferred on to the cultural and political terrain. As a result of repeated encounters with the stigmatizing gaze and as a consequence of the internalizing of negative self-images or group images, the development of a healthy cultural identity is affected. Within this perspective, the politics of recognition through sport is mobilized as a potential strategy in the repair of self-dislocation or group dislocation by affirmative action that challenges derogatory or demeaning pictures of the group. The argument is that members of misrecognized groups, or groups suffering from a lack of identity, can jettison such images in favour of self-representations of their own making and collectively produce a self-affirming culture of recognition. Add to this public assertion and the gaining of respect and esteem from society at large and a culture of distorted misrecognition changes to being one of positive recognition.

This model of how identity politics in sport may operate contains some genuine insights into the effects and practice of racism, sexism, colonization, nationalism, imperialism and other forms of identity politics. Yet the model is theoretically and politically problematic in that such an approach leads to both the reification of group identity and the displacement of resource distribution. The problems of displacement and the reification of social and political identities in sport are serious insofar as the politics of recognition displaces the politics of redistribution and may actually promote inequality. In the 1970s and 1980s the identity politics of sport was imbued with emancipatory promise and potential, and yet at the turn of the century it has been transformed into a reified school of thought that recognizes identity as an end in itself rather than recognition accompanied by resource redistribution. Those who promote identity politics in sport, as opposed to the politics of recognition, run the risk of encouraging separatism, intolerance, chauvinism, authoritarianism and forms of fundamentalism. This then is the problem of reification, which will be discussed further in this chapter. What is being argued here is the need to develop accounts of recognition which can accommodate the full complexity of social identities instead of promoting reification and separatism. This means developing accounts of recognition in sport that allow for issues of redistribution rather than displacing or undermining such concerns in relation to sport, culture and society.

By way of summary, it might be suggested that some or all of the following arguments have been utilized in an examination of identity politics in sport: (i) essentialist arguments view identity in sport as fixed and unchanging; (ii) sporting identities are linked to claims about culture, self and/or nature; (iii) sporting identity is relational and differences are established by symbolic marking in and around sport, i.e. sport contributes to both the social and the symbolic process involved in the forging of identities; (iv) sport simply reflects the changes that have accompanied the age of identity and, in this sense, identity in sport may refer to a phase or period in history; (v) identity politics in sport is reproduced or maintained through changing social and material conditions; (vi) identity in sport involves classifying people into different permutations of us and them; (vii) identity in sport involves both the promotion and obscuring of certain differences; (viii) identities in sport are not unified and contradictions within them involve negotiation; (ix) identity politics in sport, when reified, may lead to forms of fundamentalism, and (x) the quest for identity through sport involves the quest for recognition.

Bodies, identities and differences

The study of the body is a further area of work that offers endless possibilities and points of entry and exit from historical, geographical and contemporary examinations of sporting identities and differences. Even the most cursory glance at the critical academic literature on sport and related activities such as exercise, physical culture and health provides the reader with an array of bodies: the athletic body, the sporting body, the fascist body, the racialized body, the black body, the oriental body, the engendered body, the civilized body, the body-builder, the female body, the male body, gay and lesbian bodies, disabled bodies, the body habitus and the African body, all of which have been invested in as a basis for telling stories about different identities, differences and representations. The rise of identity politics, and the place of the body and sport within what Balakrishnan (2002) refers to as the age of identity, may have increased our understanding of embodiment in some societies but such an approach also contains certain risks.

The remainder of this chapter limits itself to commentating upon three central ideas in this field, hence the discussions that follow are necessarily succinct. The first of these is the notion of identities in relation to the body and sport. Although the term 'identity' has a long history deriving from the Latin root *idem* implying sameness and continuity, it was not until the twentieth century that the term came into popular usage. The use of the term in relation to body, sport and society has taken many forms, all of which have attempted to reinforce and challenge *essentialist* understandings of sport, body and society. Essentialism refers to that which is a core identity or identities after everything else has been peeled away and the extent to which sport and body cultures reproduce and reinforce essential identities. This historical contribution has highlighted the invented or constructed character of identity associated with many sporting traditions and body styles. The historical approach, as with other approaches, views identity as essentialist but also *contingent* in that the identities are associated with body change over time and are therefore contingent upon particular histories. The psychodynamic approach to identity, body and sport has attempted to answer the question, 'Who am I and to what extent are the sporting and bodily practices I am involved in a reflection of self in a psychodynamic sense?' The sociological approach to identity also has links to a theory of self in that a sociological tradition of identity theory has been linked to the symbolic interactionism associated with George Herbert Mead, Erving Goffman and Peter Berger. In this sense, body identities have been explained through the process of socialization, communication and body language. This process has attempted to reconcile the inner, subjective, creative, bodily 'I' with the outer, partly determined and objective 'me'. With respect to the sporting context, discussions of national identity have drawn upon the notion of sport helping to construct an imagined community, while developmental or process sociologists have asserted that sport and the body are but vehicles for an overall quest for identity.

The notion of *identity crisis* has been evoked on a number of occasions to imply that identity only really becomes an issue when a particular culture, social group or nation is facing a crisis of identity. The idea of the body or sport reflecting an identity crisis is problematic in that it reduces discussions of body identity to being simply reactionary rather than enabling. More importantly, the framing of debates about the body and/or sport in this way is not sensitive to particular identity crises unique to sport or body culture at a particular point in time. Did the impact of football hooliganism in the 1980s and 1990s, and beyond, pose a particular crisis of identity for English football, or was English football simply reacting to broader social and cultural forces? On the other hand, if sport is viewed as a key component for the expression of national identity, then the fragmentation of different parts of the world may pose a particular crisis of identity for particular body cultures at local, national and international levels. The notion of identity in crisis can contribute to an understanding of sport and body cultures in different parts of the world experiencing large-scale political upheaval or in places where new social forces attempt to dilute, replace or marginalize national identities. For example, to what extent have body cultures helped to reassert a new European identity that threatens national identities, or to what extent has sport reflected or enabled forms of reconciliation or a hardened militancy amongst various ethnic identities who were part of the former Yugoslavia? Thus, identities that are forged through sport, body and society may matter more if there is a real or perceived crisis of identity, globally, locally, personally and politically.

The second concept that I wish to deal with here is that of *difference* in relation to the body and sport. The marking of difference is crucial to the construction of identities in sport, body and society. Identities tend to be formed in relation to other identities and thus essential differences are used to signify or represent them. At its simplest this unsatisfactorily lends itself to binary forms of classification such as: 'us and them'; 'insider and outsider'; 'women and men'; 'black and white'; 'Arab and Jew'; 'Protestant and Catholic'; 'Serb and Croat'. All of the aforementioned depend upon differences marking particular forms of identity that, in turn, symbolize or represent forms of social exclusion and political difference. The notion of difference is integral to the understanding, the construction and, in some cases, the invention of identities, all of which tend to be used to legitimate a particular social order or ways of being. More positively, the recognition/acceptance of change and differences involving the body and sport may be seen as progressive in that it signifies an acceptance of a rich, diverse, perhaps previously excluded set of body cultures such as gay and lesbian sporting culture; a sporting Olympiad rather than the able and disabled Olympics; and a secure place for Muslim Pakistani women in sociological accounts of sport and body cultures rather than a predominance of white feminist accounts of sport and the body. In this sense differences in and between sport and body cultures and identities may be viewed as a celebration of bodily diversity, heterogeneity and hybridity. Yet the notion of identity is not the same as difference in that one helps in the construction and legitimation of the other.

The final concept that I wish to comment upon here is that of *representation* in relation to the body and sport. Representation refers to the ways in which images and texts such as articles, books and radio or television programmes reconstruct an account of sport, body and society. Thus, a painting, a photograph or a written text about sport and the body is never just about the actual sport or physical activity but is also about how the painting, the photograph or the written text has represented sport and the body. Writers about gender and the body argue that representation is continually creating, challenging, re-creating and endorsing stereotypical images, stories, and ideas about identity, sport and the body. The areas of historiography and representation are crucial to developing post-colonial accounts of the sporting body. The work of Bale (2000) and other geographers of sport, and Dimeo (2002) and other historians of sport, offer alternative epistemological systems or ways of thinking about the sporting body which dislocate Eurocentric or colonial sporting histories and geographies.

Representing accounts of sport identities and the body can never be a neutral activity. Critical representations of sport and the body attempt to wrestle with and provide answers to questions such as: Who am I? What could I be? Who am I like and who do I want to be? Writers such as Bale and Dimeo could do a lot worse than take their lead from Edward Said (1993) who argued in *Culture and Imperialism* that studying the relationship between the West and its dominated cultural other is not just a way of understanding an unequal relationship between unequal stories but also a point of entry into studying the formation and meaning of Western cultural practices themselves. Thus, Said implied that the discrepancy of power between Western and Non-Western sport necessitates that any analysis of global, international or local sport must take such a disparity into account if we are accurately to understand sport, body and society in its totality rather than having an illusion of totality. It is worthwhile exploring the issue of other sporting bodies in more detail if for no other reason than that they have made a profound contribution to the story of sport, body and society. The politics of representation are such that all accounts of sport and the body that are promoted as authentic, valid and true need to be closely questioned in order to ascertain just exactly where the authority and coherence for such claims may be located.

From identity politics to recognition through sport

I have suggested here that those exploring identity politics in sport need to avoid decoupling the politics of identity in sport from social issues relating to the redistribution of wealth and power in sport. Identity in sport should not be viewed as an end in itself and, by the same token, it is not being suggested that recognition in sport can be remedied by the redistribution of resources. Properly conceived struggles for recognition in sport can assist in the redistribution of power and wealth and should be aimed not at a promotion of essential fundamentalism but at interaction and co-operation across gulfs of difference.

There is no neat theoretical model that can be used to resolve the dilemma of identity and recognition in sport. However, this dilemma can be softened in various ways by acknowledging in part that the status model at least continues to recognize that social justice and a redistribution of wealth provides a social framework for thinking about sport, culture and society. The status model recognizes that not all distributive injustices in sport can be overcome by recognition alone, but it at least leaves the door open for a politics of redistribution. Unlike the identity model in sport, the status model continues to strive to understand recognition alongside distribution. The status model of identity politics in sport works against tendencies to displace struggles for redistribution. It recognizes that status subordination is often linked to distributive injustice and therefore notions of identity in sport would be closely aligned with notions of injustice and social change. The model also avoids the problem of reification of group identities because the status of individuals and subgroups within groups is part of the total pattern of recognition and social interaction. Thus, identity in sport can invoke notions of social and political solidarity without masking forms of authority and power within such a collective form of identity.

It is not unrealistic to see such issues being played out in the world of sport. Following the collapse of apartheid in South Africa in 1992, the chief executive of the country's newly formed Department of Sport and Recreation argued that sport and recreation in the new South Africa had to meet the needs of the people and the nation. Identity through sport in the new South Africa was not enough. Another question facing the Department of Sport and Recreation and the Government of South Africa was how to compensate their black athletes for the decades of injustice inflicted upon them as a result of apartheid policies. Speaking in Edinburgh in 1997, the department's chief executive asserted, 'From that premise of recognition of past injustices, we should be able to move forward to say: how then can we address and redress this legacy of denial and deprivation in sport for the majority of athletes in South Africa?' (Department of Sport and Recreation, 1997, p. 4). At the same time, it was suggested that sport in South Africa should be the concern not just of the Department of Sport and Recreation but also of the Supreme Council for Sport in Africa and the South Africa Truth and Reconciliation Commission. In this way sport in South Africa may be able to contribute to the renaissance of sport in Africa. It was this notion of sport in Africa that was behind Cape Town's (ultimately unsuccessful) bid to host the 2004 Olympic Games and the 2010 Football World Cup. Thus, as argued above, such an example can be viewed as being illustrative of the fact that identity in sport can invoke notions of social and political solidarity without masking forms of authority and power within such a collective form of identity. Clearly the initial phase of policy development in post-apartheid sport in South Africa practically illustrates that recognition in sport in the new South Africa was a collective effort but also that the international community should compensate South Africa for past injustices in some way, shape or form.

Today's struggles for recognition often assume the disguise of identity politics in sport. These are usually aimed at countering demeaning cultural representations of social, cultural, national or local groups in sport. The result of misrecognition in sport is that by emphasizing differences the struggle for identity has enforced forms of separatism, conformism and intolerance and displaced struggles for economic justice with the formation of reified identities. What is required is not the rejection of the politics of recognition in sport but rather an alternative politics of recognition that can remedy misrecognition without fostering displacement and separatism or reification. The forgotten notion of status can provide a possible basis for examining recognition and struggles for redistribution with the help of sport. The status model of sport tends to reject the view that misrecognition is free-standing and accepts instead that status subordination is often linked to distributive justice. Identity in sport cannot be understood in isolation nor can recognition be abstracted from distribution.

Cultural recognition, then, should not displace socio-economic redistribution as the remedy for injustice in sport even in a post-socialist age (Mair, 2006; Therborn, 2007). It is possible to think of one world of sport with many worlds inside of that world of sport. The goal for sport should not be identity as the end game but a framework that is not fearful of close-up local democracy in sport and on the ground. Even the academic left in sport, the traditional guardians of social inequality, have lost interest in the commonalities that underpin differences and identities as if the logic of global sport has arrived in every corner of the globe. It has not, but to talk of identity in sport as if nothing else matters is to accept a zero-sum game that only serves to recognize and consolidate separatism and injustice in global sport.

From recognition to redistribution and social justice

It is perhaps necessary to leave sport for just a moment to emphasize the understanding and link between recognition, redistribution and social justice as a basis for thinking more widely about aspects of sport in society. Three different understandings of recognition are worth mentioning. The first of these is a holistic conception of culture in which recognition means a commitment to redistributive ambitions, which are often subsumed beneath weak forms of social democracy and social liberalism. The consequence for sport would be the need to embrace cultural diversity and identity as an authentic, liberal, moral imperative. The second understanding regards recognition as an on-going process and one that is integral to developing relations of political inclusiveness and a more democratic polity. The implications for sport are that recognition and the democratization of sport do not imply an end-game but are in fact part of the process that may contribute to a greater/lesser degree of recognition, which may have the unpredictable effect of benefiting or disadvantaging rival groups in unforeseen ways. A final notion of recognition, and the one advocated in this chapter, is to view recognition as but one important dimension in the broader struggle for justice. It is not charity that is the hallmark of any resource that is redistributive but justice. Thus, recognition is closely tied to a relationship with recognition and justice.

Current normative understandings of what constitutes the politics of identity have their roots in earlier periods or debates. The national tradition in sports research is at times all-too-pervading and needs to be balanced by a more transnational or international approach to the importance of social identity, the belonging of individuals, freedoms and rights in and through sport. Today the relationship between identity, recognition and redistribution cries out for examination. The struggles over gender, religion and nationality that are embedded in sport makes the question of recognition impossible to ignore. References to difference and representation are often so intensely political that the question is likely to remain with sport for some time. At the same time the need for redistributive justice and sporting injustice has not disappeared. Economic inequalities in sport continue to grow, and neo-liberal forces promoting corporate globalization continue to brush aside the question of distributive justice in sport.

It is precisely this notion of the relationship between recognition, redistribution and justice that needs to be placed at the heart of the normative debate about social identity. That is to say, the tendency to date, and this is certainly true of much of the sports research in this area, has been to place too much of an emphasis on the notion of identity at the expense of the social. Research and teaching into identity and sport that reifies sporting identity (or identities) does little to determine or redress the cultural harm that is caused by reified models of identity. It is crucial that such representations promulgated as authentic or true accounts of identity in sport be questioned, their authority and coherence closely examined, and alternative and altogether more socially orientated models of intervention provided.

Conclusion: the challenge to global sport

The real challenge to global notions of sport in the twenty-first century is to take on board issues of recognition, redistribution and calls for social justice. Global sport, if nothing else, needs to be framed in terms of democracy, accountability, transparency, trust and justice. At first glance the notion of global sport would seem to provide possibilities and opportunities for regulating sporting governance and finance to ensure a more equitable redistribution of sporting wealth. Any clear template for how sport in the world should be governed has not accompanied the transition towards a more global notion of sport. The governance of global sport is multilayered, complex, national, local and international but, amidst all of this, states, sporting agencies, the sports market, civil societies and governing bodies of sport, have suffered from shortfalls with respect to popular participation and access rates, consultation and debate, inclusion and representation, transparency and accountability. Forms of global sporting governance through market-driven channels would seem to imply deep inequalities and the rule of efficiency overriding democracy. Supra-state sports organizations would appear to suffer from severe democratic deficiencies. At the moment it is unclear whether and how democracy can be adequately realized in a more global sporting world. Above all, Western sport embedded within national and increasingly European sporting governance, as well as the continuing dominance of American sporting capital, seems incapable of showing the historical imagination needed to grasp the radical challenges facing world sport. If global sport means recognizing common situations, sharing a single world of sport, then the gaps between West and non-West, rich and poor, democratic and democratizing will need a different kind of consciousness.

Global sport cannot make a significant difference to globalization, but it can make a contribution. The enduring deep challenge for forms of global sporting democracy might involve some or all of the following ideas: (i) global sport must advocate a distinctive social agenda for sport; (ii) social democracy must become a distinctive feature of global sporting reform; (iii) global sporting organizations need to recognize that they have limited but significant powers to redistribute resource and wealth to where it is most needed; (iv) global sport should institutionalize a framework for mobility and migration and monitor child labour and the production of sporting merchandise; and (v) global sport should recognize that the national identity model of sport can be dangerous if it leads to forms of reification.

Perhaps the emergence of a more socially committed approach to sport has to start from actively acknowledging the huge differences in opportunities, wealth, democracy, sporting tastes and models of professional sport that divide the world. The deep challenge facing sport is to outline the mechanisms by which it can actively be seen to contribute to social and economic welfare on an international scale. At the international level, the more powerful sporting nations would seem to have the power to enforce many of the rules and decisions affecting world sport and yet there are perhaps unprecedented opportunities in the twenty-first century in that sport is free from the Cold War politics of the past. Perhaps the most obvious and disturbing concern is the extent to which the core institutions of sport are trusted and sensitive to ways of addressing the interests of the majority in the non-Western world. The chief causes of inequality in sport remain two-fold: the transformation of global sport by financial capital and the displacement of democratic political power in sport by unaccountable market power. As has been argued throughout this chapter, identity or recognition through sport is enough. If the point of recognition is going to be a meaningful power for social good in the world of sport then those interested in covering the politics of identity in sport need to acknowledge that a redistribution of wealth is an important, if not crucial, aspect of any quest for recognition at any level. This is the challenge not just for sport but for those public intellectuals who also see sport as a power for social good.

References

Balakrishnan, G. (2002) 'The age of identity'. *New Left Review*. 16, 130–142.

Bale, J. (2000) 'The rhetoric of running: The representation of Kenyan body culture in the early twentieth century', in J. Hansen & N. Nielsen (eds) *Sports, Body and Health*. Odense: Odense University Press.

Department of Sport and Recreation (1997) *Pulling it Together: Developing a Sport and Recreation Policy that Meets the Needs of the Nation*. Cape Town: South African Department of Sport and Recreation.

Dimeo, P. (2002) 'Colonial bodies, colonial sport: "Martial" Punjabis, "effeminate" Bengalis and the development of Indian football'. *International Journal of the History of Sport*, 19, 72–90.

Fraser, N. (2000) 'Re-thinking recognition?, *New Left Review*, 3, 107–120.

Hargreaves, J. (2000) *Heroines of Sport: The Politics of Difference and Identity*. London: Routledge.

Jarvie, G. (1997) 'Sport and social problems in unprincipled societies', in P. Nardis, A. Mussino & N. Porro (eds) *Sport, Social Problems, Social Movement*. Milan: Edizioni Seam.

Klein, N. (2001) 'Reclaiming the commons', *New Left* Review, 19, 81–90.

Mair, P. (2006) 'Ruling the void and the hollowing of Western democracy', *New Left Review*, 43, 25–51.

Said, E. (1993) *Culture and Imperialism*. London: Chatto & Windus.

Therborn, G. (2007) 'After dialectics – Radical social theory in a post-communist world', *New Left Review*, 43, 63–114.

Woodward, K. (2002) *Identity and Difference*. London: Sage.

2
The Paralympic Movement: Identity and (Dis)ability

P. David Howe

Much of the literature surrounding sport for the disabled[1] treats the impaired population as a homogenous group in spite of social theorizing about identity that has taken place within the poststructuralist turn. Poststructural thinkers have emphasized that, far from possessing a single fixed identity, individuals are constantly engaged in negotiating plural identities. This chapter highlights the centrality of the body in identity formation. Drawing upon the work of Bourdieu, particularly the concept of habitus (1977, 1984), and the work of Foucault surrounding governmentality (1975, 1977), my intention here is to flag up the distinctive nature of the bodies that practise Paralympic sport and how the specific cultural environment in which they operate impacts upon identity formation. The combination of Bourdieuan habitus and Foucauldian governmentality as a way of conceptualizing identity dovetails nicely with the work of Jenkins (2008), since he expresses identity as the relationship between external and internal influences on the individual.

Within this chapter, I make a semantic distinction between impairment and disability. Impairment is a phenomenological concept that is embodied and, as such, it is more useful in understanding identity, since impairment is the physical manifestation of difference (Hughes & Patterson, 1997). Disability on the other hand, following the scholarship of Oliver (1990), is a socially constructed response to the physical difference that is impairment. Impairment therefore facilitates a better way of distinguishing members of the Paralympic community and, in turn, is central to the formation of identity. Of prime importance then is the manner in which impaired bodies are categorized, or rather classified, within the Paralympic movement. Long-term ethnographic research highlights the importance of classification as a key signifier of identity within the context of Paralympic sport (see Howe, 2008). To this end, this chapter highlights how a marriage of the disability studies and sport for the disabled literatures can increase our understanding of how the body may be of central concern within identity formation.

Initially this chapter focuses upon the concept of habitus that is central to practice theory to highlight the importance of the habitual nature of understanding oneself as a member of a particular group. Following this the categorization of (dis)ability will be explored to illuminate the importance which external influences have upon identity formation. The structural constraints of Paralympic sport will be explored through Foucauldian governmentality, as the act of classifying the impaired body is a necessity if individuals are to gain access at this level as competitors. While many Paralympians are not happy with being consigned to the identity of their classification, and often rail against the stereotypes associated with their impairment category, it is important in establishing the athletes' identity vis à vis others within the sporting movement.

Habitus and identity

The conceptual understanding of habitus, outlined by Pierre Bourdieu, is useful in examining the cultural milieu surrounding the production of (dis)abled identity. For Bourdieu, habitus informs action as grammar structures language, and can allow for multiple forms of expression through the body whether it is how the body moves or how it is covered (Bourdieu, 1984). The social agents involved in the production of the Paralympics, (be they athletes, officials or administrators) are 'players' in a game actively working towards achieving a goal with acquired skills and competences. The related processes take place within an established structure of rules, which are gradually transformed over time. Habitus predisposes action by agents but does not reduce them to a position of complete subservience.

In *Outline of a Theory of Practice*, Bourdieu (1977) explores the philosophy behind gymnastics and from this it can be ascertained that other structured sporting activities are cultural products developed over a long period of time by those who are involved in their practice. The embodiment of these products is distinctive to the practice community. In other words, for Bourdieu an agent's habitus is the embodied sediment of every encounter they have had with the social world. It can be used in the present to mould perception, thought and action to the extent that it has an important role to play in the decisions that an agent might make in future encounters. In this sense actors (athletes, officials and coaches) can be seen not simply to be following rules, but also to be bending them, in much the same way as the work of Merleau-Ponty (1962, 1965) high-lights improvisation as being fundamental to an individual's disposition. Dispositions, or more generally forms of social competence, may be seen as a product of well-established social environments. While society may be seen to be shaping agents, it needs individuals' improvisations from time to time if it is going to evolve. Therefore, in the post-industrial society in which we live, it is as important to see the body as much as a product of the self, as it is of society. It is the self that provides improvi-sation by drawing upon the sediment of previous social encounters. In this way the sediments of social encounters become the foundation for the formation of an identity.

The theory of practice developed by Bourdieu (1977, 1990a) identifies the nexus between the body and its surrounding social environment. In a sporting context, then, the games metaphor that is employed by Bour-dieu (to both sporting and non-sporting milieu) highlights the nexus between capital and field. The multiplication of the players' disposition, their competence (habitus) and the resources at their disposal (capital) in relation to the social environment, highlights the social actors' posi-tion in the world. In the particular environment that is elite sport, it is the embodied disposition or doxa that enables a social exploration of the distinctive character of sporting practice and body hexis; that is, the performative aspect of habitus. In a sense, embodied sporting practice is made up of the habitual disposition established through the training drills (either as athlete, administrator or coach) that might be part of a traditional training regime and the actual desire to play the game. Paralympic practice is therefore structured at a number of levels, with improvisation grounded in sediments of previous activities that are central to the formation of individual identity.

The structure of Paralympic practice is also imposed in the form of rules and regulations that have been codified over time by various sport-ing federations. Rules are imposed upon individuals who fall under the authority of the federations, and this includes athletes, coaches and officials. The social environment of the sport is determined by these structural elements but this still allows room for improvisation on the part of the participant. In turn, this field or network configuration (Bourdieu & Wacquant, 1992, p. 97) allows the social scientist to see beyond the body purely as an object and to consider appropriate con-ceptualizations within the sporting environment. Capital, on the other hand, allows for the exploration of the issues associated with assets both economic and cultural, which a disposition may have in a particular social field (Bourdieu, 1990b, p. 63).

The physical action of a participant within the Paralympic practice community is strategic and the better it is the more embodied cultural capital or physical capital a participant possesses (Shilling 2003; Wacquant, 1995). The greater the cultural capital an individual athlete has within Paralympic sport, the more of their identity is likely to be invested in this particular cultural environment. For example, the qualities that are associated with elite sporting bodies, such as the ability to perform under pressure and to focus on training body habit in order to get to the high performance arena in the first place, are not distinctive to Paralympians. However, the capacity to propel a state-of-the-art wheelchair around an athletics track is central to the habitus of a wheelchair racer and will impact upon that individual's identity. When a Paralympian achieves highly in training or competition they accumulate physical capital in the sporting environment (field) where those qualities are revered. The physical act of working within the social environment of the Paralympic Games requires the athlete to perform (hexis) in this world. This structure of the social environment is a fundamental component of a Paralympian's habitus and, as a result, impacts upon identity formation. A new member of the Paralympic practice community may also see the importance of acquiring good skills as part and parcel of this social environment. Within this social environment the impaired are not a homogeneous group. They are categorized, since the sporting practice of the Paralympic Games would not be possible without a system of classifying embodied ability as it is this that facilitates equitable sporting practice (Jones & Howe, 2005).

The categorization of (dis)ability

Categorizing the bodies of impaired athletes, based on degrees of functional difference, creates a continuum along which one trait may make an individual less marginalized than another who exhibits a different trait. While categorization is seen as unproblematic within the Paralympic movement, it has impacted negatively upon the wider disabled community. The notion of the categorization of impairments that leads directly to a marginal position in society stems from the work of Erving Goffman. Goffman's (1963) *Stigma: Some Notes on the Management of Spoiled Identity* was one of the first studies to draw attention to the nature of the problem of the stigmatization of people with impairments. Some critics have argued that investigations into stigma were an attempt to medicalize disability in order to classify it in respect of the predominant views expressed by society (Barnes, 1991; Oliver, 1990). For this reason, Goffman's work in this area is useful when exploring the categorization, (or rather classification), of athletes with an impairment. After all, the practice of classifying for sport is largely a medical one that can lead to stigmatization and alienation because it ultimately creates a hierarchy of bodies (Howe, 2008; Sherrill & Williams 1996). Such hierarchies may negatively impact upon the identities of impaired individuals involved in sport and throughout life more generally (Deal, 2003).

Of course, there are problems with seeing people with impairments as being entirely marginalized, since this suggests that the social position of the disabled community hinges upon concepts such as 'symbolic order' (Douglas, 1966). However, the culture of Paralympic sport is not so clear-cut. In this regard, the work of Hall (1996) is important in unpacking the position of athletes within the social environment of sport for the disabled because key to identity formation is the ability to identify with others. Hall (1996, p. 2) suggests that

> identification is constructed on the back of a recognition of some common origin or shared characteristics with another person or group, or with an ideal, and with the natural closure of solidarity and allegiance established on this foundation.

In other words, as outlined in the Introduction, identification is a social construction, which is never a completed process. The establishment of a (dis)abled identity, then, is not concrete; rather it is something that is continually transformed. Identification is important within the context of Paralympic sport, since through the process of classification athletes are forced to accept their place within the organizational structure of the sport itself and are placed in a position where they inevitably begin to draw up similarities and differences between themselves and others (i.e. those within their category). Hence, impaired sportspeople's bodies are controlled by the process of classification that is a requirement for the participation within sport for the disabled.

The culture that surrounds the practice of sport for the disabled, and the knowledge participants have of their bodies and their self identity, means that to work towards achieving goals on an individual level is just as important as the work done through and by institutions. Through work on and with the body, we experience, establish and extend our limits and abilities, while placing them in the context of a number of rules and styles that make up our social circumstances. This is not simply a matter of doing exercises, but of monitoring and refining, keeping training records and making confessions, taking up and giving up different behaviours (Smith-Maguire, 2002).

This, in a sense, is a form of self-surveillance that all elite athletes go through (Markula & Pringle, 2006). In this regard, the world of elite sport for the disabled is indistinguishable from the sporting mainstream, except for the process of classification. While other sporting practices have forms of classification (such as age and weight), because the general population varies across such categories they are less restrictive than the protocols established within sport for the disabled. Within the majority of Paralympic sports, classification of the bodies focuses upon the functional specificity of the sporting practice. This is commonly referred to as the integrated functional classification system. Critics of this system suggest that some impairment groups may be at a systematic disadvantage and in some cases may no longer be able to compete (McCann, 1994; Richter, 1994). Specifically, the system may be more difficult to classify because of the need to consider a large number of impairments simultaneously, and many of the tests used have not been statistically validated (Richter *et al.*, 1992). There is a fear that some athletes will 'cheat' the system by fooling the classifiers because the classification tests have not been validated statistically. Within the specific context of swimming, Wu & Williams (1999, p. 262) note that:

> Misclassification is an interesting and perennial problem in disability sport. As with many others, it is the root cause of much frustration and anger (a) among swimmers who feel they have been disadvantaged by losing to a competitor who should be in a higher class and (b) among coaches and swimmers who may believe that they have been disadvantaged by being placed in a higher class than their impairment warrants.

Perhaps more importantly, athletes may be penalized for enhancing their own performances, for training as an elite athlete is central to the habitus and identity of the majority of Paralympians. If athletes train and improve their technique in swimming (or any other sport that adopts an integrated functional classification system), they may be reclassified on their new ability. As Vanlandewijck & Chappel (1996, p. 73) have pointed out, this is a key concern:

> The concept of athletic excellence can only be fully appreciated when the performance is related to the functional physical resources

available to the athlete in competition. These resources represent the athlete's performance potential. Whether such a potential is fully utilized by the athlete is one crucial determinant of excellence. An acceptable classification system would allow the definition and measurement of performance potential. The definition of *potential* in this way is the cornerstone of the classification process.

In practice the determination of sporting potential is almost impossible to achieve through any of the current classification systems in place in Paralympic sport. Yet the aim of achieving as fair a competition as possible is still the goal of the classification process, and the place an individual's body occupies within a category may impact significantly upon his/her identity. In order to control classifications, the International Paralympic Committee (IPC) has launched a classification code. The IPC states that: 'The classification code will aim to synchronize all sport specific classification processes and procedures, in much the same way that the world Anti-Doping Code has done for international anti-doping rules and regulations (IPC 2004, p. 11). In order to make conceptual sense of the structure of classification imposed within sport for the disabled, we now turn our attention to the work of Michel Foucault.

Foucault's governmentality

Foucault's offerings on governmentality can be used to explore classification within sport for the disabled. The work of Foucault has been shown by scholars in the field of sport studies to provide an appropriate critique of the objectification of the sporting body, particularly as it relates to scientific classification and dividing practices (Markula & Pringle, 2006). The process of classifying an athlete for involvement within the Paralympic Games, for example, may be seen as the scientific classification of an organism that ultimately leads, in some way, to its marginalization (being separated from its social environment because of the distinctive nature of classification and the manner in which Paralympic sport is practised). This act of classification is overtly political, since the processing of the body into a particular category is a form of segregation. As the bodies of impaired athletes are classified, then their positions within the system will have a certain amount of influence upon their identity.

Governmentality is a term used to link the body of work regarding technologies of discipline found in Foucault's *The Birth of the Clinic* (1975) and *Discipline and Punish* (1977). This concept is a useful way of exploring the control that social institutions have over individuals within society, since governmentality 'incorporates both techniques or practices of self-government and the more apparent forms of external government – policing, surveillance and regulatory activities carried out by agencies of the state or other institutions for strategic purposes' (Lupton 1995, p. 9). In other words, society uses individual consciousness to perpetuate the system. Individual choice is as important as the structure of society. More explicitly, for Foucault, governmentality 'refers to a "mentality" or way of thinking about the administration of society, in which the population is managed through the beliefs, needs, desires, and choices of individuals' (Smith-Maguire, 2002, p. 307). Applying this concept to the present discussion, it can be argued that impaired athletes who are already part of the classification system may adopt the 'mentality' of their particular category as part and parcel of their social identity.

The process of classification within sport for the disabled is perhaps the most important way in which athletes are governed and, as a result, it is central to the identity of Paralympic athletes. Before the establishment of the IPC, sport for the disabled was organized internationally by a number of sporting federations. Each of these had a responsibility to a constituent body of member nations and structured a sporting calendar for impairment-specific groups, from grassroots to international level (DePauw & Gavron, 1995). Collectively these federations are known as the International Organizations of Sport for the Disabled (IOSDs). It was the IOSDs and their predecessors which helped to organize the Paralympic Games between 1960 and 1988. The early Paralympic Games were run on a much smaller scale than those under the influence of the IPC. The rapid growth of the IPC in recent years has enabled it to establish an extensive network of 160 national affiliates that in some cases replicate or have replaced the national governing bodies of the federations.

The approaches taken by individual IOSDs vary, partly because some impairments are sensory and others are physical. However, the principles behind the advent of each system of classification is the same. These classification systems were created to provide an equitable sporting environment. Detailed discussion of the systems of classification, within the sports of athletics and swimming, have occurred elsewhere (see Howe & Jones, 2006) but the influence of these systems on identity formation has not. The work of Foucault, and that of scholars who have engaged with it, can help address this lacuna (Andrews 1993; Cole *et al.*, 2004; Markula, 2003; Markula & Pringle, 2006; Rail & Harvey,

1995; Smith-Maguire, 2002), since classification within sport for the disabled can be seen as a good example of a technology of dominance.

Technologies of dominance

In the wider social sciences, conceptualizations of the individual body as a vessel ripe for manipulation, the social body (Turner 1992, 1996) and the body politic (Lock 1993; Scheper-Hughes & Lock, 1987), are all influenced by Foucault. Because of the habitual nature of training within sporting environments, whether individuals train and compete as a member of a team or perform in sport which is individual in nature, such as track and field athletics or golf, the elite performer often has a support team (including medical staff, coaches, etc.) which provides a social environment distinctive to that sport (Shogun, 1999). The social environment where the training of sporting participants takes place, then, is where the disciplined body can be seen to be developed. The conceptualization of the socially disciplined body that Foucault (1977) articulates has for generations also been, in one form or another (and perhaps unconsciously), a focus for good coaches' training procedures (Park, 1992). Because Paralympians spend so much time working on their bodies, both consciously and unconsciously, the act of discipline has an important role to play in identity formation.

The need for coaches to control training regimes, so that embodied athletes perform to the best of their ability, is something that increased as the practice of sport for the disabled went from being considered a leisure pastime to becoming a professional concern where winning was linked to economic gain (Howe, 2004). Following a rigid training regime to develop the sporting body can be seen as an extension of the genealogy[2] that is the foundation of the Foucauldian method. Archaeology is an elementary form of Foucault's method of genealogy (a moment of interpretation) which both examines historical antecedents and analyses the emergence of discourse. The genealogy is an interpretative strategy that is distinctive from traditional history. As Andrews (1993, p. 156) suggests, the development of disciplinary practice:

> revolved around the emergence of a cluster of disciplinary institutions which, in terms of structure and ideology, promoted the ethos of discipline. Institutions such as prisons, hospitals, and schools increasingly came to the fore, augmented by complementary structures of knowledge and related human sciences that rationalized and legitimated the agenda of social discipline.

Sport today, particularly the way in which coach–athlete relationships are structured, can clearly be seen as a disciplinary institution where the athlete's body is, at least in part, controlled through the training process (Pronger, 2002). This control can impact upon the identity of athletes with regard to others and, as such, the act of discipline is important in examining sporting contexts such as sporting practices for the disabled because it develops a distinctive form of power that may be seen as a tool which controls the body – not in an oppressive manner but rather with the aim of normalizing it (Rail & Harvey, 1995, p. 165). As Cole *et al.* (2004, p. 12) state,

> bodies are never simply trained but are subjected to normative judgments (which include an ethical dimension), or what Foucault called divided practices. At least dividing practices are forces of 'normalisation' that produce and exclude through reference to a norm. Techniques of normalization distinguish the normal from the pathological, or the normal from the threatening.

This act of normalization, which is part of society more generally, has had an influence on research within the field of disability studies, particularly in relation to service provision for people with a disability (Tyne, 1992) where normalization can be seen as a social good, provided that it leads to the empowerment of members of the disabled community. The adoption of 'care in the community' as a primary vehicle for the assimilation or normalization of people with impairments can be seen to have an impact upon the way in which sporting practices for the disabled have developed. Research conducted by Williams (1994a, 1994b) suggests that sporting practice is a useful way to socialize individuals with disabilities. But the question is: socialization to what end? The process of normalization to someone who physically lacks normality can be problematic.

It is clear that impaired 'bodies are invested with power relations, making them the legitimate target of the interventions of medicine, education and economics' (Smith-Maguire 2002, p. 299). Such interventions have an important impact upon the identity constructed both through the process of governmentality and the development of a distinctive habitus. In other words, technologies of dominance, and the habitus that they help to create, shape the world in and around sport for the disabled. While this may be the case, in some respects the key technologies of dominance in the world of sport for the disabled is the classification system that illuminates the nexus between the means of disciplining the individual body and those of the population as a whole.

Governmentality, identity and the Paralympic movement

Ludwig Guttmann, the father of the Paralympic movement (Scruton, 1998), was clear in his view that it was classification which was the distinctive component of governance within sport for the disabled:

> [R]ules must necessarily be combined with correct classification according to the extent of physical deficit to ensure fair play, and such classifications have been compiled over the years in co-operation with panels of medical and technical experts ... in the various fields of disablement (Guttmann, 1976, Preface)

The pace of transformation of sport for the disabled, from its roots in rehabilitative medicine to high-performance sport, has been dramatic and, as a result, the identities of athletes currently involved within the Paralympic movement will be more diverse than those of high-performance athletes in well-established sporting institutions. The social environment in which sport for the disabled exists has been transformed more rapidly than any sporting practice in history. Since 1989, when the IPC was established, there has been a constant push within the organization to achieve a level footing with the International Olympic Committee (IOC) (Howe & Jones, 2006; Mason, 2002). Rapid developments within sport for the disabled have, in many cases, led Paralympic athletes to question the importance of sport in their identities. The transition from a foundation in rehabilitation (DePauw & Gavron, 1995; Seymour, 1998) into the realm of achievement sports (Bale, 2004) can been seen to have shaped the development of sport for the disabled, not only at the level of the international sporting spectacle but right the way down to the grass-roots level. There are athletes involved in Paralympic sport who treat it as a recreational pursuit. Their habitus reflects this. More and more, however, athletes are embodying a habitus akin to the able-bodied Olympians. Within this rapidly transforming culture, Wu et al. (2000, p. 420) have suggested that '[c]lassification, sociologically, can be conceptualized as a mechanism for positive social control in that it provides both the structure and the process for operationalising' sport for the disabled. This functionalist understanding of classification belies the fact that social control can also have negative connotations. While research does suggest that classifiers undertake one of the most important roles in the sport (e.g. Richter, et al., 1992; Sherill, 1999; Vanlandewijck & Chappel, 1996) the assumption that the control they exert is altogether positive needs to be examined further.

Politically speaking, classification was, and still is, a contested terrain. Within sport for the disabled, competitors are classified by their body's degree of function and, therefore, it is important that the classification process is robust, thereby achieving equity across Paralympic sporting practice and enabling athletes to compete on a 'level playing field'. As Sherrill (1999, p. 210) has noted:

> A basic goal of classification is to ensure that winning or losing an event depends on talent, training, skill, fitness, and motivation rather than unevenness among competitors on disability-related variables (e.g. spasticity, paralysis, absence of limb segments).

Ultimately, classification acts, as both a barrier, to keep others out and as an environment where an identity may be forged.

Paralympic classification and identity formation

Paralympic classification systems are one of the key identifiable elements for participants who are just entering the world of sport for the disabled. However, entry into the world of Paralympic sport is not unique. As Hall (1996, p. 4) has suggested, 'Precisely because identities are constructed within, not outside, discourse, we need to understand them as produced in specific historical and institutional sites within specific discursive formations and practices, by specific enunciative strategies'. By being categorized as a particular class, within a distinctive impairment group, the athlete's identity is shaped by the cultural baggage that goes along with that particular classification. This act of being labelled as a member of a particular class has an impact upon individual habitus.

Sport is an embodied practice and a hegemonic battlefield for those with imperfect bodies. As such, many people who possess less-than-normal bodies may shy away from the masculine physicality associated with sporting practice (DePauw, 1997). It could be argued, therefore, that sport and athletic prowess are constructed in such a way as to alienate those, especially the impaired, who can neither aspire to nor achieve such standards. The complete and strong, aggressive, muscular body is the most tangible sign of maleness (Seymour, 1998). Sporting bodies represent a pivotal form of physical capital, because physicality has traditionally constituted an admired trait. Muscularity has high physical capital. Locating physicality as a key component of identity, this chapter has thus far attempted to establish a link between the degree of impairment and the liminal position (Turner 1967) of an individual within the

Paralympic communitas. In other words, the degree to which an athlete is impaired may impact upon their habitus and identity, which, in turn, may impact upon their position within the community.

Having a 'good' physique has a currency or value within wider society. Someone with an impairment, who uses a wheelchair for example, may not have the ability to develop a physique that is highly sought after in society at large. Not every 'able' individual can do this either, but they do possess a body that is 'normal'. Athletes with an impaired body become aware of their difference, if for no other reason than because they compare their own physical performance to that of their 'able' peers. However, as an impaired sporting culture develops, new image ideals of the body are beginning to become apparent. The chiselled torso of champion T^3 wheelchair racers is a fine example of this. On the one hand, this is a positive step forward because it shows an acceptance of the impaired form. On the other hand, more severely impaired individuals may continue to be marginalized because they cannot meet this ideal and may be 'forced' to question their status as a Paralympic athlete. As Seymour (1998, p. 120) suggests,

> The preferencing of physicality in spinal injuries rehabilitation may disenfranchise the very people who most need its services. The creation of sporting heroes as rehabilitative triumphs obliterates from view the many severely damaged people for whom such activities will always be an impossibility.

The habitus of Paralympic sport thus places a great deal of emphasis on physical capital (as do all sporting cultures) and this can impact upon identity formation.

By their very nature, sports celebrate physical skill and prowess. Impairments, however, are often exacerbated in an environment such as the competitive sporting arena. Work in the field of disability studies has suggested that individuals with impairment are pushed to the margins of society (Oliver, 1996; Thomas, 1999) and, as a result of their involvement in sport, could be seen as liminal to the practice. Media coverage of sport for the disabled perpetuates the liminality of these athletes by measuring their sporting endeavours in light of their disability. Their ability to overcome disability, rather than their athletic ability, often becomes the focus of praise and admiration (Howe, 2008). Achievement cameos lead to a 'super-cripisation' of Paralympic sport that ultimately clouds an accurate representation of the culture of the Paralympics by acting as a catalyst for the many errant images that are portrayed by the media (see Howe, 2008). Thus, new athletes who develop in recreational environments may not get an accurate picture of Paralympic sporting culture and could adopt a habitus and identity that does not fit with the 'reality' of the Paralympic Games.

DePauw (1997, p. 423) examines how sport marginalizes the impaired and argues that we need to re-examine the relationship between sport and the body as it relates to disability:

> Ability is at the centre of sport and physical activity. Ability, as currently socially constructed, means 'able' and implies a finely tuned 'able body.' On the other hand, disability, also a social construction, is often viewed in relation to ability and is, then, most often defined as 'less than' ability, as not able. To be able to 'see' individuals with disabilities as athletes (regardless of the impairment) requires us to redefine athleticism and our view of the body, especially the 'sporting body'.

Individuals who have been successfully acculturated into Paralympic habitus, in spite of the overriding control of the classification system, have identified that as impaired athletes they have abilities that require the acquisition of a high-performance identity. This identity is needed if they are successfully to compete in sport for the disabled at the international level. For those who cannot effectively establish an elite sporting identity, classification can be counterproductive and has the facility to lead to marginalization.

Marginalized by classification

The IPC has attempted to shift expectations and change the views of society in relation to people with a disability by presenting a 'normalized' view of sport for the disabled. Explicit attempts to streamline athletic classification are a product of this normalization (Howe, 2008). The act of classification may be seen as a crucial mechanism for controlling sport for the disabled communitas but it should also be seen as a means by which to control individual bodies and (ultimately) individual identities. Closer alignment with the Olympic Movement has, in part, been responsible for the pressure to streamline classification systems by reducing the number of competitive categories available for participants. This shift has had a significant impact upon the elimination of the more severely impaired athletes. One of the goals of the IOSDs is to champion the cause of these groups, which already lack competitive opportunities (Howe & Jones, 2006).

As a result of streamlining within the classification system, more severely impaired competitors are being marginalized within the Paralympic programme. Events for the more impaired athletes are excluded because at times neither the event nor the athlete fits the image that is associated with athletic competitions or the ideal athletic body. The elimination of competitive opportunities has an impact upon the identity formation of future generations of severely impaired individuals who may be interested in, and indeed beginning to establish, a habitus that embodies elite sporting practice. These events are seen as less marketable and narrower in their appeal. Severely impaired elite participants are being given sporting opportunities in events like boccia, which is removed from the environs of the athletics stadium and swimming pool that are the focus of most media attention during the Games. Boccia is a game of skill, similar to lawn bowls, played by athletes with severe cerebral palsy, yet in the context of the Paralympics it is confined to an indoor gymnasium. This shift away from the main stadium, where either swimming or athletics take place, could imply that the competition in boccia is liminal to the larger spectacle of the Paralympic Games. The involvement in competitive sport of impaired performers is, in effect, accepting the social definitions of the importance of physical prowess. For this reason it is, in essence, disabling them (Hahn, 1984).

Concluding thoughts

My initial hope when setting out to write this chapter was that the research on which it is based would reveal a sense of communitas between elite impaired athletes, that is, a 'communion of equal individuals who submit together to the general authority of the ritual elders' (Turner 1969, p. 96). The IPC can be seen as a form of ritual elder; an institution to which athletes must pay heed. Athletes with a disability are far more differentiated than a simple communitas, since they distinguish themselves both by the degree of difference which they exhibit from the able-bodied norm and, as previously mentioned, in terms of established social relations on the back of a hierarchy of difference (Sherrill & Williams, 1996, p. 48). Over forty years ago Goffman (1963, p. 47) stated:

The more the child is 'handicapped' the more likely he is to be sent to a special school for persons of his kind, and the more abruptly he will have to face the view which the public at large take of him. He will be told that he will have an easier time of it among 'his own', and thus learn that the own he thought he possessed was the wrong one, and that this lesser own is really his.

In spite of the dated terminology that Goffman deploys, this statement is an accurate reflection of much that I have observed in relation to the marginalization of differently classified bodies within Paralympic sport. Such marginalization practices impact upon identity formation whether as a result of habitus or of a violent hierarchy. Many of the athletes who were involved in sport for the disabled during the 1980s were the product of 'special' schools, although most of these educational establishments were not just for one specific impairment group. As a result, the socialization of these individuals was distinct from that of those who have impairments but are products of contemporary inclusive education. One fact remains, wherever the impaired are educated their bodies marginalize them in relation to physical education. In special schools physical education adaptations are 'normal' but in the world of inclusive education today adaptations within sport actively 'other' and stigmatize the impaired student. This suggests that special schools may actually be advantageous for the recruitment of Paralympians, since greater numbers will be engaged in the practice of sport. Whether students at special schools will be appropriately socialized in high-performance sport remains to be seen. Certainly many of my observations from the mid- to late 1980s suggest that the special-school environment encourages participation but by and large steers clear of the fact that there is a possibility for students in their adult years to become high-performance athletes.

Many Paralympians become impaired later in life and so educational segregation does not affect them directly. However, they will be aware in part from the act of re-embodiment (Seymour, 1998) that the Eurocentric rhetoric of integration and inclusion does little to ease feelings of marginality associated with sporting practice. Certainly there is presently a good deal of discussion amongst Paralympic athletes that highlights the distinctions both between and within impairment groups (Howe, 2008).

The formation of a social identity occurs amidst the balance of what we are and what we are not. Within the cultural context of sport for the disabled, it is the athletes' impairment that is of central importance to the identification process. In order to compete in Paralympic sport, impaired athletes must be classified. Impaired bodies of athletes need to be classified in an equitable manner if the practice of the Paralympic games is to function smoothly. The process of classification highlights the body as the vehicle that facilitates entry into the field of Paralympic sport. A classification category is in fact demarcated by the type of bodies it encompasses and whether or not the particular impairments are considered 'acceptable' within society at large. Within the Paralympic habitus, then, the process and act of classification is of prime importance. As a result, within Paralympic culture there is a hierarchy of acceptance that impacts upon identity formation. Being classified into a particular category may say a great deal about what one's body is not and this will have consequences when it comes to identity formation.

Identity is also determined by what those with impaired bodies do with their lives. According to Bourdieu, those who engage in a particular sporting practice will inevitably begin to embody the habitus of that particular culture. Their habitus will be distinct from that of a mainstream or 'able' sports participant but often only as far as their impaired bodies require the training and competitive environment to be adapted. Importantly, some impaired athletes require a greater or lesser degree of adaptation. Ultimately, both able and impaired high-performance athletes within the same sporting culture share, by virtue of the rules and regulations that govern practice, a great deal in common.

Notes

1. I use the phrase 'sport for the disabled' instead of 'disability sport' because through my research it has become clear that sporting provision for the disabled is part of what might be called the disability industry. Therefore, because Paralympic sport is largely run by the 'able' the phrase 'sport for the disabled' seems appropriate.
2. See Andrews (1993) for an excellent review of Foucault's genealogy.
3. This is the most 'able' or least impaired class of wheelchair racing.

References

Andrews, D. (1993) 'Desperately seeking Michel: Foucault's genealogy, the body, and critical sport sociology', *Sociology of Sport Journal*, 10, 148–167.

Bale, J. (2004) *Running Culture: Racing in Time and Space*. London: Routledge.

Barnes, C. (1991) *Disabled People in Britain and Discrimination*. London: Hurst and Co.

Bourdieu, P. (1977) *Outline of a Theory of Practice*. Cambridge: Cambridge University Press.

Bourdieu, P. (1984) *Distinction: A Social Critique of the Judgement of Taste*. London: Routledge.

Bourdieu, P. (1990a) *The Logic of Practice*. Cambridge: Polity.

Bourdieu, P. (1990b) *In Other Words: Essays Towards a Reflexive Sociology*. Cambridge: Polity.

Bourdieu, P. & Wacquant, L. (1992) *An Invitation to Reflexive Sociology*. Chicago: University of Chicago Press.

Cole, C., Giardina, M. & Andrews, D. (2004) 'Michel Foucault: Studies of power and sport', in R. Giulianotti (ed.) *Sport and Modern Social Theorists*. Basingstoke: Palgrave MacMillan.

Deal, M. (2003) 'Disabled people's attitudes toward other impairment groups: A hierarchy of impairments', *Disability and Society*, 8 (7), 897–910.

DePauw, K. (1997) 'The (in)visibility of disability: cultural contexts and "sporting bodies"', *Quest*, 49, 416–430.

DePauw, K. & Gavron, S. (1995) *Disability and Sport*. Leeds: Human Kinetics.

Douglas, M. (1966) *Purity and Danger*. London: Routledge.

Foucault, M. (1975) *The Birth of the Clinic: An Archeology of Medical Perception*. London: Vintage Books.

Foucault, M. (1977) *Discipline and Punish: The Birth of the Prison*. London: Hammonworth.

Goffman, E. (1963) *Stigma: Notes on the Management of Spoiled Identity*. Englewood Cliffs, NJ: Prentice Hall.

Guttmann, L. (1976) *Textbook of Sport for the Disabled*. Aylesbury: HM & M.

Hahn, H. (1984) 'Sports and the political movement of disabled persons', *ARENA Review*, 8, 1–15.

Hall, S. (1996) 'Introduction: Who needs identity', in S. Hall & P. du Gay (eds) *Questions of Cultural Identity*. London: Sage.

Howe, P. D. (2004) *Sport, Pain and Professionalism: Ethnographies of Injury and Risk*. London: Routledge.

Howe, P. D. (2008) *The Cultural Politics of the Paralympic Movement: Through the Anthropological Lens*. London: Routledge.

Howe, P. D. & Jones, C. (2006) 'Classification of disabled athletes: (Dis)empowering the Paralympic practice community', *Sociology of Sport Journal*, 23, 29–46.

Hughes, B. & Patterson, K. (1997) 'The social model of disability and the disappearing body: Towards a sociology of impairment', *Disability and Society*, 12, 325–340.

IPC (International Paralympic Committee) (2004) *The Paralympian: Official Newsletter of the International Paralympic Committe*, No. 1.

Jenkins, R. (2008) *Social Identity* (3rd edn). London: Routledge.

Jones, C. & Howe, P. D. (2005) 'The conceptual boundaries of sport for the disabled: Classification and athletic performance', *Journal of Philosophy of Sport*, 32, 133–146.

Lock, M. (1993) 'Cultivating the body: Anthropology and epistemologies of bodily practice and knowledge', *Annual Review of Anthropology*, 22, 133–155.

Markula, P. (2003) 'The technologies of the self: Sport, feminism, and Foucault', *Sociology of Sport Journal*, 20, 87–107.

Markula, P. & Pringle, R. (2006) *Foucault, Sport and Exercise: Power, Knowledge and Transforming the Self*. London: Routledge.

Mason, F. (2002) 'Creating image and gaining control: The development of the cooperation agreements between the International Olympic Committee and the International Paralympic Committee', *VI International Symposium for Olympic Research*.

McCann, B. (1994) 'The medical disability – Specific classification system in sport', in R. Steadward, E. Nelson & G. Wheeler (eds), *Vista '93: The Outlook. Proceedings of the International Conference on High Performance Sport for Athletes with Disabilities*. Jasper, Alberta: Rick Hansen Centre.

Merleau-Ponty, M. (1962) *Phenomenology of Perception*. London: Routledge & Kegan Paul.

Merleau-Ponty, M. (1965) *The Structure of Behaviour*. London: Beacon Press.

Murphy, R. (1987) *The Body Silent*. London: Dent.

Oliver, M. (1990) *The Politics of Disablement*. London: Macmillan.

Oliver, M. (1996) *Understanding Disability*. London: Macmillan.

Park, R. (1992) 'Athletes and their training in Britain and America, 1800–1914', in J. Berryman & R. Park (eds) *Sport and Exercise Science: Essays in the History of Sports Medicine*. Chicago: University of Illinois Press, pp. 57–107.

Pronger, B. (2002) *Body Fascism: Salvation in the Technology of Physical Fitness*. London: University of Toronto Press.

Rail, G. & Harvey, J. (1995) 'Body at work: Michel Foucault and the sociology of sport', *Sociology of Sport Journal*, 12, 164–179.

Richter, K. (1994) 'Integrated classification: An analysis', in R. Steadward, E. Nelson & G. Wheeler (eds) *Vista '93: The Outlook. Proceedings of the International Conference on High Performance Sport for Athletes with Disabilities*. Jasper, Alberta: Rick Hansen Centre.

Richter, K., Adams-Mushett, C., Ferrara, M. & McCann, B. (1992) 'Integrated swimming classification: A faulted system', *Adapted Physical Activity Quarterly*, 9, 5–13.

Scheper-Hughes, N. & Lock, M. (1987) 'The mindful body: A prolegomenon to future work in medical anthropology', *Medical Anthropology Quarterly*, 1 (1), 6–41.

Scruton, J. (1998) *Stoke Mandeville: Road to the Paralympics*. Aylesbury: Peterhouse Press.

Seymour, W. (1998) *Remaking the Body: Rehabilitation and Change*. London: Routledge.

Sherrill, C. (1999) 'Disability sport and classification theory: A new era', *Adapted Physical Education Quarterly*, 16, 206–215.

Sherrill, C. & Williams, T. (1996) 'Disability and sport: Psychosocial perspectives on inclusion, integration and participation', *Sport Science Review*, 5 (1), 42–64.

Shilling, C. (2003) *The Body and Social Theory* (2nd edn). London: Sage.

Shogun, D. (1999) *High-Performance Athletes: Discipline, Diversity, and Ethics*. Toronto: University of Toronto Press.

Smith-Maguire, J. (2002) 'Michel Foucault: Sport, power, technologies and governmentality', in J. Maguire & K. Young (eds) *Theory, Sport and Society*. London: Elsevier Science.

Thomas, C. (1999) *Female Forms: Experiencing and Understanding Disability*. Buckingham: Open University Press.

Turner, B. (1992) *Regulated Bodies: Essays in Medical Sociology*. London: Routledge.

Turner, B. (1996) *The Body and Society* (2nd edn). London: Sage.

Turner, V. (1967) *The Forest of Symbols*. Ithaca, NY: Cornell University Press.

Turner, V. (1969) *The Ritual Process: Structure and Anti-structure*. Chicago: University of Chicago Press.

Tyne, A. (1992) 'Normalisation: From theory to practice', in H. Brown & H. Smith (eds) *Normalisation: A Reader for the Nineties*. London: Routledge.

Vanlandewijck, Y. & Chappel, R. (1996) 'Integration and classification issues in competitive sports for athletes with disabilities', *Sport Science Review*, 5 (1), 65–88.

Wacquant, L. (1995) 'Pugs at work: Bodily capital and bodily labour among professional boxers', *Body and Society*, 1 (1), 65–93.

Williams, T. (1994a) 'Disability sport socialisation and identity construction', *Adapted Physical Activity Quarterly*, 11, 14–31.

Williams, T. (1994b) 'Sociological perspectives on sport and disability: Structural-functionalism', *Physical Education Review*, 17 (1), 14–24.

Wu, S. & Williams, T. (1999) 'Paralympic swimming performance, impairment, and the functional classification system', *Adapted Physical Activity Quarterly*, 16 (3), 251–270.

Wu, S., Williams, T & Sherrill, C. (2000) 'Classifiers as agents of social control in disability swimming', *Adapted Physical Activity Quarterly*, 17, 421–436.

3
Professional Identities and the Practice of Sport Medicine in Canada: A Comparative Analysis of Two Sporting Contexts

Nancy Theberge

As the editors of this volume indicate in their introduction, the interest in sport and social identities is directed to identity formation at both individual and collective levels. One of the main focuses of sociological interest in collective identities has been professional identities. Among professions, medicine has been of particular concern, in large measure as a result of its historical status in many Western societies as the most powerful profession. Within sport, medicine has assumed an increasingly prominent role, an outcome of the combined influence of the increasing emphasis on performance and the extension of the process of the medicalization of society into the world of sport (Waddington, 1996).

The growing importance of medicine in sport has provided an interesting context in which to examine issues of professional status and identity. As Dominic Malcolm (2006, p. 377) has indicated, 'something of a paradox emerges when one compares studies of sports medicine personnel with the sociological literature on the medical profession as a whole'. This paradox lies in the contrast between the elevated status and power of medical practitioners generally and the relatively weak or subordinate role demonstrated in several studies of sport medicine practitioners (Safai, 2003; Walk, 1997). The most developed research to date on this topic is Malcolm's (2006) own work on rugby union club doctors. Malcolm has indicated that sport medicine in Britain lacks a coherent professional identity. This observation is grounded in several features of the social organization of sport medicine and the speciality's relation to the broader medical profession. Few of the rugby club doctors

who responded to a survey which Malcolm and his colleague administered were members of the Royal Society of Medicine's sport and exercise
medicine section; there was disagreement over the specific skills that the
speciality should encompass, and some rugby club doctors indicated that
the most important qualification for this position was an affinity for the
sport. Few physicians in the sample described their primary emphasis as
sport medicine, and financial reward for practice as rugby club doctors,
if it existed at all, was meagre.

Malcolm's (2006) research indicates that this weak professional identity has important implications for the experiences of rugby club doctors.
His analysis focuses in particular on the relationship that physicians
have with clients, both athletes and coaches, and with other health
care providers (specifically physiotherapists). In both relationships,
physicians have diminished authority and control.

Key to Malcolm's (2006) analysis is his argument that professional
roles and relationships are worked out in the context of both structural
arrangements and the conditions that exist in particular worksites. The
structural features include both the marginal position of sport medicine
in Britain, and the centrality of performance, 'an important part of the
raison d'être of contemporary sports medicine' (Waddington, 2000, p.
382). The interest in performance, which co- exists in an uneasy relationship with health concerns (Theberge, 2007), diminishes sport medicine
practitioners' authority to define clients' needs and consider how they
may be met.

In the discussion of his findings, Malcolm (2006) emphasizes that
a fuller understanding of the professional practice of sport medicine
requires investigation in additional settings. This is a particularly salient
observation with regard to this speciality, which is marked by a variety of
practice settings. In professional sport, teams have staffs of medical and
health professionals (Kotarba, 2001; Malcolm, 2006; Roderick, Waddington & Parker, 2000) and athletes in both team and individual sports also
seek the services of practitioners in independent practice. Another context in which health care practitioners work with athletes is national
team programmes, either in a home training base or 'on tour', travelling to training camps and competitions. Another practice site is when
health care practitioners are appointed to medical missions at competitions such as the Olympics. These settings are marked by differences
in the resources available, the size, composition and working relations
of the medical staff, and even in the purpose of professional practice.
With regard to purpose, performance pressures can be particularly acute
at major competitions, whether league championships in professional

sport or World Championships and the Olympic Games. When performance pressures are diminished, greater attention and resources may be invested in rehabilitation, and even 'resting' conditions, in contrast to the focus on 'getting fit yesterday' (Roderick Waddington & Parker, 2000, p. 172) which typically prevails during a competitive season and at major events such as the Olympics.

This chapter endeavours to expand our understanding of the conditions that shape professional practice in sport medicine. In this respect, the analysis contributes to research 'concerned to explore how self and identity processes are experienced and managed across diverse work and organizational sites and management cultures' (Dent & Whitehead, 2002, p. 2). Dent & Whitehead argue that traditional assumptions surrounding the term 'professional' are facing scrutiny. They suggest that the view of the professional as 'someone trusted and respected, an individual given class status, autonomy, social elevation, in return for safeguarding our well being and applying their professional judgment on the basis of a benign moral or cultural code' (2002, p. 2) has given way to an ideology/discourse of managerialism. The underlying source of this transition is the logic of global markets, which have subjected organizational life in both public and private sectors to 'increasingly sophisticated regimes of accountability' (2002, p. 2). The blurring of the boundaries between professionalism and managerialism has led to a 'significant slippage of identity for those professionals who previously saw themselves as exclusive and privileged, and thus, somewhat removed from the messy business of managing resources' (2002, p. 2).

Dent & Whitehead identify several concepts as key to understanding processes of professional/managerial identification. Particularly salient in the analysis of the professional identity of sport medicine practitioners are the 'twinned concepts' (2002, p. 11) of accountability and autonomy. Within the ideal typical model of professions, status has carried with it authority to decide upon clients' needs and how they may be met in a manner that is autonomous, or independent of external control. What makes this feature especially salient to the practice of sport medicine is the centrality of the performance principle in sport, which sets powerful parameters on the exercise of professional authority by health care practitioners (Theberge, 2007). As indicated above, one of the main findings of Malcolm's (2006) research is the diminished authority of sport medicine physicians, in relation both to their athletes/patients and to physiotherapists.

Ideal types are of course abstractions, and always approximated in some measure and fashion in concrete instances. The analytical task is to identify the conditions that shape the autonomy and accountability of professionals and the manner in which these features of professional life are experienced. Accordingly, this analysis explores how the accountability and autonomy of physicians and physiotherapists are configured in the practice of sport medicine in two different worksites, which are differentially influenced by the global market for commercial spectator sport. The analysis seeks to understand how location in this market interacts with the status of sport medicine to configure the roles and relationships of sport medicine practitioners.

Setting and methodology

This chapter provides an analysis of the practice of sport medicine in two of the main sites within Canadian sport. The first is 'major games', which are multi-sport competitions. The best-known example is the Olympics. Other major games in which Canada competes include the Pan American, Commonwealth and World University (FISU) Games, and the Jeux de Francophonie. The second context under examination is when Canadian national teams are 'on tour' at training camps and other competitions away from their home base. As subsequent discussion will show, each of these sites is characterized by some specific features that condition professional roles and relationships.

The analysis focuses specifically on professional practice and the working relations of physiotherapists and physicians. These two professions, along with athletic therapy (Walk, 2004), have historically comprised the system of sport medicine professions in North America.[1] In recent years, there has been increasing involvement of additional professions, most notably chiropractic, psychology and massage therapy. While the expanding composition of the system of sport medicine professions is represented in the medical missions at major games such as the Olympics, the majority of health professionals in Canada who travel with national teams are physiotherapists and physicians. Thus, this comparative analysis of the practice of sport medicine, at major games and travelling on tour teams, focuses on these two professions.

Data for the analysis are taken from interviews with twelve physicians (four women and eight men) and ten physiotherapists (five women and five men). All of the participants have worked with top-level athletes and at major international competitions, including, in most cases, the Olympic Games. The sports in which the participants have worked are varied and include both contact and non-contact, team and individual, and men's and women's sports. In the interests of preserving participants' anonymity, their gender and the sports they worked with are not revealed.

Participants in the research were identified in several ways. The first was through referrals from administrators at Canadian Sport Centres, a network of eight training centres for top-level athletes, who were asked to suggest names of practitioners who work with national team athletes. Additional participants were identified from lists of practitioners at recent Olympic Games posted on the website of the Canadian Olympic Committee. A third means was a snowball technique whereby participants were asked to suggest the names of other practitioners who worked with high-performance athletes and who might be interviewed. In all cases, the manner of recruitment was to send an information letter about the research to potential participants, requesting their participation. The interviews covered a range of topics concerning the practice of sport medicine in the context of high-performance sport and of working relationships between practitioners in different disciplines and at different types of work sites. They were recorded on audio tape, transcribed and entered into a qualitative data management software tool (QSR International, 2002). A preliminary coding scheme was devised and then revised on the basis of the reading of the transcripts. Sections of interviews, based on the codes, were extracted and then examined to develop the analysis.

Practice settings in sport medicine

With regard to the analysis of professional roles and relationships within this context, there are two main distinctions between professional practice at major games and when teams are on tour. The first is visibility, including both public interest and media coverage. This is, of course, most extensive for the Olympic Games. In contrast to the Olympics, and to a lesser extent other major games, Canadian teams receive little or no publicity or media coverage when they are away on tour.

The second distinction concerns the organization and provision of medical care. One of the distinguishing features of major games is the presence of a well-equipped medical clinic staffed by a multidisciplinary team of health care professionals. The circumstances when teams are on tour are very different, given that at these times they are often accompanied by a small support staff and, in many cases, a single health professional, who is most often a physiotherapist.

Sport medicine in Canada and professional identity

In contrast to Britain, sport and exercise medicine is not recognized as a speciality by the Royal College of Physicians and Surgeons of Canada. This fact, however, is a focus of concern and lobbying by the Canadian Academy of Sport Medicine (CASM), the professional association of sport physicians in Canada, suggesting that the lack of formal recognition is itself a focus of professional identification. Additionally, and similar to the findings reported by Malcolm (2006), financial remuneration for working at major games and with national teams is minimal and often entirely absent. Many physician participants reported that the main disadvantage of working in these contexts was the loss of income while they were away from their practices. However, this is also a recognized issue within the Canadian sport system. In interviews with sport administrators, which provided background for the current analysis, there was an acknowledged concern to address this issue.

In other respects, there is a stronger sense of professional identification among the participants in this study than Malcolm (2006) reported for professional rugby in Britain. One of the main activities of CASM is the administration of an examination whereby successful candidates are issued with a Diploma in Sport Medicine. To be eligible to sit the exam, candidates must be members of CASM. In contrast to the limited membership in the sport and exercise section of the Royal Society of Medicine that Malcolm (2006) found among his participants, all but one of the physician participants in this study holds the CASM Diploma in Sport Medicine. Additionally, many of the participants are active in the affairs of CASM, having held executive positions and served as instructors at seminars and courses offered by the academy, suggesting a strong sense of identification with the speciality among these participants. In contrast to the absence of formal selection procedures in many rugby clubs, there is a formal application and selection process for members of the medical staff who work at major games. Finally, in contrast to the few participants in Malcolm's (2006) study who described sport medicine as the primary focus of their practice, a number of the physicians in this study reported that sport and exercise medicine is a main component, though rarely the exclusive focus, of their practice. A minority worked full-time in sport and exercise medicine, combining their work at major games and with individual teams with a clinical practice dedicated to this speciality. In summary, while the lack of formal recognition of sport medicine is a notable difference in the organizations of the speciality in the UK and Canada, among the sample of sport physicians examined here there is a stronger sense of identification with sport medicine than Malcolm found among rugby club doctors in Britain.

Professional practice at major games: 'When there's so much on the line'

> When you leave a Major Games and if you're one of the core people that's there, you really need a holiday. 'Cause you're working (long hours) – and you really HAVE to force people to take time off, because you do see burnout of the medical staff. Because there's nothing like an Olympics or a Pan Am Games or something like that, when there's so much on the line as, you know, the pressure. Everybody. The sports administrator wants the team to qualify and they're asking you, 'Is this athlete ready to go?' You've got the COC (Canadian Olympic Committee), you've got the sport governing bodies. You've got all the photographers there and you've got to be careful who you talk to and the next thing, bam, it's blown up. And the LAST thing you want, the absolute LAST thing you want is a doping control issue. If you've got that you'll be guaranteed 72 hours of no sleep and everybody looking at you like you've got three heads because your athlete took an agent.

The preceding account was provided by a physician who has worked at an Olympic Games as the chief medical officer of the Canadian delegation. It is one of many descriptions by both physicians and physiotherapists of the ways in which working at the Olympics is stressful. The above passage refers to several specific stressors, which were also mentioned by other participants: the importance of the competition, which yields pressure to ensure that athletes are ready to compete; scrutiny by the media; and concerns about doping infractions. Similarly, another physician stated that working at the Olympics is:

> exhausting, for many reasons ... The stress level's high for everyone. You can't make a mistake on medication or diagnosis or anything. You have to be available, all the time you're supposed to be available ... And there's always something happening.

The statement that 'you can't make a mistake' speaks to one of the particular pressures of practising medicine in the high-stakes atmosphere of the Olympic Games. This point was echoed by a physiotherapist who said: 'There's more pressure to not make a mistake.' When asked to elaborate, s/he said that mistakes are particularly costly in this setting

> because it becomes very, very obvious when it happens, right? So if it happened in [participant's home base], I might be able to hide in the system because he'd [an athlete] never get anywhere, but if this guy's already picked on the team, all this money's spent on him, he's signed up on charts or on programs to compete in [a specific sport] and he's medically disqualified or doesn't progress and other kids have [progressed] with the same injury [this reflects on the therapist].

The preceding discussion indicates the various ways in which practising at major games, and in particular the Olympic Games, places health care practitioners in a position of heightened accountability, which is experienced as scrutiny by several audiences: athletes, administrators, sport organizations and the media. This point featured most prominently in the accounts of physicians, who have the ultimate authority among the members of the health care team and thus are called to account when issues such as doping infractions or mistakes in diagnosis or treatment occur. Accountability in this practice context also takes the form of media scrutiny, which is intensified when mistakes occur. Doping infractions are cited as particularly damaging because of the additional publicity they incur. One of the most notable features of the costs of mistakes in this context is that they may have nothing to do with the health of athletes/patients. Rather, they concern competitive costs and, additionally in the case of doping infractions, the extensive negative publicity.

The multidisciplinary context: 'We go there as a team'

The presence of a multidisciplinary medical staff at major games provides the context for one of the main issues in professional practice in this setting: the negotiation of professional authority and working relationships. Elsewhere, I have explored this process in the specific instance of the incorporation of chiropractice into sport medicine teams (Theberge, 2008). That analysis showed that, despite ongoing tensions around the location of chiropractice in the broader system of health professions (Coburn & Biggs, 1986; Willis, 1983), chiropractors themselves have gained meaningful inclusion on the medical missions at major games. This sense of inclusion is facilitated by the team approach that is emphasized in major games medical missions. This was captured by one physiotherapist who said, 'We're not going there as a physio team or an athletic therapy team or a chiropractic team. We're going there as a sport medicine team and we share ideas.' A physician provided a similar description, saying, 'it's an outstanding opportunity to rub shoulders with other professionals and to learn from them'. Other participants, both physiotherapists and physicians, described the collaborative working relations that are common at major games. One physiotherapist provided the following account of working with other manual therapists:

For the most part it works quite well. You sort of leave the expertise up to whoever can do that thing the best. I would say to the massage therapist, 'I think you need a release on X, Y and Z.' So then the massage therapist would help that and maybe the athlete would come back to me and I mobilize whatever I need to mobilize. So you're working as a team. And the same thing with the chiropractor. If I feel they can manipulate T7–8 (the motion segment between the 7th and 8th thoracic vertebrae) a little bit better then fine, I would send the patient over there. And again this is, we're looking at sort of the idealist kind of team because you normally don't have all these at your doorstep. You do at a Major Games, i.e. Olympics ... For the most part if you play one off the other – not 'play one off the other' – work WITH all of them for whatever they can do the best, then I think the athlete's getting the best care.

What is significant in the preceding account is the participant's acknowledgment that occupational practice is delegated to 'whoever can do that thing best'. In the multidisciplinary context of a major games, guided by an emphasis on working as a team, the focus is not on claiming authority over patients but on collaborating in the best interests of the athletes/patients. One feature of this is acceding to the expertise of other practitioners.

The dynamic at major games between physicians and physiotherapists was also described as collaborative. A physician provided the following account:

I don't think there's much in the way of disagreement. I think there's always a bit of a hierarchy in medicine because the buck always stops with the doctor and we're all used to working in that scenario. Most physicians, by the time they get to that level and have enough sports medicine experience behind them, appreciate what their therapist colleagues can do and know that they can't do that ... If I was at a Games and I was seeing a patient for a musculoskeletal problem ... you would finish seeing the musculoskeletal problem and then turn to the therapist and say, 'This is what I think, you have a look and see what you think', and then they talk again. I think that's very collaborative. I didn't ever feel that there was any problem there.

In support of this, physiotherapists typically indicated that working relations with physicians generally were collegial and respectful. One physiotherapist provided the following account of the value that physicians accorded physiotherapists in the working context of the Olympic Games:

It just seems to me like there's sort of like this oneness, this sort of levelness in terms of what everyone's providing because – I think this maybe changes a little bit when you get back to your different clinics and different practices where there is still that physician referral to the physio etcetera. But in this situation, the physician realizes that the physio may have a far greater role in this athlete being prepared for their competition, and there is that sort of unity in trying to accomplish that goal of getting 'em [athletes] ready [for competition].

In the preceding accounts, a physician and physiotherapist both refer to physicians' recognition of the particular – noted by the physiotherapist as greater – contribution of physiotherapists in preparing athletes for competition. There is some contrast in the two accounts of these working relations in that while the physician indicates that ultimate authority ('the buck') remains with the physician, the physiotherapist's reference to the levelling process suggests a reconstitution of the hierarchy among health professions that typically prevails in other contexts. These two accounts are not necessarily in opposition: while the levelling of authority that occurs at major games may be significant, it is not absolute.

The collaborative relations that occur among members of the health care teams at major games challenge the traditional boundaries that mark the claims to authority of health professionals. These relations, grounded in an explicit commitment to the team approach, are an outcome of the consumer-focused nature of professional practice, captured in the above account of a physiotherapist who discusses working with other therapists, so that 'the athlete's getting the best care'.

The practice of sport medicine on tour

The research for this project also included interviews with coaches of several Canadian national teams. One coach made the following observation on health concerns and staffing for international trips. This participant indicated that the team generally travels with a physiotherapist:

> We generally don't take doctors with us for first nation countries. But for third world countries we would because there's certain issues around diet and dehydration and diarrhoea that (arise when) we take them to third world countries. But in first world countries we don't travel with a doctor. I mean it's not ideal, but a lot of these decisions are budget-dependent.

This participant's reference to 'budget-dependent' points to an important issue in the provision of medical support when teams are on tour. There are variations among national sport programmes in the resources available, which determine the size and composition of medical staff. Most commonly, teams travel with physiotherapists as the need for regular treatment of musculoskeletal conditions is deemed the most pressing concern when teams are on tour. The presence of physicians and other practitioners is dependent on various considerations related to health risks and available resources.

'My focus is just with that team'

Both physicians and physiotherapists indicated that being on tour enabled them to provide enhanced care. One physician with a lengthy affiliation to a particular programme described practice in this context as 'more regular and ongoing'. S/he elaborated with the following account:

> On tour it's myself and the physiotherapist and maybe a sport psychologist. And so we will see them from soup to nuts, whatever happens to be the problem. Whether it be for diarrhoea or menstrual dysfunction or headaches or depression or an Achilles problem. . . . I just make sure that during the day I talk to each and every one of them to find out how they're doing.

References to the advantages of working on tour featured prominently in physiotherapists' accounts of this practice setting. When asked what it is like to practise while travelling with a team, a physiotherapist said 'I love it. It's fabulous.' S/he went on:

> I can see what's going on. I know what's going on with their body because I'm seeing them [while training].[2] They have no problem with

me [being present in the training site] at any point in time, ANY of the coaches, and I can see what they're doing and I can relate it to what I'm seeing when [treating athletes]. It's FABULOUS ... That's totally the best. I love it.

Several physiotherapists described circumstances where their responsibilities expanded beyond their normal practice. One participant, who travels extensively with a team in a context where s/he is the sole health care provider, said, 'I actually end up doing a lot of massage on tour.' I asked how the absence of a massage therapist affected the care players receive. S/he responded, 'If we had a massage therapist on tour there would be a lot bigger line-ups for treatment. I basically save massage treatments for the more senior players who have been banged up more or somebody with, you know, a serious problem.' I then asked about the participant's skills as a massage therapist. S/he said they were limited and explained:

We have maybe two weeks of massage training in our programme in school and then in sports physiotherapy you get some training, well you don't necessarily get training it's more by correspondence that you read about sports massage. So you don't have a lot of training in it and, and I think a lot of it, for me anyways, is just I don't use a lot of specific technique.

Other physiotherapists indicated that travelling with a team afforded enhanced opportunity to focus on athletes' needs. One participant stated that when s/he travels with a team, 'It's just me' (i.e. a physician is not present). When asked what it is like to practise in that context, s/he responded:

I find it actually EASIER for me when we're away because my focus is just with that team. I essentially take almost everything, it's like a mini-clinic that I travel with, so I'm very self-sufficient. And because we're away my time is just allotted to those athletes. So it doesn't matter what time of day or night I'm able to spend a lot of time and energy on them. Whereas when you're here [i.e., the clinic where the participant works, which is affiliated to a national training centre] even though they're centralized here and part of my mandate is to service those athletes, I'm also having to treat other athletes and look after [other] programmes etcetera.

While resource limitations dictate that teams on tour typically travel with a limited and sometimes skeletal health care team, the above comments indicate that these contexts also provide the opportunity for what many practitioners see as enhanced care. The specific advantages are the ability to focus on a small number of athletes and to tend to these athletes on a regular and frequent basis.

'You pitch in and do other stuff'

The other side of the regular and close attention possible when travelling on tour is an expansion of responsibilities. One physician noted, 'If you travel with a team, you do more than just [be] a physician. You pitch in and do other stuff too. So, I mean you might sit and do stats [i.e. game statistics].' When asked, 'What's that like for you?', the participant replied, 'It's fun. It's different ... You have to be flexible. If you just say "Okay, I'm the doctor, I'm not doing anything else" then more than likely you wouldn't get too far.' I then asked the participant to talk about the clinical practice of medicine while on tour with a team. S/he indicated,

> Well, you have limited number of supplies. You usually have what you've taken with you. I'm just thinking back to the last time I travelled with [a team to a competition] and I got there and my medical bag didn't make it on the plane. But I got there and one of the guys had been out running and put a piece of rebar [a steel bar] through his foot so he needed stitches but I didn't have the stuff till the next morning. So I had to wait till my bag got there and I had the equipment to do it. And then I had to run around to a medical clinic and find a tetanus shot 'cause he wasn't up to date in his tetanus. So you have to access the local health care, too, and you have to know how to do that. And then just as I was leaving and catching the bus to the plane to go back, another guy split his hand open and needed stitches so I borrowed the St John Ambulance van that was there for spectators and used their space and some of their equipment. You have to be flexible and able to access other resources around you.

As noted above, on many occasions teams travel with only a physiotherapist and hence the issue of expanded responsibilities figured prominently in physiotherapists' accounts of this practice setting. Most participants described a comfort level with this arrangement. One physiotherapist with a lengthy history working with a national programme said, 'When travelling on tour you're sort of the medical person that does a bit of everything, so you're the umbrella person.' When asked, 'What's that like for you as a clinician?' Reflecting the comments of the physician quoted above s/he said,

> I like it. I've been doing this for so long now I feel like I can do it and I don't have a problem with it. I go into a town, I know what I need to do. I need to establish where's the hospital, where's this, where's that. I feel I can do it.

Several physiotherapists provided examples of how their roles expanded when travelling on tour. One participant said that when on tour, 'You're everything to them, to try to keep them healthy. And that includes looking at diet, what they are taking in, trying to screen them in countries where food may be a bit suspect, what may cause them problems, etcetera.' When I asked how this fitted in with the participant's skill set, s/he said, 'I think that's part of it. I've travelled enough that I know that's part of the role of a sport physiotherapist when you're travelling without a doc [doctor]. The ideal would be to have a doc come along, that would be great.'

Another participant provided an extended account of an incident when nearly all the members of a team s/he was travelling with, including the coaching staff, became ill with what turned out to be a gastrointestinal virus. S/he was the only health professional on site and became the person 'on call'. The incident started with an athlete coming to the participant's room at 2 o'clock in the morning with a report of a room mate who had been vomiting for several hours. Following this, a succession of athletes and staff members became sick. In response to my probing about this example, the participant said his/her sport physiotherapy training provided some knowledge:

> dehydration and stuff I can deal with. If they run a fever I can take their temperature. I have everything in my kit. Like I'm not allowed to give out medication. And sometimes if they get sick, I will monitor them. Sometimes they stay in my room and we monitor them and if it gets worse we can go to the clinics.

This participant's reference to lacking authority to prescribe medication addresses a main issue of concern to physiotherapists when they are on tour with a team and a physician is not present. One participant made the following observation about travelling without a physician

It's [a concern] when it comes to medication issues or when it comes to stuff that we're not equipped to handle. So we can phone the doctor and get some input from the doctor ... But if it's an issue of somebody gets sick we don't have any real way of knowing what a person's got unless it's a simple cold or flu. We're not equipped to fully evaluate the person for anything other than a musculoskeletal [condition].

When asked how often issues arise that fall outside his/her scope of practice, the participant said,

Maybe not 95 per cent but a good portion of it is stuff that would fall under our scope of practice. I think the line blurs a little bit sometimes ... in terms of medications or in terms of, you know, diagnosing, even. But we've always got the doctor available by phone.

While some participants acknowledged concerns about the blurring of boundaries around scope of practice, a few insisted that this did not occur. One participant said, 'I would never put myself in a predicament where I am overstepping boundaries.' Another spoke more extensively on this point. S/he said,

We're training sometimes off-season and stuff like that and they're having a tough time finding a physician, those are the times that I'm thinking to myself 'This is ridiculous.' I mean, I have some basic first-responder [first-aider] knowledge and training, but I'm not equipped or trained to be putting in IVs [intravenous lines] and dealing with really significant stuff. So fortunately that doesn't happen very often, but there are times [there follows a description of a sport-specific example] you can get a head injury or lacerations, whatever that might be. And that's where it's scary.

I asked, 'Is it often the case that you're faced with situations that fall outside your skill set or what you're, as a physio quote "authorized" to do, which can be two different things.' My respondent answered,

No, I wouldn't say – because again you have to be sort of honest and knowledgeable where you, what your role is and what your capabilities are and where your boundaries are, so from that perspective I would never CROSS those boundaries. But are you put in a position sometimes where [pause] that may be an issue? I think that is true again because of the resources and the support that we have. Physiotherapists, with a lot of teams, are the only medical representative and it's unfair to them.

When teams are on tour, the routine need for treatment of musculoskeletal conditions places a particular premium on physiotherapists' presence; in contrast, depending on the circumstances, the presence of a physician may be a comparative 'luxury'. This is why, when resource limitations dictate that only one health professional accompanies a team, it is most likely to be a physiotherapist (or some other manual therapist). This results in an expanded role-set for physiotherapists who frequently act as the 'umbrella person', providing services that in different contexts, including major games, would be offered by other professionals, such as massage therapists. Yet another aspect for physiotherapists of being the only health care provider occurs when issues arise that lie outside their scope of practice; most problematic are those that are the domain of physicians, notably prescribing medications. Thus, an important issue for physiotherapists is expanded accountability in circumstances where they have limited authority. Most physiotherapists indicated that while they were conscious of the dilemma of addressing concerns that are outside their scope of practice, these occurrences were rare. Moreover, procedures for dealing with such issues typically were in place, often in the form of telephone consultations with physicians.

While the presence on tour of physiotherapists is dictated by the ongoing need for their services, the need for physicians is more incident-dependent – when an athlete falls ill or has an injury. There are, to be sure, contexts that present an increased likelihood of incidents, for example environments and climates that pose the risk of dehydration. Additionally, there are contexts, such as during World Championships, where the costs of incidents are so high as to warrant the presence of physicians as 'insurance' that medical expertise is readily available when concerns arise. Unlike physiotherapists who typically are constantly busy, the incident-based nature of medical care has the ironic outcome of 'freeing up' physicians to attend to non-medical tasks such as keeping game statistics. For physicians, the multitasking that occurs on tour thus has an element of deskilling, in the sense that they take on duties that in other contexts would be delegated to non-specialists.

Discussion and conclusion

The analysis reported here confirms one of the main findings of Malcolm's (2006) research into professional rugby in the UK: the reconfiguring of power relations between physiotherapists and physicians and the influence of this on authority and autonomy. At major games, there is a 'levelling' of the relationship between these two provider groups. When teams are on tour and a physiotherapist is the sole health care provider, the expanded responsibilities that physiotherapists assume reflect the conditions described by Malcolm in professional rugby, where 'physiotherapists do not simply assist doctors but in many cases display considerable autonomy' (2006, p. 388). As Malcolm indicates, the working relations between health care providers in rugby are in part an outcome of the types of injuries that occur. The prominence of musculoskeletal conditions in virtually all sporting contexts leads to an ongoing need for the services of physiotherapists (or other therapists) across a variety of practice settings.

There are some important differences in the relations between physiotherapists and physicians described by Malcolm and those observed in this research. While in both studies physiotherapists were shown to have considerable status and authority, Malcolm's finding that physicians were professionally marginalized was not evident in this research. On the contrary, respondent comments that the absence of a physician is 'not ideal' and it 'would be great' to 'have a doc come along' attest to the continued value placed on physicians' contributions. The contrasting results between Malcolm's findings and those reported here concerning the marginalization of physicians provide support for Malcolm's argument about the importance of professional identity in structuring professional roles and relationships. These differences are likely to be related to the stronger sense of professional identity among the sport physicians interviewed for this study, which both results from and contributes to their established place in the medical support system.

One of the questions that may be raised about the comparison between Malcolm's study and this research is the significance of the commercial context of the settings studied. That is, while Malcolm studied professional sport, i.e. sport organized to generate profit, the research reported here is located in the Canadian national sport system, which is nominally 'amateur'. This point is addressed further in the concluding discussion of the significance of commercial spectator sport for the current analysis. At this point it is noted that several of the participants in the present study also have experience working with professional sports teams. Thus, it would be incorrect to assume that there is a simple association between the professional identification of sport physicians and the commercial contexts in which they work. At least in the Canadian context, some physicians strongly identified with sport medicine work in both professional and amateur sport contexts.

These research findings indicate the impact of the global market for commercial spectator sport on features of the work setting that, in turn, condition professional practice among both sport medicine physicians and physiotherapists. This impact is evident in the contrasts between the two settings examined. Alongside the football World Cup, the Olympics are the pinnacle of the global enterprise of sport, with other major games representing localized (e.g. regional competitions such as the Pan American Games) or historically specific (e.g. the Commonwealth Games) instances of this market. With regard to the configuration of professional identities, the key elements of these work settings derive from the heightened significance of these events, both competitive and commercial. One outcome of this is the increased scrutiny that sport medicine practitioners face. This is perhaps the clearest instance of the emergence of a 'regime of accountability' (Dent & Whitehead, 2002, p. 2) in which health professionals are called to account by a variety of audiences, including athletes, coaches, sport organizations and the media. The managerial ethos that operates in these contexts is felt most acutely in the pressure to avoid mistakes.

The high-stakes context of major games is also the basis for the investment of resources in a multidisciplinary clinic, another feature that conditions professional roles and identity. Professional practice in these settings is marked by a commitment to a collaborative approach, which encourages practitioners to defer to the expertise of 'whoever can do [a task] the best'. Physiotherapists share authority as manual therapists with other practitioners. Relations between physiotherapists and physicians at major games are also affected, in that the commitment to collaboration results in a 'levelling' of the hierarchical relations that may be present between these two professions in other settings.

In contrast to the heavy investment of resources in medical support at major games, the limited medical staffing to support teams when they are on tour is the key determinant of professional practice in these settings. While the presence of a multidisciplinary staff at major games encourages specialization, practice on tour typically involves an expansion of roles and responsibilities. The effect of this arrangement is experienced most profoundly by physiotherapists. Because of their skill in treating musculoskeletal conditions, physiotherapists are in particular demand. As a result, in contexts where limited resources dictate that only one practitioner accompanies a team, that practitioner is likely to be a physiotherapist, who then takes on an 'umbrella' role of increased responsibility. Another way in which working conditions on tour affect physiotherapists is that, in practice settings where physicians are not present, physiotherapists may face dilemmas when concerns arise that are outside their scope of practice and (hence) authority. The most challenging instances of this concern the prescribing of medications.

Physicians are also affected by the working conditions on tour. Like physiotherapists, they encounter situations where they must be 'creative' in identifying and marshalling resources. In addition, physicians may be called upon to contribute in ways that in some instances require no specialized knowledge. Physicians' responses to this expanded role-set, which they see as appropriate given the conditions of the worksite, provide support for Lupton's (1997) argument that debates about deprofessionalization, in the context of expanding bureaucratic controls, need to move beyond structural concerns to a consideration of the micropolitics of everyday experiences. As with the physicians whom Lupton interviewed in Australia, the participants in the present study recognized the effects of commercial pressures on their professional practice, but did not see this as diminishing their status or authority. Lupton (1997, p. 493) suggests that the 'debate could perhaps be reoriented, moving from examining *de*professionalisation to *re*professionalisation, bearing in mind that professional power is constantly negotiated at the level of everyday practice as well as at the level of policy and organizational structure'.

The analysis provided here joins the developing literature on the practice of sport medicine (Malcolm, 2006; Young, 2004) with related work on professional identities in the new economy of global capitalism (Dent & Whitehead, 2002). This chapter has explored how professional identities of health care practitioners are configured in different practice settings. These findings indicate that while the professional identity of sport medicine practitioners is important to their working relations, professional roles and relationships also vary across the different settings in which sport medicine is practised. In more commercialized settings, such as the Olympic Games, there is heightened accountability to a broader array of audiences. When teams are on tour, limitations on resources result in expanded role-sets for both physicians and physiotherapists, with varying implications for each.

In conclusion, it should be noted that this analysis captures a moment in time in the evolution of both the professional identity of sport medicine in Canada and the integration of Canadian sport into the global enterprise of commercial spectator sport and its attendant competitive and commercial pressures. One indication of the latter is the staging of the 2010 Winter Olympics in Whistler, near Vancouver, which has brought an infusion of resources into the Canadian sport system, including support for sport medicine services. As medicine and other allied health professions work to solidify their professional status, and the Canadian sport system seeks to improve performance on the international sport scene, it will be interesting to track the convergence of these two developments in order to further our understanding of professional identities and practice in sport medicine.

Acknowledgement

This research was funded by a grant from the Social Sciences and Humanities Research Council of Canada.

Notes

1. Athletic therapy is the designation in Canada for the profession known in the United States (and formerly in Canada) as athletic training. The Canadian Athletic Therapy Association defines the scope of practice of a certified athletic therapist as 'the assessment, prevention, immediate care, and reconditioning of musculoskeletal injuries' (Canadian Athletic Therapy Association). The roots of the profession, and its continuing base, lie in university athletic programmes and on professional sports teams in the United States and Canada (Walk, 2004), where athletic therapists (or trainers) historically were the primary providers of site coverage of athletic events, including immediate care of athletic injuries.
2. This excerpt has been edited to remove references which would identify the sport that the participant is discussing.

References

Canadian Athletic Therapy Association: www.athletictherapy.org/main.html (accessed 23 Aug. 2006).
Coburn, D. & Biggs. C. (1986) 'Limits to medical dominance: The case of chiropractic', *Social Science and Medicine*, 22 (10), 1035–1046.
Dent, M. & Whitehead, S. (2002) 'Configuring the "new" professional', in M. Dent & S. Whitehead (eds) *Managing Professional Identities*. London: Routledge.
Kotarba, J. (2001) 'Conceptualizing sports medicine as occupational health care: Illustrations from professional rodeo and wrestling', *Qualitative Health Research*, 11 (6), 766–777.
Lupton, D. (1997) 'Doctors on the medical profession', *Sociology of Health and Illness*, 23 (4), 480–497.
Malcolm, D. (2006) 'Unprofessional practice? The status and power of sport physicians', *Sociology of Sport Journal*, 23, 376–395.
QSR International. (2002), QSR NVIVO2 Users' Guide. Melbourne.

Roderick, M., Waddington, I. & Parker, G. (2000) 'Playing hurt: Managing injuries in English professional football', *International Review for the Sociology of Sport*, 35, 165–180.

Safai P. (2003) 'Healing the body in the "culture of risk": Negotiation of treatment between sport medicine clinicians and injured athletes in Canadian intercollegiate sport', *Sociology of Sport Journal*, 20, 127–146.

Theberge, N. (2007) ' "It's not about health, it's about performance": Sport medicine, health and the culture of risk in Canadian sport', in J. Hargreaves & P. Vertinsky (eds) *Physical Culture, Power and the Body*. London: Routledge.

Theberge, N. (2008) 'The integration of chiropractors onto sport healthcare teams: A case study from sport medicine', *Sociology of Health and Illness*, 30 (1), 19–34.

Waddington, I. (1996) 'The development of sports medicine', *Sociology of Sport Journal*, 13 (2), 176–196.

Waddington, I. (2000) *Sport, Health and Drugs*. London: Routledge.

Waddington, I., Roderick, M. & Parker, G. (1999) *Managing Injuries in Professional Football: The Roles of the Club Doctor and Physiotherapist*. Leicester: Centre for Research into Sport and Society, University of Leicester.

Walk, S. (1997) 'Peers in pain: The experience of student athletic trainers', *Sociology of Sport Journal*, 14, 22–56.

Walk, S. (2004) 'Athletic trainers: between care and social control', in K. Young (ed.) *Sporting Bodies, Damaged Selves: Sociological Studies of Sports Related Injuries*. Oxford: Elsevier.

Willis, E. (1983) *Medical Dominance: The Division of Labour in Australian Health Care*. Sydney: George Allen & Unwin.

Young, K. (2004) (ed.) *Sporting Bodies, Damaged Selves*. Oxford: Elsevier.

4
Shaping up to the Men: (Re)creating Identities in Women's Football

John Harris

Women's football is one of the fastest growing sports in the world and there are more than an estimated thirty million players globally (Cox & Thompson, 2000). Yet in countries where the game assumes a central place in contemporary culture it is also imbued with notions of masculine identity. This chapter analyses and interprets notions of identity and style within the (sub)cultural context of a women's football team based at a college of higher education in the South of England. It addresses gendered identities within football as seen and experienced by the players themselves. Focusing on events both on and off the field of play, it provides insight into the lives of the respondents through reference to the discourse(s) employed by them when talking about their involvement in the game. In so doing, it addresses the ways in which these women both colluded in, and challenged, the (re)production of male hegemony in English football. The research highlights how the women used the male model of football as something that they aspired to and provides insight into the strengths and weaknesses of the female game as perceived by the athletes themselves. In critically exploring how the respondents constructed their gendered identities, the chapter analyses the performative aspects of their sporting lives within a context that is central to notions of hegemonic masculinity in contemporary English society.

The views of women football players in England have been presented in the works of a number of scholars during the past decade (e.g. Caudwell, 2002; Lopez, 1997; Scraton, Caudwell & Holland, 2005; Williams, 2003). These writers have highlighted the trials, tribulations and progress of females entering a sport that was, for many years, an exclusively male domain. Football occupies a prominent position in the sporting hierarchy in the UK and is seen to link closely to notions of hegemonic masculinity where the domination of men and the subordination of women is central (see, for example, Clayton, 2005; Parker, 2001). Drawing upon Messner's (1988) description of the female athlete as a site of 'contested ideological terrain', it would be fair to suggest that, in England at least, the female football player has entered this realm as a consequence of the rapid development of women's football in the last twenty years. Such events make it an appropriate time to apply and analyse such a descriptor in relation to this particular sport.

Background to the study

The data presented in this chapter was collected over a period of two years during the mid- to late 1990s and encompassed extensive ethnographic observations together with in-depth, semi-structured interviews. Nine interviews were undertaken lasting an average of one and a half hours. Ethnographic data was collected at a range of venues including match fixtures, the student union bar, a campus cafeteria and other sites on and around two campuses at a college in the South of England. All members of the squad were white and the nine female players interviewed were between 18 and 21 years of age. The women came from all parts of the UK and many were studying courses within a faculty of leisure and tourism.

The chapter analyses the way in which the women located their sport in relation to wider conceptualizations of the male game. By adopting an inductive, interpretive analytical framework, emergent research themes are highlighted whereby the everyday experiences of respondents are explored in-depth. The account provides a particular (re)presentation of those experiences, although it is acknowledged that all accounts can only ever be partial and that what is presented here is merely a snapshot of life within this particular context at a specific point in time. Elsewhere I have suggested that this research may contribute alternative (re)presentations of women's football to those put forward in much of the existing literature on the game in England (Harris, 2004, 2005). Although it is beyond the scope and focus of this particular chapter to dwell on this point, those findings relating to issues surrounding (re)presentations of sexuality inside women's football offer a somewhat different perspective to those advocated by other researchers (see Caudwell, 2002; Cox & Thompson, 2000).

In inductive research, alternative accounts often emerge from the primary data. A theoretical 'label' is not placed upon the study before any data is gathered but emerges through the process of data collection.

Mills (1959) argued against an adherence to any particular theoretical 'model' and urged researchers to work from, and reflect upon, their own role in the research process. Woodward (2002, p.163) notes how phenomenological approaches 'which give high priority to description of direct experience' have now superseded the creation of theories that put forward causal explanations of how identities are formed. As researchers we are central to the research process and as a male researcher carrying out research into women's football my experiences may have been quite different to those of a female researcher undertaking a similar study (although, of course, other variables such as 'race', social class and age would also need to be considered here). We must additionally note the specific cultural context of various research projects. What the above highlights is the important role of social identities within sociologically informed scholarship.

In much social science research, particularly from within disciplines less sympathetic to the positioning of interpretive findings, social identity is presented as an 'all or nothing' term simply differentiating between insiders and outsiders (see the introductory chapter to this volume). In reality, identities are much more complex than this and the role of individuals within any given group are likely to change over time. Identities are also multidimensional, hence we may choose to prioritize a particular aspect of our selves at any point in time. Identities involve an active and continual process of construction and reconstruction and the particular form that identities take is centred upon power relationships. Castells (1997) suggests that there are three main types of identity involved within these power relationships: (i) legitimizing identity which supports systems of domination; (ii) resistance identity which highlights the struggle of marginalized individuals/groups; and (iii) project identity which encompasses the construction of new identities that transform the social structure. In different ways each of these is visible within the stories of the women footballers featured here.

Male football looms large in the governance of the women's game throughout the world. In many countries, including England, the female game is subsumed under the dominant umbrella of its male equivalent. Because women's football now constitutes an integral part of the business of the (English) Football Association (FA), many proponents of the game argue that female players in England now have greater access to facilities and resources. Yet football is far from being an equally gendered institution, for the governing bodies that control the game are historically, socially and culturally masculinized. The leading teams in women's football in England often form a very small part of larger professional male clubs. It is important to note that the FA only took over the administration of the English women's game as a result of pressure from the Union of European Football Associations (UEFA) in 1993. The current positioning of women's football in England, and some of the main obstacles to its future development, are considered in this chapter. Before looking further at the governance of the game and exploring how a group of female football players understood and constructed their (gendered) identities both on and off the pitch, I will briefly outline the wider cultural positioning of football in England.

(Re)positioning women's football

Tracey: When you watch the boys' game and then ours
          it is quite funny.
JH: Why is that?
Tracey: (laughs) 'Cos you can see the complete differences.
JH: What differences, I don't see any differences?
Tracey: The communication, like passing it [the ball]
          around, whereas we [women players] all see the ball
          [laughs] and charge after it.

Tracey's words provide a clear example of the way in which many of my respondents viewed their enactment of football. A number of the women whom I interviewed, when comparing themselves to male professional football players, identified issues such as high financial earnings, mass spectatorship, and extensive media coverage as being the most significant differences between their own sporting exploits and commonsense perceptions of the sport as a whole. When I then asked if they thought that the women's amateur game differed from that of their male counterparts within the collegiate environment, the overwhelming consensus was that it was 'totally different'.

Highlighting and exploring such differences between male and female college football must not be interpreted as an attempt to discredit or devalue the women's game. Football the world over is characterized by its multitude of styles (Critcher, 1991). A marked difference I had noticed in some of my earliest field observations was that the playing style of the women's team was noticeably slower than that of amateur male players of similar age. The slower pace of the female game appeals to followers of the sport (e.g. Davies, 1996), in that it may allow more room for skilful players to express themselves. Again, this should not be read as a criticism, for some of the most highly rated forms of male football in the world, such as that played in Italy's *Serie A*, are a much slower affair than that played in the English Premier League. In recent years Italian teams have been more successful than their English counterparts in major club and international team competitions and towards the end of 2007 the Football Association appointed an Italian as head coach of the England team.

A number of authors have commented on the 'British' style in (male) football. Davies (1990, p. 169) noted at the World Cup Finals in 1990, 'We've got skilful players. But if you look overall, yes – we are technically inferior, and our game's played at a much greater pace. It's a generalization, but it's pretty true.' Critcher (1991, p. 71) supported this view, suggesting: 'Compared with overseas players, British players are technically deficient in the finer points of the game: ball control, passing, balance and positional sense.'

Of course, since Critcher (1991) wrote this there have been many changes within English professional football. One of the most significant of these has been the considerable increase in the number of overseas players and coaches entering the English game. Arguably this development has further highlighted the technical deficiencies of English players when compared to many of their overseas counterparts. What is important to elucidate from the above is that, within English[1] culture, spectators of the professional game often expect football to be played at speed. Traditionally, pace, rather than technical ability, has been one of the most important criteria when judging team and player performances. Therefore, when discussing the experiences of a group of female football players in England it is important to bear in mind the qualities of the (male) professional game that are most valued.

Doing and performing gender in sport

Much research has looked at the way(s) in which gendered identities are (re)constructed (e.g. Butler, 1990, 1993; Hargreaves, 1994, 2000; Messner, 1988; Young, 1990). Butler's (1990, 1993) research has been particularly influential in framing the work of a number of scholars, in relation to issues of gender, including those within the sociology of sport (see, for example, Caudwell, 2002). Butler (1990) suggests that gender is not the expression of what we are but is something that we 'perform'. For Butler (1990, 1993), gender is not 'naturally' ascribed but is a changing social construct that demonstrates fluidity and multiplicity. Individuals actively negotiate this performance within a particular socio-cultural context. Yet, this is not necessarily an active choice, for social learning perpetuates gender norms and prioritizes 'appropriate' behaviour which, in turn, reinforces certain cultural norms. Butler's (1990, 1993) work is important in terms of discrediting essentialist ideas about gender. It must also be noted that, with reference to doing or performing gender, there are numerous roles that we can adopt. Likewise, we may move between different roles dependent on the situation or context in which we find ourselves (see also Ussher, 1997). In the next two sections of this chapter, I look at how my respondents constructed their gendered identities both on and off the pitch.

Gendered identities on the pitch

My early observations regarding the playing style of the team and, in particular, the pace at which they played, resonated closely with the views shared by many of the women themselves, as the following comment from Hannah shows:

> Ladies football is much slower, theirs [men's] is much faster. It is surprising how quick they get from one end of the pitch to the other. I am not saying it is a bad thing, it should just be seen as a different sort of game.

Often the way in which respondents talked about this particular difference indicated that it was perceived by them as something negative. For example, three of the women believed that the reason why their enactment of the game was slower was because 'boys have been playing longer' (Lorna). As Tracey suggested, 'Well most of the boys have been playing from, say, all of their life, from a young age up until now ... whereas most of the girls have either just started or have only been playing for a few years.'

Mary demonstrated a similar line of thought:

> I think it is a lot slower cause we have found when we have gone down for a kick-about on a Wednesday afternoon and a lot of the lads are there and we say: 'Do you fancy a kick-about', and we have been knackered [tired] after ten minutes [laughs].

Mary attributed the slower pace of the women's amateur game not just to the relative fitness levels of males and females, but also to the fact that:

> At this level I think it is, I hate to say it, but it [the women's game] is a lot less skilful. It is a bit more pot-luck [ad-hoc] [laughs] to be honest. In a lot of cases some people don't know what they are doing.

In general, it would be fair to say that the women viewed their own game as an inferior version of that played by their male counterparts at the college. With reference to the work of Castells (1997), this may be understood as a way of legitimizing identity by reflecting the perpetuation of existing structures. Football is positioned and perceived in English culture as a 'man's game' and the women felt that their version of the sport was an inferior one. A wide range of reasons was offered for this. The actual set-up and organization of football at the college itself was highlighted by Hannah as an example of this when she noted: 'Well they [men] have got loads of teams, and we have one team of all abilities . . . it's just a different game.'

In turn, the perceived physical differences between the sexes were also cited by some as significant: 'We have not got the same power and agility. I mean we have just got the agility, but men are less afraid of jumping and dropping on the floor. I would never do that' (Rebecca).

As Rebecca was one of the most physically committed players in the team, her comment came as something of a surprise to me. Earlier in the interview Rebecca had described herself as an '[h]ard un', a characteristic by which she differentiated herself, and some of the other players, from a number of respondents commonly known amongst team members as 'the girlie ones' (see also Harris, 2004). This distinction challenges the notion of a homogenous footballing identity often put forward in stereotypical portrayals and caricatures of a female football player as 'butch' and/or masculine. These contrasting identities evidence the dynamic and changing relations within and between social groups. Many of the players expressed caution regarding some of the more physical aspects of the game. It became apparent that all of the women viewed the male game as being in a culturally exalted position and that every aspect of their own performance was inevitably judged, by themselves and others, against this marker.

Elsewhere I have suggested that, through their perceptions of their own enactment of the game, these women both colluded in and challenged the (re)production of male hegemony in football (Harris, 2001), in some ways making them complicit in the maintenance of that hegemonic position (see Connell, 1987, 2002, 2005; Connell & Messerschmidt, 2005). Through their very participation in the game these women could be viewed as challenging such hegemonic norms and values. Yet by using the male game as a model to aspire to, and by continually comparing their own enactment of the game to that of their amateur male counterparts, they may also be viewed as supporting and reinforcing traditional gender norms.

From the first couple of competitive fixtures that I went to watch, what stuck in my mind most of all was the friendly nature of the contests. As I recorded in my field notes at the time, 'I can't believe how friendly it all is – what a change from the male game. I don't ever recall a male game I have seen where I haven't heard a player swear.'

This is not to say that I did not witness the use of foul language throughout the duration of the fieldwork period. However, such occurrences were rare. The playing style adopted by the team was one that exhibited a 'clean' and fair approach to the game, devoid of many of the harsh and deceptive aspects of the contemporary male game such as 'play-acting' and cynical fouls. Patricia stated: 'No-one has ever been booked in one of our games'. In describing the differences between the male and female game, she further noted:

> Some of the blokes [male spectators] said it was a lot friendlier a game, there is no … not like rivalry. But this one guy said it is completely different to a bloke's game, as the ref [referee] is not blowing [awarding] for so much of the fouls, as our knowledge of the game is new i.e. the laws of the game, we don't know all of the rules.

In this sense it could be argued that the women were developing their own version of the game played in a particular 'style'. Yet this was not positioned, or perceived, to be in opposition to the male game. Rather, aspects of it were taken as a point of departure for many of the women in (re)positioning their own game. In stark contrast to men's football, Jane suggested that in women's football:

> If you hit [physically knock] them down some say 'Sorry'. The blokes would not do that. Like, the girls would sometimes have a chat, but we do not do that as much now. But the blokes don't do that, you know, ask the opposition how long they've been at college [laughs] do they? But girls are more friendly.

For the majority of the women in the team, football was played for fun, and the issue of competition was not always deemed to be important, although a number of players clearly possessed a more competitive attitude than the others, as the following quote from Mary highlights: 'When I am on the pitch I want to get people moving, I don't want to talk to the opposition about knitting patterns.'

So, although there were subtle (and, at times, not so subtle) differences between the women in terms of how competitive they were on the field of play, all agreed that referees tended to be far more lenient with them (as women) than those who officiated the male game. This became especially evident as regards the more technical aspects of play, such as throw-ins. Patricia stated that 'the referees allow girls to get away with more, like not throwing in properly'. Such leniency, the players suggested, was a regular occurrence. As Donna recalled:

> I mean I was telling a few of the lads [male collegiate football players] that Sonia did a handball on Monday, and it was in the penalty area, and they asked, 'Oh, was she sent off?' And, like, no-one has ever been booked in one of our games, and, like, could have been [for this offence], and I think that the referees and everyone think that there is no point, because if someone [one of the teams] lost one person [player] then that would be it – you know it wouldn't be a game.

The referee's (in)actions here could be interpreted as somewhat condescending, and may imply that female players should forego punishment as 'they are only girls' (Donna). Throughout the fieldwork, I rarely observed any of the women question a decision made by an official. On occasion I did witness an opposing player look on in disbelief at some of the decisions made. It is also worth noting that over the course of the two seasons I did not once witness a female officiate in any of the games that I observed. Over this same time period the team commissioned the services of male coaches. These illustrations of the heavily gendered nature of English football are reflected at the higher levels of the women's game where the majority of the successful club sides are coached by men.

However, the view was also expressed that this level of leniency had the potential to hinder the development of women football players. As Donna suggested:

> 'Cos I mean they [the referees] are a bit more lenient with us, and for throw-ins and stuff [laughs], a lot of people don't throw-in properly – I used to do that as well. You know, if you watch matches and stuff, I know it's professional, but if you watch (men's) matches and stuff they can throw it over half-way [length of the field], and ours like [laughs] it goes over there [laughs and points a couple of yards away].

It was also noticeable that there were quite clear differences in the playing ability of members of the team. This appeared also to be true of all the other female teams that I saw the college play against and it seemed more evident than it was in the male collegiate game. It was often the case that if a team had one outstanding player, then she was easily able to dominate the game. Never did I witness anything similar in the male game at the collegiate level where the numbers of highly skilled players seemed to be more balanced and their pending threat more easily negated. Within the context of amateur male football, it is often the case that should a particular player be controlling a game, an individual is deployed in an attempt to 'kick' [nullify the effect of] an influential player out of the game. Not once did I witness this during my observations of the women's team. Here, it seemed, was evidence of these women (re)creating identities as football players and playing the game in a somewhat different way to that which was (and is) commonly accepted.

In all cases, the male game was viewed as *the* model of how football should really be played, and the slower pace of the female game was viewed as an additional sign that they were somehow inferior to their male counterparts. This surprised me, for I had initially envisaged that the women might be critical of the male game, and that an altogether more 'feminist' outlook would be prevalent. Instead, a strong resistance to feminism emerged at various stages during the research. Largely this was delineated by the majority of respondents wanting to distance themselves from what they perceived as culturally entrenched (sexuality-based) connotations regarding lesbianism, which have historically been attached to certain forms of female sport (see Gilroy, 1989; Hargreaves, 1994), and was more of a resistance to this particular kind of inference than to any explicit understanding or articulation of feminist principles (see also Harris, 2005).

The potential for one woman to dictate the course of a collegiate game was emphasized in a conversation that I had with one of the team's male coaches after the college had lost an away match 4–3. The primary difference between the two sides, he suggested, had been that the opposition had fielded one player who had the capability of scoring goals, and was 'so good, she wouldn't have looked out of place in a men's game' (Paul). Although, within the context of this particular conversation, the coach concerned was simply trying to articulate how good a player this woman actually was, and framed his comment solely as a compliment, it is worth noting that the highest praise he could afford the player was that she could have played amongst and alongside men. It is the case that compliments like these can carry a double meaning. The view that a woman 'plays like a man' may, on the one hand, be seen as praising the football skills of the female in question. However, it may also be suggestive of the fact that since she is so good, she must somehow 'not be a woman at all'. These kinds of assumptions are further exacerbated when such displays of competence are evidenced amidst traditionally 'male' activities.

As a male with some background in football, I have played and understood the game in an environment where traditional gendered roles were clearly in place. Hence, my initial observations of women's collegiate football in England linked closely to Tracey's comments presented earlier in this chapter. As I stated in my field notes:

It reminded me of a primary school match. There seemed to be a general desire to run after the ball. I'm sure we'll see a big dirt track right up the middle of the pitch tomorrow, and barely a blade of grass moved out of place on the wings.

Going back to these notes I felt somewhat guilty about the way in which they clearly illustrated my failure to move beyond a set of preconceived ideas of what I thought football should be like, which, in turn, made me question what I was comparing the footballing style of my respondents to. As it turned out, the women themselves had similar views. Donna, one of the most experienced players on the team, noted:

I mean we bunch up a lot when we play. I think that's because we can't pass very far, and our throw-ins don't go very far, and ... everyone goes after the ball. It's like experience again, because lads have been playing football since they were little – like you – but girls have sort of only just come into it.

Extending this argument further, Sonia speculated as to the differences between the way in which male and female participants play the game and how these might be due to wider socialization processes:

[T]he actual skill and ability of those [women] taking part is not of the same standard as the men, because the men, when they go to school, they go with a football, and the boys set up their coats [as goalposts] and they play from the age of zero. So it is built into their psyche. And then in secondary school, the boys play football, rugby ... they [the teachers] put it into boxes that girls are to do this, and the boys are to do that. So the time the women get to knock the football about is hugely less than the lads. Thus, they have had, the men's first team football will have been playing for fifteen years, whereas ladies football team, we have a total of three years. So, the skill level, the ability to get out of tackles, to move the ball around, and direction of the ball in the air is less than the men.

In addition to what Sonia says here, we must not lose sight of the fact that young women have historically been less encouraged than boys to develop their motor skills in childhood (see Hargreaves, 1994). It has been argued elsewhere that young women in England are still consciously steered away from football (see also Harris, 2002; Renold, 1997). These findings suggest that this had similarly been the case for the majority of my own respondents.

Gendered identities off the pitch

Away from the field of play, differences between male and female football players also seem representative of the location of football within the wider culture and its status as a highly masculinized game. Lorna suggested that there is 'an ego factor present in male football'. Such a suggestion may be traced to early childhood experiences of physical activity, where male competence in sport (and specifically, in the UK, in football) often constitutes the focal point of individual identity (see Mac an Ghaill, 1994; Parker, 1996; Renold, 1997; Swain, 2000, 2006). Of course, the influence of sporting competence as a marker of identity should not be seen to be confined to childhood. To borrow Messner's (1988, p. 202) description of American Football, it could be that 'football's primary ideological salience lies in its ability, in the face of women's challenges to male dominance, to symbolically link men of diverse ages and socio-economic backgrounds'. Lorna did not think that females achieved any sort of status through playing football nor that the sport itself had a particularly significant meaning to many women: 'I don't think it's the same in women's football. I've never turned round to any of the girls to say: "I'm better than you are"'.

This view is also supported by Tracey's thoughts on how male professional football players behave off the field of play. She talked of a friend who went out with a football player from an English professional league club. Despite not being a particularly successful player, the very fact that he was a professional footballer was, she felt, something that many women found attractive: in her words, 'a kind of status thing' (see also, Clayton & Harris, 2004; Parker, 2001). As a consequence of the masculine 'status' attached to the English professional game, Tracey's opinion was that such players 'think they can get anyone don't they?' Indeed, autobiographical accounts of professional footballing life frequently demonstrate that this is the case, with such attitudes also being highlighted by player and ex-player recollections of off-field activities (see, for example, Dunphy, 1976; Best, 1990). Parker's (2001) study provides evidence of a similar environment in the professional ranks in more recent times and Clayton's (2005) work on the collegiate game highlights an environment where everyday discourse centres largely around academic study, the consumption of alcohol and the (somewhat obligatory) pursuit of women (see also Clayton & Humberstone, 2006).

However, Tracey did not feel that the same principle applied to female players (even those associated with one of the prestigious English women's league teams) as, in her view, most men would not recognize either the players concerned or the name of the team for which they played. Tracey also suggested that if a woman introduced herself as a female football player, 'most blokes would probably think she was a lesbian anyway' (see especially Caudwell, 2002; Cox & Thompson, 2000; Harris, 2005). Again, this points to the strong link between 'masculinity' and sport, particularly within organized team games. This stands in stark contrast to the relationship between sporting prowess (especially in 'male' sports) and femininity, which is still often perceived as oppositional, contradictory and rarely achievable (see Choi, 2000; Harris & Clayton, 2002; Vincent, 2004).

Despite the tensions evident in the views of respondents with regard to the gendered nature of English football, the women generally spoke positively about the male players at the college. They respected them as football players and in some cases articulated an admiration for the speed and power of the male game. A number of the male collegiate players applauded the fact that these women were prepared to play the game at all. During informal conversation, two first-team (male) players told me how surprised they were at the ability of some of the women. One of them, Robert, said: 'Of course, you've got some who haven't got a clue, but others, I mean they are like, you know, they are not bad players. I think if they had a bit more practice they could really be quite good.'

Amidst their taken-for-granted assumptions concerning biological sex and sporting competence, others argued that any member of the women's team 'could never be that good at football' because they were girls (Pete). This evidences the fact that although both femininity and masculinity are socially constructed, they are often mistakenly associated with innate abilities. By challenging traditional conceptions of femininity, which in this case refers not so much to playing football but to ascending towards a certain level of competence, a woman may render the whole notion of her femininity as problematic.

At the college a sense of mutual respect between both groups of players was, on the whole, apparent. The women aspired to be as good as the men, and some of the men admired the fact that the women would 'give it [football] a go' (Steve). Furthermore, some of the male players admitted that the women were 'not as bad as' they might have initially presumed. However, the views expressed by a number of male students in various informal (primarily social) settings (i.e. the student bar) displayed negative connotations regarding the sexual orientation of members of the women's team, and the suggestion that all female football players were necessarily lesbians (see also Clayton, 2005).

There was also positive support for women's football from other men. I had noticed early on in the fieldwork that when women's matches were being played at the same time as other games, there were more spectators (mostly male) watching the women's games than there were watching any of the men's. Three of my respondents believed that a number of male spectators came to watch because of the 'novelty value of it all'. As I observed and conversed on the sidelines with various spectators, it was apparent that some men had come to watch the game because they were dating one of the female players (or were hoping to be doing so soon). Of course, this represents a reversal of the way in which professional football is often portrayed at the popular cultural level where celebrity male figures play the game while their wives or girlfriends watch and are depicted as fulfilling a largely supportive role (Clayton & Harris, 2004).

As for the female players themselves, some suggested that one of the main reactions which they had encountered when people first found out that they played football was that of complete surprise. This did not relate so much to the fact that the women played this particular sport but more that they did not 'look like' people who would do so. As one respondent commented, 'A lot of people can't see why I play football as I wear glasses and have long hair, like [they say] "*You* play football?" I mean, they know I am sporty, but they can't see with my stance and physique that I would play football.' Tracey also experienced similar reactions: 'That's the thing though with women's football ... people are really shocked when I say I play.'

As one of the most 'feminine-looking' players on the team (certainly in relation to conventional images of femininity), Tracey differed markedly from the negative stereotypical image often presented of sportswomen (see Hargreaves, 1994). From my two years 'in the field', I noticed that the perceived attractiveness of certain women did much to legitimize their status as football players (to both males and females) and their 'acceptance' into the wider footballing culture within the institution. Although this cannot be stated with any certainty, it seemed that if a female football player showed that she was still 'feminine', then this meant that she was more readily accepted as a football player by men. Beyond this, many of the women football players themselves also highlighted that the maintenance of their femininity was an important factor in their own identity construction and the promotion of the game as an 'appropriate' activity for females (see Harris, 2004).

Exploiting the attractiveness of female athletes to market sport is nothing new (see, for example, Hargreaves, 1994; Harris & Clayton, 2002; Vincent, 2004). However, in team sports there continues to be an imagined association between participation and perceived sexual deviance and/or unattractiveness (Gilroy, 1989; Cox & Thompson, 2000; Harris, 2005). In attempting to reinvent hockey as a vibrant and 'sexy' activity, the English Hockey Association (EHA) used a picture of one of its younger players in a black dress under the caption '8.30 p.m. my place' to promote a forthcoming fixture. Monica Pickersgill, the then president of the EHA, said that the Association wanted to show that 'normal, sexy, boy-interested girls play hockey and you don't have to look like a horse' (Midgely, 1998). The Football Association have also more recently attempted to develop women's football under the slogan 'A more beautiful game' (Football Association, 2005). Certainly, further research is needed to explore the role of the governing bodies in 'sexing' their sport and examining the ways in which social identities are (re)constructed in sport governance initiatives.

There were, of course, others at the college who found the whole notion of women playing football quite humorous, and voiced this opinion at matches. These individuals, however, were in the minority and, in some ways, many of the women football players accepted (and indeed expected) this. As Sonia perceptively recognized, 'A few of the lads snigger, but I think that if the lads were playing netball, you would get the same snigger.'

Mary noted that 'some do take the Mick [tease and mock], but they soon stop with a fist in their mouth', highlighting how she would not be frightened to threaten anyone who made fun of the sport. Here again is an example of different players perceiving, and understanding, their participation in and enactment of football in diverse ways. Some players simply accepted, that their participation would be frowned upon and made fun of, while others, like Mary, were less tolerant.

Talking football: (re)creating identities

Discourses surrounding women's football at the college necessarily impacted upon governance structures as well as participation. For example, one of my respondents talked about her role as 'chairman' of the Women's Football Club and I asked her why she used the term 'chairman' as opposed to 'chairperson'. When first deciding to undertake the research I suspected that female football players themselves would adopt a broadly 'feminist' outlook. I was very much mistaken as the following extract shows:

Donna: I mean if you asked some of the girls to run the line, to be linesman, a lot of them wouldn't know which way to point the flag.
JH: Linesman?
Donna: Oh, linesman, yeah. But that's just, you know, you've got to have a chairperson now instead of chairman [laughs]. We have a chairman for our club, it's not a chairperson.
JH: OK, but why did you say linesman for a woman?
Donna: 'Cos that's what they are, just 'cos you say linesman it hasn't got to be a man – well that's the way I see it. I don't see why people have to change 'man' just to be politically correct, 'cos people know what it means anyway.

Patricia also reflected upon the discourse used by the officers of the club and noted: 'That is quite funny, 'cos ... when you go to pick a chairman that is just what they called it, like in a game you shout 'man on', you can't say 'woman on' [laughs]. It takes too long to say [laughs].'

The above comments are indicative of my respondents' dismissal of issues relating to 'political correctness'. All considered the heavily gendered terminology that they used as unproblematic. This may also be interpreted as a further sign of the way in which group practice upheld the stereotypical ideals surrounding male football as *the* cultural model to which they should aspire. More than this, it seemed that the female players were attempting to avoid anything even vaguely associated with feminist approaches or perspectives. As highlighted earlier, their views were not based upon a considered rejection of feminism but more in accordance with a perceived lifestyle and ideology that they imagined to have an implicit link to sexual orientation (see especially Harris, 2005).

Concluding remarks: social identities and the place of women's football in contemporary society

The findings of this research demonstrate how important male football might be to the furthering and development of the female game. Hargreaves (1994) has noted how women's sport may struggle to flourish when it is developed and administered within the context of predominantly male organizations. Within the social setting featured here the exalted position of male football, and the identities of male football players (both in terms of their access to facilities and resources and in relation to how they were perceived by the female football players themselves) provides a visible signifier of the perceived maleness of the game in contemporary English society. By locating their own enactment of football against the backdrop of the male game (both amateur and professional), the women seemed constantly to be trying to legitimize their involvement in football and to provide a suitable point of reference for their own sporting development. In shaping their footballing identities in this way, these women were enmeshed in well-established (and heavily masculinized) power structures that are common to both football and to the wider sporting world. However, what this study also highlights is the complex inter-relationship between traditional binaries of gender and the way(s) in which individuals are able to create new identities within any given social structure.

The great future predicted for women's football in England has yet to materialize. Indeed, the Football Association's (2001) stated aim of having an English professional women's league in place for the start of the 2003/04 season failed to come to fruition, and, perhaps more significantly, in recent years many English professional clubs have withdrawn their funding of women's teams. In 1995, the head of the Fédération Internationale de Football Association (FIFA), Sepp Blatter, claimed that 'the future of football is feminine' but, more than a decade on, such a view looks decidedly quixotic. Even in the USA, one of the leading and most progressive nations in terms of women's football, a much-heralded professional women's league fell into financial difficulty and closed within three years of its inception (see Southall, Nagel & LeGrande, 2005).

Of course, the women whose views and experiences are presented in this chapter are from one particular club and are not necessarily representative of all female collegiate football players in England. Indeed, given the dynamic and shifting nature of identities it may well be that women now playing in the same institution have very different experiences to those featured here. Nevertheless, this account demonstrates the way(s) in which identities may be shaped and constructed in a specific social setting. Through their many references to the male game of football, the women highlight how difference and sameness is implicated in the marking of gendered boundaries and also how boundaries may be redrawn in the identity making process.

Note

1. The terms English, British and the UK are often used interchangeably in much research on sport, with little consideration of the differences between them. The findings presented in this chapter relate to women's football in England although some of the quotes presented from published works may use the term 'Britain'. Sometimes this may refer to football in Scotland and Wales as well but many times the real focus is on the English game.

References

Best, G. (1990) *The Good, The Bad, and The Bubbly*. London: Simon & Schuster.
Butler, J. (1990) *Gender Trouble: Feminism and the Subversion of Identity*. London: Routledge.
Butler, J. (1993) *Bodies that Matter*. London: Routledge.
Cashmore, E. (2004) *Beckham* (2nd edn). Cambridge: Polity.
Cashmore, E. & Parker, A. (2003) 'One David Beckham ...? Celebrity, masculinity and the soccerati', *Sociology of Sport Journal*, 20, 214–232.
Castells, M. (1997) *The Power of Identity*. Oxford: Blackwell.
Caudwell, J. (2002) 'Women's experiences of sexuality within football contexts: A particular and located footballing epistemology', *Football Studies*, 5, 24–45.
Choi, P. (2000) *Femininity and the Physically Active Woman*. London: Routledge.
Clayton, B. (2005) Tales from the pitch: An ethnography of male collegiate football masculinities. Unpublished Ph.D. thesis, BCUC, Brunel University.
Clayton, B. & Harris, J. (2004) 'Footballers' wives: The role of the soccer player's partner in the construction of idealised masculinity, *Soccer and Society*, 5, 317–335.
Clayton, B. & Humberstone, B. (2006) 'Men's talk: A (pro)feminist analysis of male university football players' discourse', *International Review for the Sociology of Sport*, 41 (3), 295–316.
Connell, R. (1987) *Gender and Power*. Cambridge: Polity Press.
Connell, R. (2002) *Gender*. Cambridge: Polity Press.
Connell, R. (2005) *Masculinities* (2nd edn). Cambridge: Polity Press.
Connell, R. & Messerschmidt, J. (2005) 'Hegemonic Masculinity: Rethinking the Concept', *Gender and Society*, 19, (6), 829–859.
Cox, B. & Thompson, S. (2000) 'Multiple bodies: Sportswomen, soccer and sexuality', *International Review for the Sociology of Sport*, 35, 5–20.
Critcher, C. (1991) 'Putting on the style: Aspects of recent English football', in J. Williams & S. Wagg (eds) *British Football and Social Change*. Leicester: Leicester University Press.

Davies, P. (1990) *All Played Out*. London: Heinemann.
Davies, P. (1996) *I Lost My Heart to the Belles*. London: Heinemann.
Dunphy, E. (1976) *Only a Game*. London: Kestrel Books.
Football Association (2001) *The Football Development Strategy 2001–2006*. London: Football Association.
Football Association (2005) 'Playing the game' (online). Available from http://www.thefa.com/Womens/GettingInvolved/HowToGetInvolved/Postings/2002/05/10905.htm (accessed Dec. 2007).
Gilroy, S. (1989) 'The embody-ment of power: Gender and physical activity', *Leisure Studies*, 8, 163–171.
Hall, S. (1996) 'Introduction: Who needs identity?', in S. Hall & P. du Gay (eds) *Questions of Cultural Identity*. London: Sage.
Hargreaves, J. (1994) *Sporting Females*. London: Routledge.
Hargreaves, J. (2000) *Heroines of Sport: The Politics of Difference and Identity*. London, Routledge.
Harris, J. (2001) 'Playing the man's game: Sites of resistance and incorporation in women's football', *World Leisure*, 43, 22–29.
Harris, J. (2002) 'No you can't play, you're a girl: Some primary school reflections of female football players', *The Bulletin of Physical Education*, 38, 161–178.
Harris, J. (2004) 'Still a man's game? Women footballers, personal experience and tabloid myth', in S. Wagg (ed.) *British Football and Social Exclusion*. London: Routledge.
Harris, J. (2005) 'The image problem in women's football', *Journal of Sport and Social Issues*, 29, 184–197.
Harris, J. (2006) 'Ahead of the game?', *Recreation*, May, 32–34.
Harris, J. & Clayton, B. (2002) 'Femininity, masculinity, physicality and the English tabloid press: The case of Anna Kournikova', *International Review for the Sociology of Sport*, 37, 397–413.
Lopez, S. (1997) *Women on the Ball*. London: Scarlet Press.
Mac an Ghaill, M. (1994) *The Making of Men*. Buckingham: Open University Press.
Messner, M. (1988) 'Sport and male domination: The female athlete as contested ideological terrain', *Sociology of Sport Journal*, 5, 197–211.
Midgely, C. (1998) 'Hockey sticks image jollied up', *The Times*, May 9.
Mills, C. W. (1959) *The Sociological Imagination*. Oxford: Oxford University Press.
Parker, A. (1996) 'The Construction of Masculinity within Boys' Physical Education', *Gender and Education*, 8(2), 141–57.
Parker, A. (2001) 'Soccer, servitude and subcultural identity: Football traineeship and masculine construction', *Soccer and Society*, 2, 59–80.
Renold, E. (1997) 'All they've got on their brains is football: Sport, masculinity and the gendered practices of playground relations', *Sport, Education and Society*, 2, 5–23.
Scraton, S., Caudwell, J. & Holland, S. (2005) 'Bend it like Patel: Centring race, ethnicity and gender in feminist analysis of women's football in England', *International Review for the Sociology of Sport*, 40, 71–88.
Southall, R., Nagel, M. & LeGrande, D. (2005) 'Build it and they will come? The Women's United Soccer Association: A collision of exchange theory and strategic philanthropy', *Sport Marketing Quarterly*, 14, 158–167.

Swain, J. (2000) 'The money's good, the fame's good and the girls are good: The role of playground football in the construction of young boys' masculinity in a junior school', *British Journal of Sociology of Education*, 21(1), 95–109.

Swain, J. (2006) 'The role of sport in the construction of masculinities in an English independent junior school', *Sport, Education and Society*, 11(4), 317–335.

Ussher, J. (1997) *Fantasies of Femininity: Reframing the Boundaries of Sex*. London: Penguin.

Vincent, J. (2004) 'Game, sex and match: The construction of gender in British newspaper coverage of the 2000 Wimbledon championships', *Sociology of Sport Journal*, 21, 435–456.

Williams, J. (2003) *A Game for Rough Girls? A History of Women's Football in England*. London: Routledge.

Woodward, K. (2002) *Understanding Identity*. London: Arnold.

Young, I. (1990) *Throwing Like a Girl and Other Essays in Philosophy and Social Theory*. Bloomington, IND: Indiana University Press.

5
Split between Nations: Tracking the Transnational Identity of Sydney Maree

Theresa Walton

Whereas a number of the chapters in this book explore collective identities in and through sport, this chapter looks at sport and social identities by focusing on the life of one athlete. With reference to a range of print media accounts, it considers the case of the middle-distance runner Sydney Maree, and critically assesses transnational identities in the international sports arena. McDonald & Birrell (1999) advocate focusing on a particular athlete as a site for exploring the 'complex interrelated and fluid character of power relations as they are constituted along the axes of ability, class, gender and nationality' (p. 284). Throughout the chapter I draw on the work of philosopher Anthony Appiah (2005) in examining the ethics of identity to explicate more fully the broader questions raised by Maree's particular case.

On 16 December 1838 several hundred Afrikaner migrants killed thousands of Zulus in the Battle of Blood River, thereby taking control of the South African Transvaal.[1] This was, according to many, a turning point in the country's history. These events established Afrikaner settlements outside of British jurisdiction, a framework for complicated racial divides, and minority white control, the consequences of which were to be played out in the coming centuries. Celebrated each year by Afrikaners, the day was declared a national holiday in 1910.[2] Many events commemorate the battle, including, on 15 December 1976, a major national track meet in Port Elizabeth where ironically, given the reason for the holiday, Sydney Maree, the only black participant, won a mile race that changed the course of his life when he became the first, and to date only, South African schoolboy to run this distance in under four minutes (3:57.9). Maree's performance took place during a time of transition for South Africa. Apartheid laws, which had maintained a strict racial segregation and subjugation in every aspect of life since the late 1940s, had been loosened slightly in athletics in the hope that the country would be able to re-enter international competition. Yet these changes also served to create a sense of uncertainty for Maree in terms of his identity. As he said in 1979, 'I am nothing in South Africa. I am nothing outside of it. I don't have a home, really. I am an outcast wherever I go' (Jordan, 1979, p. 16). My aim within this chapter is twofold: first, to draw attention to Maree's story through recounting his personal and sporting history; secondly, to use this example to try to explicate complicated understandings of how social identities take shape. In so doing, I focus primarily on US media representations of Maree as an example of public discourse about him. I begin with a brief discussion of identity construction. I then go on to explore Maree's place in various narratives of social identity: within the geographic space of apartheid South Africa; within the social construction of 'race' in South Africa and the United States; within the discourse of the international sporting boycott of South Africa, and Maree's peculiar position within it; and finally within the frameworks of 'American' and transnational identities. My overall objective is to explicate complicated understandings of how social identities take shape, and to draw attention to Maree's story by recounting his personal and sporting history.

Philosophies of identities

In modern conceptions of identity, scholars have considered the tensions between individual agency and cultural constraints. While some academics favour a focus on agency and resistance, most concentrate on the ways in which we are each individually constrained by the economic, political and ideological systems within which we are embedded. Significantly, when we consider the way in which people navigate their identities, the particular circumstances of any one individual are uniquely multifaceted. In other words, within the social and cultural constraints into which we are born, it can be argued, in one sense or another, that we make specific choices about our lives and the pathways that they follow. Of course, there is no agreement, theoretically or practically, about the extent to which we are subjective agents of our stories. Appiah (2005, p. 22) writes that 'we should acknowledge how much our personal histories, the stories we tell of where we have been and where we are going, are constructed, like novels and movies, short stories and folktales, within narrative conventions'. Embedded in those narrative conventions are ideas of collective identities which provide frameworks for understanding individual identities. Importantly, some might see such conventions as constraints or limits, while others might see them simply as parameters (Appiah, 2005). In other words, parameters denote the edge of an identity, but not as a limit on individual freedom. However, such boundaries are always already limiting, in terms of both inclusion and exclusion. As Appiah (2005, p. 112) argues,

> The limit parameter distinction helps us see why 'identity' has become a locus of warring political institutions. Black, woman, gay, aboriginal – so many of the identity categories that are politically salient are precisely ones that have functioned as limits, the result of the attitudes and acts of hostile or contemptuous others. Each of these categories has served as an instrument of subordination, as a constraint upon autonomy, as, indeed, a proxy for misfortune.

Moreover, Appiah (2005, p. 112) argues, 'Some identities were *created* as part of a classificatory system for oppression', a statement which could be aptly applied to Maree's blackness within the political legal system of racial apartheid in South Africa, or anti-immigrant rhetoric within the United States.

Yet this debate over limits and parameters with regard to identity is not only pertinent for explicating Maree's individual identity, it is also important in understanding the social construction of identities themselves. Thus, Appiah (2005, p. 21) explains:

> We are all members of broader collectivities. To say that *collective* identities – that is, the collective dimensions of our individual identities – are responses to something outside ourselves is to say that they are products of histories, and our engagement with them invokes capacities that are not under our control. Yet they are social not just because they involve others, but because they are constituted in part by socially transmitted conceptions of how a person of that identity properly behaves.

So, Maree's geographically, historically and culturally migrating placement as: a black South African; a stateless expatriate; a 'South-African-born US citizen' and a world-class runner, has collective dimensions which play out in particular ways in his media-constructed and self-constructed identities.

Migration itself is central to modern track and field competition, and therefore to the identities of runners. As Bale (2004, p. 132) has noted,

> The migratory movements that runners may experience range from local to global. Such a range of geographical scales is central to the hierarchal nature of sports organization. A runner starts a career by representing a school or club against other schools or clubs. As a runner's career progresses, he or she may become good enough to represent the country, state or nation.

The traditional career high point, representing one's nation, became the main source of contention in Maree's national and athletic identities. Bale (2004, p. 140) notes, with regard to national identity, 'sources of identity have increasingly included the region, the local, multiculturalism and fundamentalism. Sport is another cultural form that has been claimed to build group identity, as discussed in connection with patriotism and topophilia.' Yet, just as sport and sporting figures bring people together, such processes exclude others, such as Maree as a South African. Likewise, individuals who come to represent a nation – such as Olympic athletes – are not always accepted as representative of national identity, as was the case with Maree in the US. Even Bale seems uncertain of exactly how these processes work. As he notes,

> Although the vast majority of those who represent their countries in such events continue to be citizens of that state from birth, there is today an increasing and not insignificant minority who seem to have little, if any, commitment or relation to the nation they superficially *appear* to represent. (2004, p. 140; emphasis added)

History, however, shows that running, at least since its modern inception, has always been globally integrated. For example, athletes born of other nations have represented the United States in the Olympic Games. From Irish-born US citizens in the 1896 Athens Games to Russian-born swimmer Lenny Krayzelburg at the 2000 Sydney Games, part of US national identity is the story of the 'great American melting pot' immigrant nation (Dyreson, 2003). Similarly, as Jarvie (1993, p. 72) reminds us, 'multiculturalism is embedded in virtually all states and any claims that people have to a single culture or a single identity becomes almost impossible to maintain'. In sum, then, just as sport is globally integrated, so too are the nations for which athletes compete.

Appiah (2005, p. 181) states that, 'insofar as identities can be characterized as having both normative and factual aspects, both can offend against reason: an identity's basic norms might be in conflict with one another; its constitutive factual claims might be in conflict with the truth'. Such is the case with systematic identification based on 'race' which we can clearly see as culturally created and, in the cases of South Africa and the United States, often arbitrarily determined on an individual basis. Yet that is not to say that the effects of such irrational identity are not real in terms of their impact upon both individual and collective identities. As Appiah (2005, p. 139) reminds us, 'cultural norms are, after all, constituted not only by what they affirm and revere, but also by what they exclude, reject, scorn, despise, ridicule'. Appiah (2005, p. 137) also argues that having a shared history 'cannot be a *criterion* for being members of the same group, for we need something by which to identify the group in order to identify *its* history; and that something cannot, on pain of circularity, be the history of the group'. Thus, while sporting narratives may contribute to ideas of national identity, it is a process rather than an end point, as there is constant negotiation, with competing narratives of which people and which sports are included as well as what meaning to make of them in relation to national identity. Jarvie (2003, p. 541) argues that we must acknowledge that 'the nation is a process that is neither fixed nor immutable'.

In terms of national identity, in particular, we must acknowledge both Anderson's (1983) conception of the 'imagined community' and also how powerful the human imagination can be. Appiah (2005, p. 245) cautions that if nationals are connected, it is through 'language, law, and literature' as well as shared events 'not in propria persona, but through their shared exposure to narrations of those events: in folktale and novel and movie, in newspapers and magazines, on radio and television, in the national histories taught in modern national schools'. As Jarvie (1993, pp. 74-75) notes, 'Sport itself often provides a uniquely effective medium for inculcating national feelings ... It is as if the imagined community or nation becomes more real on the terraces or the athletics track.' Sporting narratives, then, which remind 'us' of 'our' past through the stories of particular athletes or events, are not merely descriptive of who 'we' are, but are constitutive as well. Thus, Appiah (2005, p. 239) notes, it is 'important to remember how abstract a thing the nation really is'.

Furthermore, in this context of the limits and parameters of identity, it is clear that we do not have complete control over our choices and we are further constrained by our capacities, both in embodiment and in development. For Maree, the limits and parameters of his choices were tied to his physical ability, his sport, his nation of origin and his adopted country (not to mention such issues as 'race', gender, sexuality and religion in each of those contexts). Thus, to understand Maree's individual identity, as a South African, without the rights of South African citizenship, and the choices he made with regard to his athletic career, his education and later his US citizenship, requires some explanatory discussion of the land from where he came.

Geography, placement and identity: South Africa

Born on 9 September 1956, the eldest of five children, Sydney Maree spent his first seven years in Cullinan, where both his mother's (the Marees) and father's (the Mutules) extended family owned and farmed land. As part of the apartheid government policy to remove 'black spots' of settlement from desirable land (Beck, 2000; Kunene, 1979; Thompson, 2000), Maree's family was forcefully removed to Hammanskrall in the early 1960s. After a few years there, Maree grew up in Atteridgeville, a black township outside of Pretoria. His running career started at Vlokfontein Technical High School in Mamelodi, which was part of a movement towards semi-skilled training for blacks across South Africa (Mathabane, 1998; Thompson, 2000). The groundwork for Maree's success later in the US was laid in South Africa, and media accounts highlight the hard work he put in as a young runner and student. He earned high grades in his academic work, despite running 45 minutes each morning and then the two miles to catch the train for school, followed by training with his coach, James Makoka, back in Atteridgeville (Smith, 1983).

His first sub-four-minute mile came just six months after the Soweto riots, when black students protested the 1974 Afrikaans Medium Decree, which mandated that black schools should teach in the language of the oppressors: Afrikaans. On 16 June 1976 a rally turned violent and police fired upon the student protestors, killing hundreds. This began a year of particular unrest, violence and fear in South Africa, which witnessed severe disruption to the country's education system. After the Soweto riots Maree's already difficult life became even more troubled – he could no longer run as and when he wished, for example, because he feared for his safety. As *Sports Illustrated* writer Gary Smith (1983, p. 65) notes, 'Maree sank back onto the couch. He couldn't run now, not when a streak of black flesh through the gray of the predawn could draw fangs or bullets, and so he waited.'

The cultural construction of 'racial' identities

The apartheid laws in place from 1948 to 1994 in South Africa were based on complicated racial designations around four key categories: (i) 'African' for blacks, which included all indigenous ethnicities; (ii) 'coloured' for those of 'mixed' racial heritage;[3] (iii) 'Indian,' for those of Asian descent;[4] and (iv) 'whites', which included Afrikaners, primarily of Dutch descent, and English speakers of Anglo descent.[5] While nearly 80 per cent of South Africans are 'black', the 'white' minority have traditionally controlled the government and fiscal resources.[6]

During the years of apartheid, laws kept black people from voting and owning land in many parts of the country, regardless of economic success. Apartheid laws also forced black South Africans to carry identity cards or 'passes', limiting where they could travel and live in their own country. Blacks travelling without their 'passes' were regularly rounded up and arrested. As historian Douglas Booth (1998, p. 128) has noted, 'between 1980 and 1984 nearly one million Africans were arrested for pass offenses'. This happened to Maree on two occasions but the arbitrary enforcement of the law and the privileges of being a well-known athlete meant that he was recognized and released on both occasions (Burfoot, 1986; Smith, 1983).

Apartheid laws established separate and below-par facilities and resources for non-whites (i.e. in education, health and sport), and limited opportunities for work (Thompson, 2000). Like the majority of black South African families, Maree's was systematically fragmented by apartheid laws and oppression. Maree's father, Ambition Mutule, who was involved in the Pan African Congress resistance movement, left the family when Maree was an infant. He was later arrested and sent to prison on Robben Island. Sometimes individuals could live in white areas as employees, as was the case with Maree's mother, but they could not bring their families with them. As a child, Maree stayed with his extended family in Cullinan and Hammanskraal, seeing his mother only once a month for a day until he was 11 years old, when he went to live with her in Atteridgeville (Smith, 1983). It could be argued that these separations had an influential effect on Maree's individual identity. Though Maree was officially categorized as 'coloured', one writer described him as 'a deep polished ebony' and recounted how other black boys taunted him with '*Montsho! Montsho!*', a Sotho word meaning 'black boy' (Smith, 1983, p. 70).

Maree's coach, James Makoka, remarked, 'He had been training so hard because he thought whites were superior' (Smith, 1983, p. 72). South

African medical student and activist Steve Biko (Arnold, 1978 p. xix) said about the process of racial oppression,'The most potent weapon in the hands of the oppressor is the mind of the oppressed.' Labels of identification, then, are not simple reflections of our lived identity, but are rather constitutive of them. Appiah (2005, p. 66) points out that 'once labels are applied to people, ideas about people who fit the label come to have social and psychological effects. In particular, these ideas shape the ways people conceive of themselves and their projects.'

Such events and circumstances clearly have the potential to influence individual identity. As Maree stated in 1983,

> Subconsciously, I have a mission. When I started doing well, I started wondering why black people in South Africa are limited. Why we couldn't train at the same facilities, why we couldn't use the same bathrooms, why we couldn't sit in the same restaurants. I said, 'Does it mean we are inferior?' I wanted to prove, no; given an opportunity, we can excel. (in Leavy, 1983, p. D1)

Maree also argued that his experiences at Villanova University taught him 'that white men are just as human as I am, they work as hard as I do. Before that, I thought God had given them all the good things in life' (in Leavy, 1983, p. D1). In 1992 he recounted,

> At Villanova, where 97% of the students are white, I shared a dormitory with a white student – the closest I had ever been to a white man. I used to lie awake, just watching him breathing, to see if he was different. (in Gillon, 1992, p. 25)

Indeed, Maree indicated many times in media accounts that he hoped, through his running and academic success, to influence both blacks and whites to think differently about people of colour. In this sense, one might argue that Maree provided a ray of hope for black South Africans within apartheid. As one of Smith's (1983, p. 70) respondents declared:

> I feel I'm on the path of Sydney Maree. Since I too go to Vlakfontein Technical High School. Every time I run I think, 'What would Sydney Maree be thinking now?' Before I go to sleep I read articles about him. We blacks in South Africa lack persistence and determination. We say, 'Oh, we are beaten.' Sydney Maree doesn't know when he's beaten. And the teachers here keep telling us he was just a kid like us.

Appiah (2005, p. 65) is careful to remind us that identities 'are brought into being by the creation of labels for them'. Tellingly, in these accounts, Maree's success lay not in 'natural' ability, but in determination. Yet even this aspect of his life was understood in racial terms within this time period. As the athletic director of Maree's high school, Friedemann Stut, stated, 'It was discipline that made Sydney Maree. I think I know where he got it. There was white blood in his family, you know' (in Smith, 1983, p. 73). This contrasts sharply with the rising claim of the 'natural black athlete' within the US context which shows the arbitrary designation of 'racial' differences (Miller, 1998). In this connection, Appiah (2005, p. 23) argues persuasively that

> The main reason why personal dimensions are different is that they are not dependent on labeling: while intelligence, in our society, is of the first social importance, people could be intelligent even if no one had the concept. To say that race is socially constructed, that an African American is a 'kind of person' is, in part, to say that there are not African Americans independent of social practices associated with the racial label; by contrast, there could certainly be clever people even if we did not have the concept of cleverness.

Thus, when a 'black' schoolboy at Vlakfontein characterizes how 'we' are, then, consciously or subconsciously, he is reinforcing the social categories of 'race'.

Apartheid: the sporting boycotts

Even though apartheid laws were put in place in the late 1940s, it was not until 1964 that the International Olympic Committee banned South Africa from Olympic competition and all qualifying competitions. The 1970s marked the beginning of the time period when the global community voiced more consistent condemnation of apartheid, and sporting boycotts represented one response to this. Protests included refusing to schedule matches, cancelling contests rather than allowing the exclusion of non-white team members, and anti-apartheid demonstrations in countries where South African teams were allowed to play (see Booth, 1998; Jarvie, 1985).

The main issue for the sporting community was the apartheid practised in sport selection, which meant that only whites represented South Africa. In the 1970s South African Prime Minister Pieter Botha began to eliminate 'petty discrimination' and thereby 'partly deracialized the state and dismantled overtly racial policies' but came nowhere near outlawing apartheid (Booth, 1998, p. 128). Some sports organizing bodies, including those concerning track and field athletics, saw this as an opportunity to offer integrated, or 'non-racial', athletics competitions and team selections, wherein participants would be chosen purely on merit. As in the case of Maree, these opportunities for black athletes were extremely limited, and many anti-apartheid protestors, including the South African Non-Racial Olympic Committee (SANROC), believed that these small concessions represented a form of tokenism rather than a genuine attempt to implement strategies for equal opportunities (Booth, 1998).

Some journalists advocated that sport should not be used as an instrument of pressure against South Africa because it was outside the scope of political debate. Yet, as the South African Council on Sport (SACOS) argued, there could be no 'normal' sport in an 'abnormal' society (Booth, 1998). Thus, the global community was asked to consider not only whether South Africa practised apartheid in sport, but how the general oppression of blacks under apartheid made equal opportunity in sport virtually impossible. Sydney Maree's case illustrates that simply having enough access to food to stave off malnutrition was a major concern for most black South Africans at this time. In describing the area where Maree trained as a schoolboy, Smith (1983, p. 67) writes that he ran

past the sign that read THIS GROUND IS DANGEROUS, CONTAINING UNEXPLODED BOMBS, SHELLS AND CARTRIDGES ... the sign standing in the middle of a pathetic corn field because the slow death of hunger terrifies more than the quick death of the trampled shell.

In 1976, the same year as Maree's first sub-four-minute mile, the International Amateur Athletics Federation (IAAF), the world governing body for track and field, finally banned all South African athletes from international competition more than a decade after the IOC had done so. In response, athletics within South Africa began to open up possibilities for non-whites to compete in order that they might gain re-admittance into international events. This provided a small window of opportunity that benefited only a few black and 'coloured' athletes, including Maree.

Yet Maree and others also faced being excluded by the boycotts by virtue of their South African birth. Indeed, because of the IAAF ban on South African athletes, Maree often could not run in international competitions – even if wearing his Villanova (American university) colours. As Jane Leavy (1983, p. D1) notes,

> Maree was taken captive by the irony of the regulation. Time after time, he came to the starting line only to be turned away. To be refused the chance to run was to deny him the chance to be himself, to continue his mission. 'In South Africa, I was punished for being black', he said. 'In the United States, I was punished for being South African.' He took his case to the press and told [coach, Jack] Pyrah he was going to quit but didn't. 'It built me and it broke me but it built me more than it broke me', he said.

Maree's place within this overall scenario (i.e. as a black South African) clearly brought into focus the complicated tensions of his own identity – in terms of nationality, athletics and 'race'. In 1977, at their London summit, the Commonwealth representatives adopted what became known as the Gleneagles Agreement, which condemned apartheid and established a formal boycott of South African athletics participation with Commonwealth countries. The agreement also went one step further by imposing a boycott extension on participants who engaged in 'major sport' with South Africa (Payne, 1991). This put in place another reason for athletes to refuse to race against Maree, ostensibly fearing sanctions by their own national sport governing bodies, the IOC or, in the case of running, the IAAF. However, when Maree was allowed to compete none of these governing bodies responded, indicating a certain sympathy for his 'in-between' status: not fully South African but also not of any other state.

According to media accounts at that time, even though the boycott caused hardship for Maree himself, he believed that it was morally right and that it could also be effective in bringing change in his homeland. But he also noted repeatedly that boycotting athletics without economic sanctions would have little impact on the South African regime, stating in 1983 for example, 'It's all so hypocritical. The countries that are boycotting South Africa in sports are trading with them and feeding their people with South African food. If they had boycotted trade, I could have accepted the sports boycott, but no, they took the easy way out' (in Smith, 1983, p. 77). This allowed the global community to place symbolic importance on athletes as representatives of South Africa, while many of those same countries benefited economically from the apartheid system.

Political identities: agent of integration or political pawn?

Thompson (2000) notes that by the late 1970s a significant amount of foreign capital had been invested in South Africa, much of which was centred on US interests. Thus, the US had a direct economic stake in the apartheid system. Relations between South Africa and the US also had a series of wider implications. Some have argued, for example, that Maree, (who began a tour of the US in 1977), was used by the apartheid government as a pawn in a political game to try to show the outside world that life in South Africa was not as bad as some had portrayed and to improve its image abroad through the use of advertising, media and propaganda campaigns (Booth, 1998). The South African newspaper *The Citizen* was the prime sponsor of Maree's initial two-month trip to the US, which, in time, became a four-year period of enrolment at Villanova University and, subsequently, citizenship and a near-20-year settlement. There is clear evidence to suggest that the originally planned two months was part of a government-funded campaign to 'show the world how a black man could flower in the garden of South Africa' (Smith, 1983, p. 73). Indeed, at least a handful of black athletes were given travel visas to go to universities in the US during this time. The importance of sport for the cultural identity of South Africa becomes clear in these attempts to influence international sentiment towards apartheid policy. When Maree arrived in New York, an employee of Sydney S. Baron and Company (a public relations firm which the South African government had hired to help manage the country's international image) met him at the airport (Smith, 1983). The company had arranged for Maree to meet with a Philadelphia track club sponsor, who introduced him to coaches at Villanova.

Black South Africans who benefited from moving out of their homeland were in a difficult position. Politically, Maree faced heavy pressure to denounce apartheid, but he knew that his family would be in danger if he did so and that he would not be allowed to return to South Africa if he spoke out against the government. According to one media account, Maree 'anguished over what the consequences of his words might be for members of his family. He could not call them; they had no phone' (Smith, 1983, p. 77). For Maree, the tensions of his position were clear:

I hated apartheid. I never felt like a human being until I left South Africa. But these groups wanted me to make statements that would be heard all over the world. I felt that was not the way. I could not start a revolution, but I could mingle with white South Africans and show them what a black could do if he got the opportunity. I could go back and be an example for the blacks who have no role models. If the South African government prevented me from re-entering the country, I could achieve nothing. (in Smith, 1983, p. 77)

As this account shows, media sources focused on notions of individual prejudice and achievement rather than the systematic oppression of blacks and the economic privileges of whites within South Africa's apartheid system. Yet, while prejudice was certainly a key component of the social and cultural fabric, it was the overarching, ideological offerings of white supremacy which served to justify and rationalize the oppression of black South Africans at an everyday level.

'American' and transnational identities

Perhaps not surprisingly, given dominant sporting tropes, media accounts in the US framed Maree's story as a tale of the ultimate 'American dream'. *Track & Field News* writer Tom Jordan (1979, p. 16) stated the irony involved in this:

here is Maree, a black, being told that he may not compete in US invitational meets because of his citizenship. Yet, in many ways, because he is black, he is not a citizen of South Africa – he cannot vote, own a house, or speak freely without fear of fine or imprisonment.

Runner's World writer Amby Burfoot (1986, p. 56) later asserted, 'For too many years he [Maree] was a man without a country. A black non-person ... he had no human rights in South Africa, no athletic rights outside. He grew more frustrated, angry.' Indeed, between 1981 and 1984, as he was applying for US citizenship, Maree travelled with documents that listed him as 'stateless' (Hackett, 1984). Then again, Maree also remained outside of stories of 'American' distance running, even after he became a citizen of and twice Olympian for the United States. One reporter noted in 1988, a year in which Maree represented the US in the 5,000 m race at the Olympics, 'And as the Games approach, once again the question is being asked: Why can't the United States produce in the middle distance?' (Bloom, 1988, p. B9).

At the time of writing, Maree has still not been inducted into the USA Track and Field Hall of Fame, perhaps the only US former world-record holder to be excluded, despite his impressive running credentials, which include having held the US record for the 1,500 m for 20 years from 1985 to 2005. At various points he was the holder of four separate US records (1,500 m, 2,000 m, 3,000 m and 5,000 m). He remains one of the top five US athletes of all time at each of those distances, even though his running career ended nearly two decades ago. He was ranked in the top ten in the world in both the 1,500 m and 5,000 m for five years between 1982 and 1989, ranked number one in the 5,000 m in the US for five years between 1986 and 1990 and ranked either number one or number two in the 1,500 m in the US for five years between 1981 and 1986. He has twice been an Olympian for the US – in 1984 and 1988 – and was placed fifth at the Seoul Olympic Games in the 5,000 m. Yet he remains outside of recent narratives of US running successes at that time. As Walton & Butryn (2006, p. 19) write, 'Notably, both the popular and running press "symbolically annihilate" (Gerbner, 1972) Maree in discussions concerning the future of US distance running'. And in fact, not one media representation among hundreds asks who will be the 'next Maree.'

Importantly in terms of the present discussion, Jackie Hogan (2003, p. 100) notes:

> Nations are more than geopolitical entities; they are discursive constructs – constructions of the character, the culture, and the historical trajectory of a people. Such constructions, by their very nature, are acts of inclusion and exclusion. They symbolically delineate membership in the national 'imagined community'.

Inclusions and exclusions from such constructions constitute the parameters of community membership. Questions over Maree's *national* identity (South African or American) are troublesome to media writers, in part because national identity is not just a matter that gives shape to Maree's own life, 'it is also that ethnic and national identities fit a personal narrative into a larger narrative' (Appiah, 2005, p. 23). Put another way, we are not solely authors of our own stories as 'we write in a language we did not ourselves make. If we are authors of ourselves, it is state and society that provide us with the tools and the contexts of our authorship; we may shape ourselves, but others shape our shaping' (Appiah, 2005, p. 156).

Clearly, citizenship and belonging to an imaginary community are not the same thing (Maguire, 1993). For Maree, the mythology of *immigrant* America remains seeped in whiteness, excluding many – the melting pot is a recipe of white, primarily European, ethnicities. As Foner

(1998, p. 87) writes of the solidification of racial exclusion in early US history, 'Even as a focus on "race" helped solidify a sense of national identity among the diverse groups of European origin that made up the free population, it drew ever more tightly the lines of exclusion of America's imagined community.' Accordingly, black migrants from African countries, like Maree, do not fit within US national mythology either in terms of a white immigrant nation, or in terms of enslaved African Americans. Therefore, in Maree's transition to the USA he remained outside of the ideal tropes of immigration and of black American experience. For even though 'the usual story of immigration doesn't apply to the descendants of African slaves, who have not had the privilege of becoming "white"' (Appiah, 2005, p. 115), neither, as a 'black' man emigrating from South Africa in the 1970s, does Maree fit with familiar tropes of black Americans as descendants of slaves. Consequently, while Maree is easily understood in terms of skin colour-based racism, his story fails to sit easily within national imaginings of 'Americanness'. Thus, a figure like Maree has no place in foundational myths of the United States, particularly in discourses surrounding distance running which, like the immigrant myth of the United States, has largely been constructed as 'white' space (Walton & Butryn, 2006). Moreover, as Dennison & Markula (2005) have argued, Western media tend to 'read' black athletes from African nations through familiar tropes of famine and civil unrest, which also fits with constructions of Maree. Therefore, even though Maree held the US record for the 1,500 m for 20 years, his adopted country has fallen short of embracing him as a representative of the nation, an issue further complicated by his continued ties to South Africa.

Concluding thoughts

In some ways the story of Sydney Maree is reflective of global changes in the 1980s when, as Maguire (1993, p. 309) argues, the 'global migration of both professional and college sports personnel was a pronounced feature of sports development'. Yet the particularities of track and field, which placed most prominence on international competitions such as the Olympic Games, where athletes represented their nations, and the ban on South African athletes, put Maree in a somewhat unique position. As a black man he was not a citizen in his native land, but the international community denied him access to competition because of his South African birth. Despite this, Maree managed to rise to the position of international competitor when he finally gained US citizenship in time for the 1984 Games. Yet, the turmoil of effectively being 'nationless' clearly came at great cost. As Maree said in 1981, 'You can't imagine what it was like all those years. Never knowing. Training for a meet but not knowing whether I'd be allowed to run. Trying to fight off one discouragement after another and keep going' (in Smith, 1981, p. B7). Such uncertainty, however, also served as a strong incentive, as Maree explained: 'When I couldn't even compete in the US, it was bad for my head. I couldn't sleep at night. In a way it broke me, but it also gave me strength to train even harder' (in Rein, 1981, p. 81).

Speaking of his time working with Maree, assistant Villanova track coach, Jack Pyrah noted, 'He sort of made a martyr of himself, but maybe he had the right to. He thought everyone was trying to use him. He came into the office one day and said, "I can't train, I can't sleep, I can't study. Maybe I should give up running" (in Smith, 1983, p. 77). Thus when *Sports Illustrated* writer Gary Smith pushed Maree to claim a national allegiance in 1983, asking, 'Do you feel like an American now, or like a South African?', Maree answered, 'I am neither' (Smith, 1983, p. 82). In 1986 he told *Runner's World* writer Amby Burfoot (p. 60), 'It's a little funny, but when I leave here [the US] I usually tell Lisa [his wife], "I'm going home." Then when I say goodbye to my mother in Atteridgeville, I tell her, "It's time for me to go back home." If you think about it, I'm fortunate to have two homes and such strong feelings about both.'

Media accounts suggest that the reason why Sydney Maree ran so far and so hard was to find a place in a world where he did not seem to belong. As Gary Smith noted, 'His documents say that he was a South African for the first 25 years of his life; by next April his passport will call him an American. Maree is searching for some deeper definition' (Smith 1983, p. 67). His running was said to fill this need: 'Maree had a hole in him that grew deeper when he didn't finish a day exhausted. "I felt I should leave my workouts crawling," he said. "I channeled all my anger into running"' (Smith, 1983, p. 71).

Maree himself acknowledged that the strength of his work ethic came from his need to gain control over his own life amidst frustrating circumstances. Neil Amdur (1983, p. B13) of the *New York Times* wrote, 'He cannot control his country's racial policies, he acknowledges, but running has become the one thing in his life that he says he can control.' Maree noted in 1983, 'So many things have happened to me that I could not control, so that whenever there was something I *could* control, I have always felt I must conquer it'(in Smith, 1983, p. 72). Thus, running was perhaps one way for Maree to attempt to author his own life, while also trying to change the narrative conventions through which his story could be told.

Clearly, Maree can be said to be neither simply an American nor a South African, but rather both and neither. He offers a resistance to normalizing tropes of the US narrative of immigration as a story of whiteness, and also to the complexities of whiteness and blackness in the extreme example of apartheid. The case of Maree opens up a complex place for what national identity means within globalization and also how that meaning changes or is erased over time. In such cases, Maguire (1993, p. 311) argues, 'the certainty underpinning notions of national cultures and identities is therefore undermined. For some migrants, an adherence to and celebration of two or more cultures and identities is possible.' Maree's case illustrates that many of the factors that drive the international movement of people – particularly out of oppressive regimes – are not necessarily a wholesale rejection of their culture/country of origin. Nor do Maree's continued feelings of connection with his homeland of South Africa mean that he is any less 'American' – even given his return to South Africa in 1994.

In asking immigrant Americans to disassociate themselves from the culture of their birth, it may well be that they are also being asked to deny something of themselves, thus pointing to differences between how identity is recognized and how identities are lived. Appiah (2005, p. 105) writes, 'we have the notion, which comes from the ethics of authenticity, that, other things being equal, people have the right to be acknowledged publicly as what they already really are'. To ask immigrants to disavow their past and to prove their allegiance to another country (i.e. the US) is to ask them to deny an aspect of themselves and, somewhat ironically, does nothing to assuage the sense of rejection proffered by the racial tropes of the country that has excluded them. Further, in this way the notion of US identity is tightly constricted and moves further away from the reality of the fluidity of human movement, particularly in 'immigrant America'.

Notes

1. In 1994, after South-Africa's first racially inclusive national elections, the former provinces and homelands were restructured, and a separate Transvaal province no longer exists. Parts of the old Transvaal now belong to the new Gauteng, North West, Limpopo and Mpumalanga provinces. The Transvaal is still used as a provincial division of the High Court of South Africa.
2. Still celebrated today, the holiday has been renamed 'Reconciliation Day' in an attempt to recognize the horror of the event for many South African ancestors.

3. In 1948 a commission was put into place to determine 'unclear' cases. Again, the arbitrary categorization of people in this way meant that some families had members from several 'racial' categories.

4. Most people included in this category were from India, but it also included some Chinese. Cultural differences clearly complicated the arbitrary 'racial' classifications of apartheid since Japanese and Taiwanese were classified as honorary whites.

5. Known as the 'rainbow' nation, South Africa includes many distinct cultures. For example, there are 11 official languages in South Africa: Afrikaans, English, Ndebele, Sotho, Swazi, Tsongo, Tswana, Venda, Xhosa, Zulu and Pedi.

6. And, as the 2001 census shows, even though apartheid officially ended in 1991, the white minority still maintains economic power. Just a few examples highlight this discrepancy: the median annual income for white males is about $12,203, while the median for black men is about $2,115; 28 per cent of black South Africans are unemployed, as opposed to only 4 per cent of whites; 87 per cent of whites have running water in their homes, compared to only 18 per cent of blacks; and while 70 per cent of whites complete high school, only 22 per cent of blacks do so.

References

Amdur, N. (1983) 'Players: Maree runs on inner strength', *New York Times*, 2 June, B13.

Anderson, B. (1983) *Imagined Communities: Reflections on the Origin and Spread of Nationalism*. London: Verso.

Appiah, K. A. (2005) *The Ethics of Identity*. Princeton, NJ: Princeton University Press.

Arnold, M. (1978) (ed.) *Steve Biko: Black Consciousness in South Africa*. New York: Random House.

Bale, J. (2004) *Running Cultures: Racing in Time and Space*. London: Routledge.

Beck, R. (2000) *The History of South Africa*. Westport, CT: Greenwood Press.

Bloom, M. (1988) 'American milers trail in race for gold', *New York Times*, 13 Sept., B9.

Booth, D. (1998) *The Race Game: Sport and Politics in South Africa*. Portland, OR: Frank Cass.

Burfoot, A. (1986) 'Home free: Sydney Maree has found his place, as a runner and a citizen, in America', *Runner's World*, July, 54–60.

Dennison, J. & Markula, P. (2005) 'The press conference as performance: Representing Haile Gebrselassie', *Sociology of Sport Journal*, 22 (3), 311–335.

Dyreson, M. (2003) 'Return to the melting pot: An old American Olympic story', *Olympika: The International Journal of Olympic Studies*, 12, 1–22.

Foner, E. (1998) 'Who is an American?', in P. Rothenberg (ed.) *Race, Class, and Gender in the United States: An Integrated Study* (4th edn). New York: St. Martin's Press.

Gerbner, G. (1972) 'Violence in television drama', in G. Comstock & E. Rubenstein (eds) *Television and Social Behaviour*. Washington DC: US Government Printing Office.

Gillon, D. (1992) 'A well that hasn't run dry for Maree', *The Herald* (Glasgow), 12 Sept., 25.

Hackett, G. (1984) 'Newsmakers', *Newsweek*, 14 May, 61.

Hogan, J. (2003) 'Staging the nation: Gendered and ethnicized discourses of national identity in Olympic opening ceremonies', *Journal of Sport and Social Issues*, 27 (2), 100–123.

Jarvie, G. (1985) *Class, Race and Sport in South Africa's Political Economy*. London: Routledge & Kegan Paul.

Jarvie, G. (1993) 'Sport, nationalism and cultural identity', in L. Allison (ed.) *The Changing Politics of Sport*. Manchester: Manchester University Press.

Jarvie, G. (2003) 'Internationalism and sport in the making of nations', *Identities: Global Studies in Culture and Power*, 10, 537–551.

Jordan, T. (1979) 'Outcast in the promised lands: Sydney Maree's unusual situation', *Track & Field News*, July, 16.

Kunene, M. (1979) 'Children of apartheid', *UNESCO Courier*, Oct., 4–11.

Leavy, J. (1983) 'Maree: The freedom runner', *Washington Post*, 14 Oct., D1.

Maguire, J. (1993). 'Globalization, sport and national identities: "The empire strikes back" ', *Leisure and Society*, 16: 293–322.

Mathabane, M. (1998) *Kaffir Boy: A True Story of a Black Youth's Coming of Age in Apartheid South Africa*. New York: Touchstone.

McDonald, M. & Birrell, S. (1999) 'Reading sport critically: A methodology for interrogating power', *Sociology of Sport Journal*, 16, 283–300.

Miller, P. (1998) 'The anatomy of scientific racism: Racialist responses to black athletic achievement', *Journal of Sport History*, 25(1), 119:151.

Payne, A. (1991) 'The international politics of the Gleneagles Agreement', *Round Table*, 1 Oct., 417–431.

Rein, R. (1981) *People*, 16 March, 77–78 & 81.

Smith, G. (1983) 'He ran, but he knew now why: Sydney Maree', *Sports Illustrated*, 18 July, 64–82.

Smith, R. (1981) 'The stepchild of apartheid', *New York Times*, 20 Nov., p. B7.

Thompson, L. (2000) *A History of South Africa* (3rd edn). New Haven, CT: Yale University Press.

Walton, T. & Butryn, T. (2006) 'Policing the race: American men's distance running and the crisis of whiteness', *Sociology of Sport Journal*, 23(1), 1–28.

6
Sport, Religion and Social Identity: Physical Education and Muslim Independent Schooling[1]

Samaya Farooq and Andrew Parker

Since 11 September 2001, stories surrounding the alleged evils of Islam have dominated Western news media. The subsequent 'war on terror' has seen the removal of Muslim governments in Afghanistan and Iraq and has resulted in mounting public suspicion about the identity of young Muslim males worldwide. Amidst all of this, key questions have arisen: How and why has a religion of peace become so closely associated with issues of hatred, destruction and violence? What might be done to stop such events happening again? How might Muslim males negotiate their identity in these highly politicized times? Against this backdrop, this chapter presents the findings of a small-scale qualitative study of identity construction amongst a group of adolescent males at a UK Muslim independent school. Exploring the interface between Islam, sport and schooling, the chapter highlights how religion provided a central mechanism through which pupils sought to negotiate their masculine identities in accordance with a series of institutional norms and expectations. In turn, physical education is posited as a means by which respondents embraced their sense of self while expressing a series of broader religious ideals.

Sport, religion and social identity

Social identities may be constructed in a variety of ways and in line with a range of social factors and forces. They are continually negotiated and renegotiated amidst the ever-changing nature of social life. Jenkins (2008) argues that spirituality can act as a channel through which individuals seek to establish their identities. The findings presented in this chapter demonstrate how Islam shaped the identities of a group of young Muslim males and how sport served as a vehicle through which these identities were physically lived out.

Islam is widely accepted as a divine ideology which was revealed to the Prophet Muhammad by God (Allah) (Ruthven, 2006). As a monotheistic religion, it is grounded on two fundamental principles: (i) the oneness of God (*Tawhid*) and (ii) the acceptance of the Prophet Muhammad as God's last and most beloved messenger (*Risalah*) (Muslim Education Trust, 1994). Literal interpretations of religious scriptures, such as the Qur'an and the *Shar'iah* (the divine law which imbues Islamic culture) are pervasive amongst Muslim communities as individuals strive to live within the guidelines set out within these sources (Mawdudi, 1989). For example, in keeping with the *Shar'iah*, Muslims often seek to dress modestly and to avoid pre-marital or extra-marital cross-gender interaction(s), and pastimes or recreations that might stimulate sexual expression between men and women (outside of wedlock). Other directives include looking after one's body, following a controlled diet, practising *Zakah* (a welfare contribution), keeping the annual fast during the month of Ramadan, and offering disciplined *Salah* (regular prayers five times a day) (al-Qaradawy, 1992).[2] Humility, respect and kindness towards others are all valued qualities within Islam and stem from its core premise of peace. Excessive individualism, selfishness, jealousy, anger and aggression are actively discouraged in line with the principle of *jihad-e-nafs*: self-control over one's negative desires and urges. Needless to say, for many Muslims, Islam is not just a faith or a religion but the central focus of their social existence.

In recent years Islam has come under increasing scrutiny as a consequence of a series of events on the broader political stage (Modood, 1990, 1997). Most notable perhaps are those of 9/11 and 7/7, and the related rise in suicide bombings and violent protests in various countries. In turn, public interest in Muslim males has increased. In the UK, for example, it is not uncommon for newspapers and other media to feature negative images of Muslim men. Certainly there exists a degree of consensus amongst social commentators that, in the aftermath of urban disturbances in a number of UK towns and cities in recent years, British Muslim males have been subject to negative media profiling, being variously labelled militant, aggressive, rebellious and fundamentalist (Dwyer *et al.*, 2008; Hopkins, 2007; Hussain & Bagguley, 2005). Academic debate concerning the alleged deviant and violent nature of young British Muslim men has also increased (see Goodey, 2001; Macey, 2002, 2007). These discourses have subsequently engendered wider conjecture as to the existence of a fundamental conflict between Western societies and the values embraced by Muslims and endorsed through Islamic teachings (Esposito, 2002; Vertovec, 2002). Likewise, speculation about the possibility of a crisis in Islam has increased, particularly in relation to the behaviour and identities of Muslim males (see Lewis, 2003). For example, Dwyer *et al.*, (2008, 117) highlight how, since the London bombings of 2005, young British Muslim males have been the targets of a 'reactive politics of fear' that necessarily delineates such men into two simple categories: 'those who support us' (those who support the West) and 'those who are against us' (terrorists, Islamists and Fundamentalists) (see also Amin, 2002; Back, Michael & Khan, 2002).[3] Amidst these descriptions, the plurality of British Muslim masculinities is largely ignored, and a male adherence to Islamic principles is over-simplistically associated with Islamic fundamentalism. With these issues in mind, it is our contention that there is a need better to understand the multiplicity of Asian masculinities amongst young British Muslim men, and more readily to recognize religion as a category of influence for identity construction.

Interest in the role and place of Islam within sport has been gathering momentum since the 1980s. This has culminated in an abundance of literature exploring the issue of Islamic teaching with regard to sports and physical activity (see Dagkas & Benn, 2006; De Knop, Theeboom, Wittock & DeMartelaer, 1996). The general consensus within this literature is the belief that Islam is an ideology that exhorts its followers to take up recreational, physical and/or competitive activities. The use of religious texts such as Qur'anic verses (*sura*) and written accounts of the Prophet Muhammad's teachings (*Hadith*) have frequently been used by some Muslims to portray Islam's positive view of sport (see Walseth & Fasting, 2003). Islamic literature, for example, stipulates that the Prophet Muhammad and the second caliph, Omar Ibn Khattab, recommended that Muslims 'teach (their) children swimming, archery and horseback riding' (al-Qaradawy, 1992, 296) as well as encouraging competitions involving physical exercise and discipline.

The juxtaposition of sport and Islamic principles regarding the physical body has also been explored. For example, the disciplined use of the body and the strict control of food and drink intake in Western sports is similar to Islam's requirement for Muslims to take care of their bodies and to monitor their health (Daiman, 1995), to acquire high levels of physical fitness and strength (Zaman, 1997) and to strive for a cleanliness and purification of the mind, the body and the soul (Mawdudi, 1989). A small number of studies have explored how physicality and the body are closely linked with Islam. Walseth & Fasting (2003), for example, have discussed how Muslims view the physical body as a God-given entity that has specific needs and that should be cared for. There are also numerous studies which locate sporting activity and exercise as an ideal means through which Muslims can fulfil the needs of their body within the precepts of Islam (Abdelrahman, 1992; al-Qaradawy, 1992).

Sport, religion and masculinity

Academic analyses of the relationship between Islam and the construction of masculinity are lacking both within and beyond the social and political sciences (Ouzgane, 2003). This is particularly evident within the sociology of sport, where it is more common to find discussions of the construction of masculinity through the relationship between Christianity and sport (Dunn & Stevenson, 1998; MacDonald & Kirk, 1999; Stevenson, 1991, 1997). A topic that occupies a pre-eminent place within this literature is that of 'muscular Christianity', an ideology which is perhaps best known for embodying the pedagogy and ideals of the Christian Socialists Charles Kingsley and Thomas Hughes (Kidd, 2006; MacAloon, 2006). Concerned about the prevalence of weak and effeminate men in Victorian society, Hughes and Kingsley merged traditional Anglicanism with a form of manliness that favoured physical and moral strength, courage and aggression above sentimentality, reflection and gentility (Tozer, 1985; Watson, Weir & Friend, 2005; Watson, 2007). Physical education and organized competitive sports were also promoted within the English public schools (Holt, 1989; Mangan, 1986; Neddam, 2004). These activities were seen as valuable social tools via which unruly boys could be transformed into disciplined Christian gentleman (Hall, 1994; Morford & McIntosh, 1993). In more recent years, of course, a plethora of work has coalesced with the notion that participating in sport immerses young men into a social institution that has its own ideology and embedded norms regarding appropriate, desirable and acceptable masculine behaviours (see, for example, Messner & Sabo, 1990).

Masculinity, sport and schooling: context and method

The present study is underpinned by a symbolic interactionist perspective of the 'self'. This approach necessarily sees the 'self' (and what individuals do) as being influenced by the social milieux in which individuals live and the expectations that such milieux hold regarding acceptable forms of identity and behaviour (Hall, 1992, 2000). Hence, in this view, identity is not solely about the 'self' but about how individuals construct themselves in accordance with broader social processes through interaction, communication and negotiation (see Jenkins, 2008; Woodward, 2002). As a specific form of identity, masculinity is situational: individuals mould the 'self' within the social, historical and political specificities of their immediate surroundings and settings. A number of researchers have identified schools as heavily gendered social institutions which facilitate the construction of particular masculinities in and through various activities, including sport (Mac an Ghaill, 1994; Martino & Pallotta-Chiarolli, 2003; Parker, 1996; Swain, 2006). Teachers are seen as active agents in this process and are believed to trigger support and guide socially acceptable forms of identity construction by controlling the gestures, movements and locations of pupils through the processes and practices of discipline, surveillance and normalization (Connell, 2005). Masculinity has come to be viewed as a social process that refers to what boys do with or to their bodies (Swain, 2003, 2006). In fact, the physical body is believed to be an integral part of self-identity (Shilling, 2005). Some researchers highlight how boys consciously locate the physical body in particular social spaces actively to develop and maintain their identities (see Frosh, Phoenix & Pattman, 2002). Likewise, sport and physical activity have, in themselves, been recognized as key sites for the construction and display of identities (Hargreaves, 2000; MacClancy, 1996; Maguire *et al.*, 2002).

The findings which follow derive from research carried out during the spring and summer (March–July) of the 2005/2006 academic (school) year at Dar-ul-Islam,[4] an all-male Islamic independent school situated in the English West Midlands. Located on the outskirts of one of the UK's most deprived urban areas, Dar-ul-Islam serves a largely Sunni Muslim clientele of predominantly Pakistani origin and, at the time of the research, had 1300 pupils aged between 11 and 23 years on roll, approximately 52 per cent of whom were residential boarders. Like many British Muslim schools, Dar-ul-Islam seeks to provide a secure and stable learning environment with a conventional Islamic ethos (Sarwar, 1994). Although the core subjects of the National Curriculum were taught during the compulsory school years (i.e. across the 11–16 age range), the post-compulsory years emphasized Islamic education. The purpose of this was to equip pupils to follow the 'path of the Right (*al-Haqq*) and the Light (*an-Nur*)' and abhor 'ignorance (*al-jahiliyyah*) and darkness (*az-zulumat*)' (Sarwar, 2001, 5). State funding was deemed neither desirable nor feasible for the maintenance of Dar-ul-Islam, since it was the freedom to prioritize an Islamic education that was celebrated by the founders of the school and those who chose to attend.[5] Annual fees were set at between £1,200 and £1,600, well below the UK average for independent schooling.[6] The empirical data presented are taken from interviews conducted with 16 British-born Pakistani Muslim males aged between 14 and 19, all of whom were boarders at the school and had attended for between three and six years. Gaining access to the school proved challenging, with both teachers and parents being concerned about the welfare of the pupils. Following various negotiations with the school hierarchy, access was granted. Letters outlining the research aims were distributed to a random sample of 50 families whose sons had been boarding at the school for more than three years.[7] Consent forms were provided with each letter. A total of 16 pupils volunteered to participate in the study. Parents expressed no further concerns.

The research utilized those methods of sociological enquiry traditionally associated with ethnography (i.e. participant observation, semi-structured interviews and documentary analysis) in order to explore the day-to-day lives of the individuals concerned. Decisions over when and where interviews took place, and which lessons could be observed, were made entirely by the headteacher. A fieldwork journal was used to record observational events and all interviews were tape-recorded and transcribed in full. Observations were carried out two to three days per week in term time. Alongside interviews with pupils, discussions also took place with a selection of the school's governors and teaching staff. In order further to enhance the data collection process (and in line with established practice with regard to respondent validation), interview transcripts were sent to all interviewees for verification and feedback (see Hammersley & Atkinson, 2007). Numerous educational studies have based their analysis on the symbolic interactionist approach (see Burgess, 1983; Woods, 1983), central to which are assumptions surrounding the potentially dynamic and creative nature of social action and the definitions which individuals attach to situations and their interactions with others. From the data analysis a series of key themes emerged relating to the way in which pupil respondents sought to construct their masculine identities and sense of self in accordance with the internal values of the school and what they saw as the predominant external (broader social) discourses surrounding Muslim men. What we present here is a discussion of the most common 'religious' identities that were evident from the data. It is not implied that these are exclusive or fixed identity types. Rather, through an exploration of the way in which these identities were constructed, we seek to demonstrate the plurality and fluidity of the various masculinities on show and frame them in accordance with three specific modes of self-identification. These comprise 'the rational self', 'the disciplined self' and 'the united self'.[8] Before considering these specific identities in more detail, we take a closer look at the internal and external factors impacting on masculine construction at Dar-ul-Islam.

Islam, schooling and masculine identity

Perhaps not surprisingly, Islamic education was the core feature of schooling at Dar-ul-Islam. Arabic lessons, Qur'anic classes and the teaching of the *Shar'iah* and *Hadith* took place every day, including weekends. The central purpose of this was to prepare pupils for life both here on Earth (*Dunya*) and thereafter (*Akirah*). An in-depth analysis of interview data revealed that religion was an important indicator of the 'self' for all respondents. By identifying as Muslims, pupils viewed Islam as a fundamental aspect of their individual identities (Nielsen, 1992). Usman, like many of his peers, expressed how he saw himself as 'Muslim before anything else in this *dunya* (world)'. Embedded within such notions was a total acceptance of the *Shar'iah* and the personal struggles to attain 'one-ness' with Allah. All pupils saw it as their duty, as devout Muslims, to follow the Qur'an and the *Sunnah* as instructive manuals for life on earth. Many held beliefs around a literal interpretation of the superior principles of the Qur'an and the *Shar'iah*, thus accepting Islamic texts and concepts such as *Tawhid*, *Risalah* and the *Akirah* as absolute truths:

Naveed: As a Muslim I...live for Allah. He is the Creator of all the universes, the most Gracious and the most merciful. I also believe that [the] Prophet Muhammad is Allah's last and most beloved messenger.

This statement highlights Dar-ul-Islam's approach to Islam, reflecting, in particular, how respondent lives were imbued with idealized discourses about the practice of Islam in very orthodox ways. Pupils were encouraged to consider religious scriptures from the Qur'an and exemplars from the *Shari'ah* and the *Hadith* when making decisions about their personal and social lives. However, a key issue to emerge during the course of the research was how participants' understandings of what it meant to be a young Muslim man were shaped by the school itself and by wider social discourse. Indeed, over time it became clear that pupils made informed decisions about themselves (i.e. about being Muslim and being male) on two distinct levels: (i) the internal level, which represented their identity within their immediate school environment, and (ii) the external level, which represented factors exterior to their everyday educational context.

Negotiating the 'self' at the internal level

The school environment was an integral part of respondent existence. It symbolized a 'second home' and, as such, provided a physical and social space in which they could fully embrace the Islamic way of life (Bilal). In fact, many said that they had chosen to attend Dar-ul-Islam simply in order to learn more about Islam. There was also a very real sense that pupils wanted to become better proponents of their faith:

> Shazad: I just wanted to become a better Muslim, I wanted to learn more about my *deen* [religion], I wanted to strengthen my *Iman* [commitment to faith]...'cos without Allah in my life, I felt like I had nothing in life, no meaning, no purpose...no direction.

Every facet of institutional life at Dar-ul-Islam was infused with Islam, from the décor in classrooms, corridors and dormitories to the volume of space designated for the public and private worship of Allah. This was also evident in the content, style and structure of lessons and in the way that pupils looked, dressed and behaved. In keeping with the precepts of Islam, a modest and simple dress code was prescribed for all pupils. This manifested itself in the form of long flowing grey robes (*thorb*), white hats and socks, and casual footwear. Elaborate designer clothing and expensive fragrances or cologne were discouraged in order to prevent feelings of jealousy or superiority amongst pupils. Those who had reached puberty were encouraged to wear a beard as this was viewed to be the most natural way for Muslim men to follow the *Sunnah* (exemplars) of the Prophet (Sarwar, 1994).

High priority was given to discipline with regard to everyday behaviour. This was intended to facilitate the moral and psychological well-being of pupils, to enhance their self-esteem, to build confidence, and to motivate them to pursue excellence in all their worldly endeavours. The headteacher, Mr Khan, spoke of the role that Dar-ul-Islam aimed to play in the lives of its pupils:

> Teaching boys how to become men of personality and character... establishing truth and goodness in their lives...(and) eradicating the temptations of Iblis (*Satan*)...is what we're all about. If the boys didn't want to become better Muslim men...they wouldn't have chosen to come here. We don't force them to attend, they choose us.

Mr Khan also believed that it was his responsibility, as headteacher, to ensure that pupils 'got what they (were) seeking', i.e. guidance in embracing Islam as a way of life by adhering to the literal teachings outlined in the Qur'an, the *Shari'ah* and the *Sunnah*. Living amidst such values and ideals meant that pupils were enveloped by religious law and culture and this, in turn, encouraged them to embrace Islam in strict orthodox ways:

Imran: Every morning we get up for *Fajr* (prayer between dawn and sunrise) and hear the *azhan* (call to prayer). The [loud] speakers are everywhere and the sound is so loud that sometimes even the walls vibrate. You have breakfast as the sun rises and all the while you think about Allah. There is a quiet satisfaction in knowing that every day you open your eyes and ears to the world, and your heart to Allah.

Implicit in Imran's statement here is that a 'God-consciousness' permeated the pupils' sense of self: 'Allah's immanence' and presence governed their every thought and action (Farooq). As Bilal explained, *deen* (faith) provided a specific medium through which participants sought to make sense of themselves and to understand their existence in the wider world. This is consistent with previous research findings which have associated spirituality with a channel through which followers can seek a particular identity (Parry *et al.*, 2007). With its emphasis on discipline and order, Dar-ul-Islam ensured that the gestures, movements and behaviours of pupils were regulated in line with institutional values and beliefs (Kirk, 1998). Strict anti-bullying policies, for example, were in place to punish those who hurt their fellow 'Muslim brothers' and the precise (and heavily policed) timetabling of classes and wider school activities ensured that elements of Islamic culture dominated both the educational and the social experiences of pupils. This was evident not only in the way that respondents were pre-occupied with the desires of Allah, but also in the rituals that they were encouraged to undertake. The following comments are illustrative in this respect:

Jameel: Living in the school we're taught how to live as Allah and the Prophet recommended. We consciously follow Islam and the Shar'iah ... We recite and interpret the Qur'an ... We learn about the *Shar'iah*, the *Sunnah* and the *Hadith* and offer our prayers on time. I couldn't achieve these things without the school environment.

When asked to explain why he felt that he could not follow Islam in this way outside of Dar-ul-Islam, Jameel talked of his everyday struggles to commit to the faith, explaining that at times when he should be praying or reading the Qu'ran, he struggled to resist watching television and simply 'having a laugh' with his friends and siblings.

Teachers were important agents in this overall process. They were the ones who, by 'always [being] there' and offering 'guidance' to pupils (Salim), ensured that individual and collective behaviour was monitored. In this way, teachers were important components in the disciplinary and regulatory regime at Dar-ul-Islam, ensuring that identities were normalized and constructed according to the belief and value structures in place. Indeed, a recurring issue which emerged from discussions with respondents was how teachers shaped pupils' understandings of what it meant to be a Muslim man. All the interviewees stated that they were taught to aspire to the Prophet Muhammad as the *Khulafah* had done[9] and to accept and revere the Prophet and His companions as setting the best example for 'mankind' to follow. Pupils talked about the 'nobility and loyalty of Hazrat Abu Bakr' (Salim), the 'justice of Hazrat Umar' (Bilal), the 'reserve and modesty of Hazrat Uthman' (Jameel), the 'bravery of Hazrat Ali' (Shazad) and the 'infallibility of the Prophet Himself' (Mohammad). Many articulated how, in their view, Muslim men should aspire to engendering such characteristics in their own lives, given that they reflected an ideal representation of Islamic masculinity. Alongside teachers, school friends and peers were identified by respondents as providing an important source of social and moral support to help individuals retain a heightened awareness of the behavioural and cultural expectations of God and Islam and, in this sense, served as inspirational role models for respondents:

> Naveed: At school you're surrounded by others who are just like you. You have your friends and companions who, as your Muslim brothers, always look out for you and make sure that you're close to your *deen* (faith).

Although it was apparent that, at the internal level, teachers and friends helped to maintain and support respondents' sense of self, what also emerged was that external factors similarly fed into identity formation. The reliance of pupils on external factors, in the negotiation and renegotiation of their identities as Muslim males, demonstrated a clear relationship not only between the self and the school but also between the self and wider society.

Negotiating the 'self' at the external level

Common during pupil discussion was concern over the ways in which the British media had portrayed Muslim males in recent times. Indeed, it would be fair to say that the role and effect of (largely) negative media discourses had significantly impacted on the personal lives of all interviewees. As Mohammed noted, there was a strong sense of awareness amongst pupils regarding the 'animosity' surrounding 'young Pakistani Muslim men living in Britain'. Moreover, there was a dominant belief that, in seemingly representing the opinions of Western society more widely, the British media was attacking the overall identity of young Muslim males, their existence in Britain and, perhaps more importantly, their 'way of life' (Ramzan). Consistent with previous research findings, participants discussed how, in their view, the media had come to portray Muslim men in an often derogatory and vilifying way (see Dwyer *et al.*, 2008; Shah, 2006; Vertovec, 2002):

> Imran: They [the British media] belittle us in every possible way . . . Everyone associates the image of a Muslim man with bushy beard and *pajri* (long-tailed turban), with the face of an Islamic fundamentalist, a terrorist or a culturally narrow-minded misogynist. It makes me so angry.

Pupils were clearly disturbed by the way in which they believed Muslim men were being portrayed in the wake of 9/11 and 7/7 (Ahmed, 2003; Esposito, 2002). This was apparent in their obvious discontent when reflecting on media reports of the turbulent cultural, political and legislative climate in the UK surrounding issues such as the profiling of Muslim males, police raids and interrogations in connection with terrorist activity, not to mention the removal 'of Muslims from planes for having beards and looking shifty' (Usman). Many pupils articulated their distress at the way in which they perceived their religion and identity to have been 'hijacked by *jahil lork* [ignorant people]' (Abdul). There was a widespread belief amongst interviewees that the brutality of 9/11 stemmed not from Islam but from 'a contradiction between the ideals' embedded in Islam and those beliefs held by 'some men claiming to follow Islam' (Mohammad). Amir expressed his own concerns at how the majority of young Muslim men lived their lives in opposition to the codified rules prescribed by the *Shar'iah*, yet still claimed to be Muslim. Ramzan too stated that, in his view, many Muslim men were caught in a 'web of confusion and sin and didn't know who they are and what they're supposed to do with their lives'. In articulating their belief that a crisis did not necessarily exist between Western societies and Islam, a number of respondents argued that the real problem for Muslim men was the inner conflict which they faced in trying to stay within the realms of Islam amidst the cultural temptations and distractions of the West:

> Mohammad: A lot of Muslim men feel they can't relate to Islam any-
> more. They're stuck between ... two parallel cultures,
> one that gives them freedom ... and the other one that
> they feel constrains them. It's a shame that what they
> see as constraining is Islam.

It became clear over time that, as young Muslim men themselves, respondents were experiencing their own sense of inner conflict when attempting to reconcile the value structures of their everyday lives with that of the broader social world (see Lewis, 2003). For Usman, this conflict was characterized by '[losing] it when people say Muslim men are violent' yet feeling 'bad' on account of this. Usman's frustration made him 'aggressive', thus confirming what 'everyone already [thought] of Muslim men'. For Usman this personal struggle (or crisis regarding his sense of 'self') was born out of 'everyone else's' discontentment with his identity, his character and his way of life. His aggression was directed towards those who violated the precepts of Islam, thereby giving 'Muslim men and Islam a bad name', and also towards the British media for portraying all Muslim men as 'radical terrorists'. This sense of conflict and crisis made it hard for Usman (and those holding similar views) to fulfil the duties of *jihad-e-nafs*.[10] The school provided a safe environment in which pupils could dress, behave, interact and exist as Muslim men. Yet where external discourses were concerned, respondents felt subject to personal attack. It was evident that, both individually and collectively, pupils were negotiating a 'self' that was more valued by themselves and the school than by the external society in which they lived. One of the central ways in which they sought further to embrace and to reinforce this sense of 'self', and to reconcile their inner conflict, was through the physical activities that they encountered in school. It is to a closer analysis of these activities that we now turn.

Identity, Islam and sport: the emergence of a valued self

Physical education (PE) and sport took high priority at Dar-ul-Islam, with PE representing the second most important subject (in terms of time allocation) in the school curriculum. Each pupil had six hours of PE per week, with an emphasis on team sports such as hockey, basketball, football (soccer) and cricket. In turn, interview discussion revealed that PE, sport and physical activity constituted the second most important aspect of respondent lives, after religious studies. All interviewees saw PE as an essential element of their school experience and as a specific time and place in their daily routine where they could apply their religious beliefs in practical ways. Adopting literal interpretations of the Qur'an and *Sunnah*, respondents argued that positively embracing physical activities and sports was important, since it was in keeping with the requests of Allah, the Prophet and the *Khulafah*. Usman, for instance, believed that his body was a 'gift from Allah' and that he was charged with the responsibility of taking care of it (see Walseth & Fasting, 2003; Zaman, 1997). Pupils utilized PE and sport as sites in which they could recreate and affirm a valued sense of 'self'. As we have seen, all respondents felt that they were under pressure to (re)negotiate the boundaries of their masculine identities in line with broader social factors. PE and sport were seen to be useful tools for achieving this. Amidst the turmoil of identity formation and the conflict which individuals experienced between the internal values of the school and external media discourses, physical activity provided a social environment in and through which the production of the ideal 'self' could be achieved.

The rational self

The ability to be more 'rational' was something that many pupils felt was integral to becoming good Muslim men, particularly those who were distressed about their persistent feelings of anger and resentment at their perceived identity. These respondents were concerned that harbouring negativity and aggression was destructive to their relationship with Allah and they wanted to resolve this. Many turned to the texts of the Qur'an and the *Hadith* for guidance on the ideal character and persona of Muslim men. Hussain, for example, referred to a *Hadith* in which the Prophet told Muslims that Allah abhorred violence, anger and aggression in human society: 'Allah calls to the home of peace and grants to *rifq* (gentleness) the many pleasures and blessings that He does not grant to *unf* (violence).' Similarly, Ali noted how he saw the Prophet's life as a practical example for 'mankind'. The majority of respondents also talked about the *Hudaibiyyah* peace treaty in which the Prophet is famously revered for accepting all the conditions of the enemy to prevent violence and mass panic in turbulent times. In fact, many respondents took this story to imply that the Prophet disliked hostility and aggression and requited evil with good intentions. This interpretation influenced respondent perceptions of the ideal character of Muslim men and had important consequences for the ways in which they viewed and utilized PE and sports.

A dominant belief which emerged both during interviews and in everyday discussion with pupils was that PE provided a neutral environment in which it was acceptable for young men to dispel negative energies and emotions (Morford & McIntosh, 1993). Referring to the cathartic effects of sport, Imran reasoned how after 'a hard game of footy [soccer] or basketball [his] mind and body [felt] refreshed'. When asked why he thought this was, Imran replied: 'Cos' in sport you can sorta get angry and be violent and by doing that you get rid of your bad feelings...your head is clearer, you're calm and at ease.' This was important to Imran because this state of being calm, peaceful and having a clearer head better enabled him to 'focus on Allah'. Similarly, Shazad and Usman discussed how their involvement in physical activity helped them to 'relax the body and mind after letting it all out' (referring here to the discharge of negative energies). Participation in sport and physical activity, therefore, constituted time spent doing good and virtuous work since it allowed for the expulsion of negative feelings, in return ensuring the replenishment of mind and body. This was reinforced in the classroom as teachers actively encouraged pupils to engage in sports in order to facilitate physical, social and mental well-being. 'Allah rewards Muslims who take care of their bodies...it is a trust from Him that we will return,' explained Shazad. For the pupils themselves these explicit endorsements of sports participation were invaluable because they helped rekindle their relationship with their faith and with Allah. In fact, many respondents reasoned that since the control of one's negative feelings was an important premise within Islamic law (as it constituted *jihad-e-nafs*), and since physical activity enabled them to do this, involvement in PE and sports was an important obligation for Muslims.

The disciplined self

Alongside the desire of some respondents to generate a sense of rationality through physical activity, a number of interviewees looked to PE and sport to help them engender a more disciplined sense of self. Bilal and Jameel, for example, identified how it was not the 'violent aspect of sport' that necessarily led them to regard it as a lifestyle priority, but the 'importance of following rules'. Jameel inadvertently made this point during a half-time break in a football game:

Jameel: The rules of sport are all about controlling yourself... controlling, disciplining your *nafs* [negative desires and urges that stem from the psyche] as opposed to letting it [the *nafs*] control you by getting angry and punching or kicking someone... this is important if we wanna be good Muslim men 'cos Allah rewards discipline.

Jameel's comments explicitly imply that sports have the potential to control and regulate the body. In particular, he viewed team sports as an important tool through which he, and others, could 'tame' or curb and control their negative tendencies as opposed to releasing them in less appropriate ways. What Jameel alludes to here is, of course, the potential of sport to immerse the body in rule-bound activity and regulate its conduct (Connell, 2005). For Jameel, sporting participation could help to restrain the physical body from exerting aggression and violence and presented alternatives to this type of conduct (such as goal-setting and learning to control one's 'inner demons', or *nafs*). According to this conception we might reasonably assume that for those respondents seeking to cultivate an altogether more 'disciplined self', a precise and strict regulation of the physical body was essential to the achievement and maintenance of their idealized masculine identities. It also highlights how the physical body was centrally located in respondent visions of the 'disciplined self'. This emerged as pupils made reference to a *Hadith* in which the Prophet states, 'a strong Muslim is better and more beloved by God than a weak one, even if both are good' (see Abdelrahman, 1992, 9). This association between 'being strong in one's faith' and engaging in physical exercise was important to this particular group of respondents simply because they identified the latter as the 'only way' in which they could achieve the former. In other words, participation in sport (or disciplined and rigorous physical exercise and training) was viewed as a practice through which boys could actively and consciously 'become' what God wanted them to be:

Jameel: Doing a sport... sorta gets you used to a routine so that eventually you become that routine... So if... we [referring to Muslim men in general] need to be strong and disciplined to show everyone that we're not savages, we have to physically and visibly show that we are everything it means to be disciplined.

Embedded in Jameel's comments here is the view that sport and physical exercise are mechanisms that can facilitate the production of a strong and muscular physical body which subsequently reaffirms the vision of a controlled and disciplined Muslim. This group of respondents believed that being muscular symbolized an image of control and discipline because it took a controlled and disciplined regime to build and construct such a body. Echoing previous research findings, these views reflect how the body can serve as a physical anchor for (socially defined) roles and behaviours (Shilling, 2003). They also portray how the physical body might act as a site of expression and appropriation for the image of a valued social self (Swain, 2006). This is because sport and physical exercise enable the social self (habits and behaviours) to become inextricably connected with visible aspects of the physical self (bodily appearance) (Shilling, 2005).

The united self

The third identity category to emerge from interview discussion, was that of the 'united self'. Respondents in this group viewed PE and sport as a mechanism by which they could embrace notions of 'unity' and cohesion. These issues were articulated by a relatively small number of interviewees who believed that there existed a crisis in Islam and that this was a consequence of Muslim men losing sight of what modern-day Islamic life should comprise. These pupils believed that a revival of Islam's most basic principles was needed to reshape the character of young Muslim men who had lost their way personally and, in so doing, had also lost their religious identity. For some of these respondents, this meant reminding Muslim men of Islam's respect for 'mercy, peace and living in unity with your neighbour regardless of [your] differences' (Mahboob). For others, it meant seeking a lifestyle where the central, if not defining, feature of Muslim masculinity was less attached to 'brutality, aggression and terrorism' and more in tune with the image of a 'kind and considerate Muslim brother' (Amir). The 'self' that these pupils advocated incorporated an identity which encouraged Muslim men to turn to 'each other for social guidance and support' (Farooq) and to 'Allah for spiritual guidance' (Amir). Such sentiments stemmed from the desire amongst this group to live in harmony with their faith, with their Muslim brothers, and with their immediate surroundings. Sports, and in particular team activities, were actively embraced for their cohesive characteristics (Carron *et al.*, 1998, 2002). Respondents identified sport as a social setting through which men could learn to turn to each other for social support and to Allah for spiritual and moral guidance. According to Farooq, this was especially possible in team sports because of the relationship between the player, the team and Allah:

> Farooq: There's a connection between you and your teams 'cos you rely on team-mates for tips and support; they rely on you because you're a part of that team, and there's a connection between you, the team and Allah.

Farooq fervently believed that this connection existed because fate rested in God's hands: 'There's only so much that you can physically do, the rest is up to Allah.' This was a recurring theme amongst those pupils who aspired to the 'united self'. The majority believed that recognizing God's control over one's fate was essential because 'it [applied] to all aspects of Muslim life'. Amir expressed how this belief was necessarily entwined with a Muslim's identity: 'Turning to Allah for guidance in times of uncertainty or struggle is a part of who you are in Islam.' The positive benefits to sport of an adherence to religion (for example instilling values such as fair play or overlooking the importance of winning) did not interest this cohort. Rather, religion was the driving force behind their identity with sport serving merely as a tool to assist that process.

Conclusions

This article has examined the production of masculine identities within the confines of an independent British Islamic boarding school. Our findings highlight how the process of making sense of the 'self' required respondents continually to negotiate the relationship between their immediate institutional lives and the wider social context. The juxtaposition of the values evident in these two different settings caused pupils to experience elements of conflict and crisis over their religious identities. This was because what respondents learned about the ideal character of Muslim men and the precepts of Islam within the school was neither confirmed by nor reflected in the external discourses to which they were party. These findings highlight how respondents sought to resolve these inner conflicts by (re)negotiating the boundaries of a series of 'idealized' masculine identities. All pupils used religion to shape their perceptions of the valued 'self', turning to the Qur'an and the *Hadith* for guidance on how their Muslim masculinities were to be constructed, in terms of being 'rational' in their behaviours and actions, 'disciplined' with regard to their emotions, and/or 'united' in their relations with each other. In a post-modern world predicated upon the dissolution of traditional and unified religious theologies, the reassertion of particular identities through spirituality highlights how, for some, religion remains a pervasive and cohesive influence in the construction of the 'self'.

We have also explored how pupils utilized physical activity to embrace different versions of their valued sense of 'self'. Evidence from interview discussion highlights how physical education and sport were used as sites through which young men could actively assume, and consciously embody, particular masculine identities. Although the respondents' general source of motivation for involvement in PE and sport was fuelled by their understanding that participation in such activities was honourable in terms of their broader religious beliefs, the specific meanings and interpretations that pupils attached to sport meant that, in reality, it served a variety of purposes, and was utilized in different ways by different individuals. To this end, participation in sport was not a neutral event; rather, it presented a physical and social space through which respondents could create, regulate and police their masculine identities. In this way, the physical body acted as an integral part of the making of the 'self'. It served both as an anchor of socially defined roles and behaviour and as a site of interaction, expression and appropriation for the social (and idealized) self. It was also a mechanism through which the social self (habits and behaviours) became inextricably connected with visible aspects of the physical self (bodily appearance). By dedicating a significant amount of time to the study of Islam, physical education and sport, Dar-ul-Islam authoritatively and selectively regulated the cultural resources available to its pupils and, in turn, necessarily shaped the contours of their identities.

What, then, of the broader relationship between sport, religion and identity? What we have attempted to illustrate here are some of the principles upon which differing masculinities might be constructed amidst a climate of social and political ambivalence towards Muslim men in the UK. Within a symbolic interactionist framework, respondent behaviours can be understood as a fundamental endeavour to construct more desirable, socially acceptable forms of the 'self'. In turn, the 'self' can be recognized as a provisional, fragmented and contingent entity, subject to constant (re)negotiation and change (Jenkins, 2008). With regard to the evidence presented, the school itself and the institutional experiences of its pupils characterize how masculinities are (re)shaped in line with both internal and external social forces and how particular identities may emerge at specific points in time. At Dar-ul-Islam, religious masculinities which embodied violence, aggression and deviance were devalued and marginalized. In contrast, masculinities which embraced rationality, self-discipline and unity were encouraged. We are not implying that 'rational' religious masculinities were in any way hierarchically located as more important or superior to 'disciplined' religious masculinities, or indeed to the 'united' masculine identities on display, nor that these three identity categories were the only ones evident amongst the pupils. There was variation in masculine construction both within and outside the parameters of these categories. In sum, the majority of our respondents constructed their masculine identity in accordance with the internal values of Dar-ul-Islam. However, this was not without its difficulties in terms of the recognition (and ultimate dismissal) of competing external discourses.

Notes

1. Adapted, with permission, from S. Farooq and A. Parker, 2009, "Sport, physical education and Islam: Muslim independent schooling and the social construction of masculinities", *Sociology of Sport Journal*, 26, 2.
2. The term *Zakah* refers to the monetary contribution which working Muslims are obliged to give to the 'poor and needy'. The expected level of contribution is 2.5 per cent of annual income. Daily prayers (*Salah*) are offered in the direction of the Kabb'a in Mecca.
3. For a similar example in the North American context, see Lieberman & Collins (2008).
4. In order to preserve anonymity, pseudonyms have been used throughout.
5. Like most mainstream state secondary schools in England and Wales, Dar-ul-Islam grouped pupils according to age. Thus, during the compulsory years of secondary schooling (11–16 years) they were taught the full range of National Curriculum subjects, alongside Arabic and various other Islamic education classes. However, after the age of 16 the educational emphasis centred more on the study of the Qur'an (*Hifaz*), and pupils were streamed according to their rate of progress. At the most basic level, (i.e. pupils who were learning the first five of the obligatory thirty chapters of the Qur'an), the age range was 16–21 years. At the highest level (i.e. pupils who were learning the last five chapters of the Qur'an) there was a mixture of pupils aged 18–23 years. Some pupils progressed faster then others, completing *Hifaz* by the age of 18. The training and qualifications which pupils attained from their post-compulsory education better enabled them to undergo professional training to become imams (Islamic priests). However, not all pupils followed this route, with some going on to further education and university.
6. According to the UK-based Independent Schools Council (2007), the average cost of independent schooling in Britain is in the region of £9,000 per academic year.
7. The decision to recruit pupils who had been boarding at the school for three years was taken because this time period was considered sufficient to enable participants to offer in-depth accounts of school life.

8. While recognizing the dangers of essentializing respondent accounts into fixed identity types, we have chosen to present our analysis in this way because these were the predominant metathemes to emerge from the data collection process in relation to identity formation amongst respondents. In turn, these categories allow us to demonstrate more fully the ways in which a variety of masculinities were constructed amidst a series of broader religious and social influences. It is not implied that these self-identifications apply to all young British Muslim men, as this would be an over-generalization which ignored the very diversity that makes up any such population.

9. The *Khulafah* were the male companions and disciples of Muhammad who became the figureheads and leaders of Islam once the Prophet had departed from Earth.

10. The term *jihad-e-nafs* refers to the need for Muslims to control their negative urges and emotions, such as anger, frustration and aggression. Control of these emotions is important because it is believed that they can potentially provoke one to behave in a manner contrary to the expected norm.

References

al-Qaradawy, Y. (1992) *The Lawful and the Prohibited in Islam*. Kuwait: International Islamic Federation of Student Organizations.

Abdelrahman, N. (1992) *Women, and Sport in the Islamic Society*. Alexandria University: Alexandria.

Ahmed, A. S. (2003) *Islam under Siege: Living Dangerously in a Post-honor World*. Cambridge: Polity.

Amin, A. (2002) 'Ethnicity and multiculturalism: Living with diversity', *Environment and Planning A*, 34, 959–980.

Back, L., Michael, K. & Khan, A. (2002) 'New Labour's white heart: Politics, multiculturalism and the return of assimilation', *Political Quarterly*, 73, 4, 445–454.

Burgess, R. (1983) *Experiencing Comprehensive Education*. London: Methuen.

Carron, A. V., Brawley, L. R. & Widmeyer, W. N. (1998) 'Measurement of cohesion in sport and exercise', in J. L. Duda (ed.) *Advances in Sport and Exercise Psychology Measurement*. Morgantown: WV: Fitness Information Technology, 213–226.

Carron, A. V., Bray, S. R. & Eys, M. A. (2002) 'Team cohesion and team success in sport', *Journal of Sports Sciences*, 20, 2, 119–126.

Connell, R. (2005) *Masculinities* (2nd edn). Cambridge: Polity.

Dagkas, S. & Benn, T. (2006) 'Young Muslim women's experiences of Islam and physical education in Greece and Britain: A comparative study', *Sport, Education and Society*, 11, 1, 21–38.

Daiman, S. (1995) 'Women in sport in Islam', *Journal for International Council for Health, Physical Education, Recreation, Sport and Dance*, 32, 1, 18–25.

De Knop, P., Theeboom, M., Wittock, H. & DeMartelaer, K. (1996) 'Implications of Islam on Muslim girl's sport participation in Western Europe', *Sport, Education and Society*, 1, 2, 147–164.

Dunn, R. & Stevenson, C. (1998) 'The paradox of the Church hockey league', *International Review for the Sociology of Sport*, 33, 2, 131–141.

Dwyer, C., Shah, B. & Sanghera, G. (2008) ' "From cricket lover to terror suspect" – Challenging representations of young British Muslim men', *Gender, Place and Culture*, 15, 2, 117–136.

Esposito, J. L. (2002) *Unholy War: Terror in the Name of Islam*. Oxford: Oxford University Press.

Farooq, S. & Parker, A. (2009) 'Sport, physical education and Islam: Muslim independent schooling and the social construction of masculinities', *Sociology of Sport Journal*, 26, 2.

Frosh, S., Phoenix, A. & Pattman, R. (2002) *Young Masculinities: Understanding Boys in Contemporary Society*. London: Palgrave.

Goodey, J. (2001) 'The criminalisation of British Asian youth: Research from Bradford and Sheffield', *Journal of Youth Studies*, 4, 4, 429–450.

Hall, D. E. (1994) 'Muscular Christianity: Reading and writing the male social body', in D. E. Hall (ed.) *Muscular Christianity: Embodying the Victorian Age*. Cambridge: Cambridge University Press.

Hall, S. (1992) 'The question of cultural identity', in S. Hall, D. Held & T. McGrew (eds) *Modernity and its Futures*. Cambridge: Open University Press/Polity.

Hall, S. (2000) 'Who needs identity?', in P. Du Gay, J. Evans & P. Redman (eds) *Identity: A Reader*. London: Sage.

Hammersley, M. & Atkinson, P. (2007) *Ethnography: Principles in Practice* (3rd edn). London: Routledge.

Hargreaves, J. (2000) *Heroines of Sport: The Politics of Difference and Identity*. London: Routledge.

Holt, R. (1989) *Sport and the British: A Modern History*. Oxford: Clarendon Press.

Hopkins, P. (2007) 'Young people, masculinities, religion and 'race': New social geographies', *Progress in Human Geography*, 31, 2, 163–177.

Hussain, Y. & Bagguley, P. (2005) 'Citizenship, ethnicity and identity: British Pakistanis after the 2001 "Riots"', *Sociology*, 39, 3, 407–425.

Independent Schools Council (2007) *Independent Schools Council Census 2007*. London: Independent Schools Council.

Jenkins, R. (2008) *Social Identity* (3rd edn). London: Routledge.

Kidd, B. (2006) 'Muscular Christianity and value-centered sport: The legacy of Tom Brown in Canada', *International Journal of the History of Sport*, 23, 5, 701–771.

Kirk, D. (1998) *Schooling Bodies: School Practice and Public Discourse, 1880–1950*. London: Leicester University Press.

Kirk, D. (2002) 'The social construction of the body in physical education and sport', in A. Laker (ed.) *The Sociology of Sport and Physical Education: An Introductory Reader*. New York: Routledge Falmer Press.

Lieberman, J. & Collins, S. (2008) *Violent Islamist Extremism, the Internet, and the Homegrown Terrorist Threat*. Washington: United States Senate Committee on Homeland Security and Governmental Affairs.

Lewis, P. (2003) *The Crisis of Islam*. New York: Modern Library.

Mac an Ghaill, M. (1994) *The Making of Men: Masculinities, Sexualities and Schooling*. Buckingham: Open University Press.

MacAloon, J. J. (2006) 'Introduction: Muscular Christianity after 150 years', *International Journal of the History of Sport*, 23, 5, 687–700.

MacClancy, J. (ed.) (1996) *Sport, Identity and Ethnicity*. London: Berg.

MacDonald, D. & Kirk, D. (1999) 'Pedagogy, the body and Christian identity, *Sport, Education and Society*, 4, 2, 131–142.

Macey, M. (2002) 'Interpreting Islam: Young Muslim men's involvement in criminal activity in Bradford', in B. Spalek. (ed.) *Islam, Crime and the Criminal Justice System*. Uffculem, Devon: William Publishing.

Macey, M. (2007) 'Islamic Political Radicalism in Britain: Muslim Men in Bradford', in T. Abbas (ed.) *Islamic Political Radicalism: A European Perspective*. Edinburgh: Edinburgh University Press, 160–172.

Maguire, B. & Collins, D. (1998) 'Sport, ethnicity, and racism: The experience of Asian heritage boys', *Sport Education and Society*, 3, 1, 79–81.

Maguire, J., Jarvie, G., Mansfield, L. & Bradley, J. (2002) *Sport Worlds: A Sociological Perspective*. Champaign, IL: Human Kinetics.

Mangan, J. A. (1986) *The Games Ethic and Imperialism*. Harmondsworth: Viking.

Martino, W. & Pallotta-Chiarolli, M. (2003) *'So What's a Boy?' Addressing Issues of Masculinity and Schooling*. Philadelphia: Open University Press.

Mawdudi, A. (1989) *Towards Understanding Islam*. Leicester: Islamic Foundation.

Messner, M. (1988), 'Sports and male domination: The female athlete as contested ideological terrain', *Sociology of Sport Journal*, 5, 3, 197–211.

Messner, M. (1990) 'When bodies are weapons: Masculinity and violence in sport', *International Review for the Sociology of Sport*, 25, 1, 203–220.

Messner, M. & Sabo, D. (eds) (1990) *Sport, Men and the Gender Order*. Champaign, IL: Human Kinetics.

Modood, T. (1990) 'British Asian Muslims and the Rushdie affair', *Political Quarterly*, 61, 2, 143–160.

Modood, T. (1997) *Ethnic Minorities in Britain: Diversity and Disadvantage*. London: Policy Studies Institute.

Morford, W. & McIntosh, M. J. (1993) 'Sport and the Victorian gentlemen', in A. G. Ingham & J. W. Loy (eds) *Sport in Social Development*. Champaign, IL: Human Kinetics.

Muslim Education Trust (1994) *Islam: A Brief Guide*. London: Muslim Educational Trust.

Neddam, F. (2004) 'Constructing masculinities under Thomas Arnold of Rugby (1828– 1842): Gender, educational policy and school life in an early-Victorian public school', *Gender and Education*, 16, 3, 303–326.

Nielsen, J. S. (1992) *Muslims in Western Europe*. Edinburgh: Edinburgh University Press.

Ouzgane, L. (2003) Islamic masculinities: An introduction, *Men and Masculinities*, 5, 3, 231–235.

Parker, A. (1996) 'The construction of masculinity within boys' physical education', *Gender and Education*, 8, 1, 141–157.

Parry, J., Robinson, S., Watson, N. J. & Nesti, M. (2007) *Sport and Spirituality: An Introduction*. London: Routledge.

Ruthven, M. (2006) *Islam in the World* (3rd edn). London: Granta Books.

Sarwar, G. (1994) *British Muslims and Schools*. London: Muslim Educational Trust.

Sarwar, G. (2001) *Islamic Education: Its Meaning, Problems and Prospects*. London: Muslim Educational Trust

Shah, S. (2006) 'Leading multiethnic schools: A new understanding of Muslim youth identity', *Educational Management Administration and Leadership*, 34, 2, 215–237.

Shilling, C. (2003) *The Body and Social Theory* (2nd edn). London: Sage.

Shilling, C. (2005) *The Body in Culture, Technology and Society*. London: Sage.

Stevenson, C. L. (1991), 'The Christian-athlete: An interactionist-developmental perspective', *Sociology of Sport Journal*, 8, 1, 362–379.

Stevenson, C. L. (1997) 'Christian athletes and the culture of elite sport: Dilemmas and solutions', *Sociology of Sport Journal*, 14, 1, 241–262.

Swain, J. (2003) 'How young boys become somebody: The role of the body in the construction of masculinity', *British Journal of Sociology of Education*, 24, 4, 299–314.

Swain, J. (2006) 'The role of sport in the construction of masculinities in an English independent junior school', *Sport, Education and Society*, 11, 4, 317–335.

Tozer, M. (1985) 'Charles Kingsley and the muscular Christian ideals of manliness', *Physical Education Review*, 8, 1, 35–40.

Vertovec, S. (2002) 'Islamophobia and Muslim recognition in Britain', in Y. Haddad (ed.) *Muslims in the West: From Sojourners to Citizens*. Oxford: Oxford University Press.

Walseth, K. & Fasting, K. (2003) Islam's view on physical activity and sport: Egyptian women interpreting Islam, *International Review for the Sociology of Sport*, 38, 1, 45–60.

Watson, N. J. (2007) 'Muscular' Christianity in the modern age: 'Winning for Christ' or 'playing for glory'?, in J. Parry, S. Robinson, N. J. Watson & M. Nesti, *Sport and Spirituality: An Introduction*. London: Routledge.

Watson, N. J., Weir, S. & Friend, S. (2005) 'The development of muscular Christianity in Victorian Britain and beyond', *Journal of Religion and Society*, 7, 1, 1–25.

Woods, P. (1983) *Sociology and the School. An Interactionist Viewpoint*. London: Routledge & Kegan Paul.

Woodward, K. (2002) *Identity and Difference*. London: Sage.

Zaman, H. (1997) 'Islam, well-being and physical activity: Perceptions of Muslim young women', in G. Clarke & B. Humberstone (eds) *Researching Women and Sport*. London: Macmillan.

7
Sport and Metrosexual Identity: Sports Media and Emergent Sexualities

Ben Clayton and John Harris

This chapter looks at a relatively recent identity marker to appear in the media – the metrosexual. In examining how the media frame sporting identities in and around contemporary masculinities, we consider the ways in which celebrity athletes feature in discourses of metrosexuality. Newspaper accounts have positioned the metrosexual in the following ways:

> He loves children, is faithful to his woman and knows Gucci from Gap – meet the metrosexual man, the latest incarnation of the male species.
>
> (*Daily Mail*, 18 June 2003)

> There was a time when male grooming was all about a basin of luke-warm water, a blunt razor and a quick splash of Hai Karate. A blotchy complexion, sandpaper lips and unkempt hair were all acceptable. Fast forward to 2004, however, and the unthinkable has happened. Super-toned and hyper-groomed, the metrosexual man is now offi-cially spending longer in the bathroom than female counterparts.
>
> (*Scotsman*, 19 March 2004)

In the summer of 1998, a widely publicized photograph of England's most famous football player of recent years, David Beckham, sporting a sarong, was presented to the English nation's tabloid-reading public amidst a goading undertone of emasculation. In the decade that fol-lowed, emasculation turned to detestation, back to emasculation and to acclamation and imitation, in what appeared to be the dawn of a transformation of male footballing identity (see Harris & Clayton, 2007a). Notwithstanding its conception in the public schools, football in its modern form was quickly imbued with a working-class masculine value system, which differed markedly from the accustomed middle-class Christian standards of language and gesture. The 'working-class-shop-floor' culture of football (Parker, 2001) has vehemently defended these values through its structures, collective practices and everyday routines at all levels of participation (see, for example, Clayton & Humberstone, 2006; Parker, 2001). Beckham, however, has in some ways continued to resist the traditional values of male team sports and their respective sub-cultures, which, when coupled with media exploitation of his transcendence (see Cashmore & Parker, 2003; Clayton & Harris, 2004; Harris & Clayton, 2007a; Whannel, 2002) has given rise to a new form of sporting identity – the *metrosexual* identity. This does not mean, of course, that metrosexual identity is only applicable to sport, for it has been used in a number of other contexts. Our focus within this chapter, however, is on how the term has been used in relation to high-profile athletes.

To this end, we examine media representations of athletes who are positioned as metrosexual sport stars. Figures such as the Los Angeles Galaxy and England footballer David Beckham and the Welsh rugby player Gavin Henson receive significant media coverage not just because of their performances as athletes but because of their appearance, lifestyle and 'celebrity' image. The cultural politics of sporting celebrity has received much attention in recent years (see, for example, Andrews & Jackson, 2001; Smart, 2005) but there is little work on more contemporary conceptualizations of the way in which superstar status and masculine identity come together. Within this chapter we try to address this subject by introducing and explaining the place of metrosexual identity in sport media coverage and other social spheres. The media has long been recognized for its role in shaping and maintaining cultural norms and values, and for its influence on the culture of sport in particular (see Whannel, 2002). It is, for most of us, the only available means for understanding and interacting with the world of professional sport, and the sporting identities it creates inform the reality of the social dynamics of sports. This chapter brings to the study of social identities visible examples of how masculine identities, and in particular sporting masculinities, are moulded within the print media. It begins by mapping out some of the cases of metrosexual identities in male sport.

The rise of the metrosexual athlete

The term 'metrosexuality' is usually attributed to UK journalist Mark Simpson (1994) as a reference to male narcissism or, more specifically, the commodity fetishism created by the increasingly male-orientated marketing of certain products and services (see also Simpson, 1996). The metrosexual man is said to indulge in daily routines that might previously have been labelled effeminate, such as male grooming and dressing for style. During his initial writings on this subject, Simpson (1994) described the metrosexual as

> a young man with money to spend, living in or within easy reach of a metropolis – because that's where all the best shops, clubs, gyms and hairdressers are. He might be officially gay, straight or bisexual, but this is utterly immaterial because he has clearly taken himself as his own love object.

The masculine world of male team sports has not escaped this metrosexual trend, despite often being perceived as oppositional to it. The official website of the Entertainment and Sports Programming Network (ESPN), for example, provides 'photographic evidence' of eight well-known metrosexual athletes, including such diverse characters as former NBA star Dennis Rodman, ice-hockey legend Mike Modano and ex-tennis professional, Patrick Rafter (ESPN, 2007a). Rodman's association with effeminacy has been well documented (Lafrance & Rail, 2001). His modes of self-presentation have incorporated the kinds of behaviour and embellishment that would challenge even the most inclusive of Western discourses of heterosexual masculinity. Indeed, Rodman has been described as a disruptive force vis-à-vis gendered power relations for his performances of transvestism (Barrett, 1997). By contrast, Modano and Rafter's metrosexual qualities could go unnoticed but for the attention drawn to them by this particular website. Modano, it seems, has a narcissistic obsession with his hair, and Rafter a fixation with skin care (ESPN, 2007a). Tennis is located on this website as a sport at the centre of the metrosexual movement. Players such as James Blake, Feliciano López and Fernando Verdasco couple on-court appearances with internet exhibitions of fashion, while the long-time men's world number one, Roger Federer, strolls imperturbably on to Centre Court dressed in a custom-made white suit, with matching shoes, sweatshirt and baseball cap (*Sun*, 10 July 2006). The *Sun* (10 July 2006) said that Federer's outfit looked 'a bit dodgy' and the *Guardian* (29 June 2007) described it as a 'fashion controversy'.

The cynicism of the press and others, however, appears to be as interchangeable with celebration as Federer's dandy-licious white cap with 'gold Swoosh' bandana that was highlighted in a number of popular publications during Wimbledon fortnight. Amid frequent calls for a 'Menaissance' (*Daily Mail*, 12 July 2006) are the not quite so frequent eulogies to the moralities of metrosexual man. David Beckham, as he so often is in discussions of metrosexuality, is a case in point. To this end, the *Sun* (30 August 2003) was moved to write:

> He is the perfect role model for every generation. A clean-living, honest, decent, caring, gentle bloke. He doesn't smoke, he doesn't drink, he doesn't do drugs. To his children Romeo and Brooklyn, he is a dad to be hero-worshipped. To older boys he has soccer skills to be envied and emulated. To parents, he is a shining example of gentleness and love. To older people, he is an admirable possessor of old-fashioned values they thought had been lost. How many young men would wait until the fourth date before kissing a new girlfriend, as he did with Victoria? David Beckham is a remarkable character. On the outside he is 21st Century man personified, a glamorous, handsome fashion icon. On the inside he is from a world long past, of gentility, manners and consideration.

In many ways Beckham has become a 'poster-boy' for metrosexuality. His fame and prominence on the international stage can be attributed, in no small part, to his atypical football marriage (see Clayton & Harris, 2004), his ever-changing hairstyle and his courageous fashion choices. His marketability knows few bounds, sharing the billboard on Time Square with the Calvin-Klein-clad crotch of Swedish football player Freddie Ljungberg (Coad, 2005). While Beckham may have fired-up the winds of change in terms of footballing identities (albeit with more than a little help from the mass media), such advancements have now developed into a full-blown metrosexual tornado, enveloping the most unlikely of victims. Even the dowdy, thick-set persona of Manchester United and England football player Wayne Rooney has not escaped the metrosexuality tag as he 'donned a brown zip-up cardigan while enjoying the teeny-bopping sounds of Christina Aguilera at her Manchester gig' (*Sun*, 25 November 2006). Rooney, too, has joined in the conspicuous endorsement that has come to define top-flight football, with a range of designer clothing in his own name. As Coad (2005) has noted, fashionable football players and the subsequent discussions about gender and sexual identity are the most visible manifestation of metrosexuality – a far cry from the working-class values of times gone by. So perhaps one of the most pertinent and timely questions to ask is whether we are truly in a new and feminized age of male sporting identity?

Emergent sexualities? A critique

In recent years the popular press has attempted to establish metrosexuality as a new brand of masculinity. Like all other manifestations of masculinity, metrosexuality is a social construct created and maintained within a patriarchal society, largely attributable to the forging and sanitizing powers of the mass media (see Connell, 1987, 2005). However, unlike other masculinities, metrosexuality has been branded and commodified in a cognizant mercantile movement, originating with Salzman, Matathia & O'Reilly's (2005) primarily North American perspective on male identity and its meaning for the male advertising market.[1] Not content with their self-proclaimed reinvigoration of Simpson's (1994) term, Salzman *et al.* (2005) take their marketing rhetoric 'beyond metrosexualmania'. The 'übersexual' man for instance, is both ruggedly macho and compassionate, more focussed than the metrosexual upon his demeanour and never invites questions of homosexuality. At the other extreme, 'emo boys' (the term 'emo' is borrowed from a particularly emotion-inducing genre of music) are men who have 'learned some very positive lessons from their feminine sides, but at the expense of their backbones' (Salzman *et al.*, 2005, p. 74). For these writers at least, the differences between these groups of men are subtle; indeed barely visible to the enquiring, sociological eye. All appear to be men whose displays of gender, (though not necessarily their conceptualizations of gender), differ to varying degrees from the familiar Western form. However, the emergence of emo boys and metrosexual and übersexual men has impacted enough to give rise to 'retrosexuality', comprising a deliberate rejection of all things feminine and the simultaneously active pursuit of patriarchal masculinity. The *Sun* (16 May 2005) reported on a Sport England survey (Tomlinson *et al.*, 2005) and found that 57 per cent of men were now enjoying adrenaline sports, such as karting and wing-walking, in an effort to claw back some masculine identity.[2] Trends such as these, according to the article in *The Sun*, are a sign of the preening metrosexual being overtaken by the new 'adrenosexual' – a particular form of retrosexual man, 'proving' his manhood in pursuit of risk and danger. Participation in male team sports would seem to be central to the identity of retrosexual men, exaggerating their claim to masculinity with largely forgotten hegemonic attitudes, behaviours and characteristics. The ESPN website, to complement their list of metrosexual athletes, offers some more 'photographic evidence' of athletes who do not fit the metrosexual bill (ESPN, 2007b).

The criteria for the retrosexual man seems equally as vague and rangy as that for their metrosexual counterparts. The rugged facial hair of National Football League (NFL) quarterback Brett Favre and baseball's Eric Gagné appears to be enough to locate them firmly within the retrosexual camp. Equally, the 'mullet' (a hairstyle short at the front, top and sides but long at the back) of major league baseball's Randy Johnson, coupled with his height and aggressive pitching style, and the craggy dentistry of NFL's Edgerrin James are extolled by ESPN as the antithesis of metrosexuality. Not all retrosexuality is associated with physical appearance. Retired basketball legend Karl 'the Mailman' Malone is included in ESPN's list for his rejection of the tradition in professional male sport of purchasing sleek cars, choosing instead an eighteen-wheel truck (ESPN, 2007b).

Few feminist or pro-feminist scholars have entertained any of these supposed emergent sexualities. Part of the problem here is that scholars have maintained, and been satisfied with, the explanation that metrosexuality, and its successors, are terms imposed upon the social world by a mass media in the service of a market in flux. This, in itself, is difficult to refute. Simpson's (1994) original use of the term 'metrosexuality' indicated the changing retail habits of single men with a high level of disposable income, and its subsequent usage has remained largely in the domain of the popular press and marketing rhetoric. This should not, however, detract from the very real existence of the behaviours that attract these media connotations.

Metrosexuality, and its numerous derivatives, are labels attached by the media to various states of masculine identity (see Harris & Clayton, 2007b; Parker & Lyle, 2008). We believe that while they do not represent discrete brands of masculinity, they are important portrayals of the multiplicity and mobility of gender relations and masculine and feminine identities. The theorizing of Connell (1987, 1995), which has characterized many studies of gendered identities, does not mention metrosexuality or metrosexuals. This should come as no surprise because the position of metrosexuality as something new and pioneering which should inspire a fresh academic outlook on gender relations is a falsehood. The label might be new but the state of masculinity that it represents is age-old and well documented. Utilizing Connell's (1987) concept of hegemonic masculinity, the retrosexual is a more familiar form of maleness, embodying attitudes and behaviours which are taken to guarantee the dominant position of men and the subordination of women.

Male team sports have long been associated with the legitimation of male hegemony, where orthodox sporting masculinities include the expression of overtly heterosexist attitudes and behaviours, aggression (even violence), a fierce competitiveness, and an outright rejection of effeminacy (Messner, 1992; Parker, 2001; Schacht, 1996). Historically, this has been a position that the sports media has been keen to preserve. Harris & Clayton (2002a) note the media's emphasis on traditional male traits in their reporting on men's sport, utilizing phraseology which highlights those characteristics which associate men with power, while maintaining that women do not display the same attributes (see also Kane & Lenskyj, 1998). Retrosexuality, then, may be seen as cognizant with the heteronormative definition of heterosexual masculinities, which is problematized by the emergent characters of metrosexual and übersexual, in much the same way that the notion of hegemonic masculinity is disrupted by subordinated, marginalized forms of masculinity (see Connell, 1995, 2005).

Metrosexuality and übersexuality, however, also exhibit hegemonic masculine characteristics. In the last few years, for example, David Beckham, has attracted much academic interest as a sports star who manages simultaneously to conform to and resist orthodox sporting masculinities (see Cashmore, 2004; Cashmore & Parker, 2003; Clayton & Harris, 2004; Whannel, 2002). He is, in Connell's (1995) terms, complicitly masculine – sustaining a largely traditional masculinity while avoiding a total adherence to hegemonic norms. Beckham's football talent has regularly been the cornerstone of the sports media's construction of his macho image. This was particularly evident in the build-up to the 2002 World Cup finals in Japan and Korea, amidst fears that the England captain would miss the opening three matches with a foot injury. The *Mirror* (4 June 2002) noted that 'England are a quiet team screaming out for our leader, David, to organize them and keep the ball.' This was in stark contrast to reporting four years earlier when Beckham was vilified and emasculated for a sending-off offence against Argentina. At that time he was largely castigated by the British media, framed as a hate figure and routinely mocked for his effeminate indulgences. As *GQ* magazine (May 1999) sardonically noted, Beckham and his wife, Victoria ('Posh'), could regularly be seen out in 'their hers and hers wardrobe'. Later articles to address Beckham's sexuality were to take an altogether different perspective, with the *Sun* headlining, 'Becks: I'm an animal in bed' and announcing how 'he and Posh had plenty of romps before she fell pregnant for the second time' (29 April 2002).

Whannel (2001, 2002) has mapped the media spectacle of 'punishment' and 'redemption', in which Beckham's gender role cataclysms are set against his thoroughly masculine contributions to sporting successes at a national level and, equally, the rumours about his sexual behaviour and alleged extramarital relations. Going by media definitions, Beckham's lifestyle would seem more akin to that of the übersexual than to that of the metrosexual which he has been labelled and has even quintessentialized. Indeed, discerning the two concepts is not always easy, especially because the former appears to be little more than a consciously articulated extension of the latter for the purposes of further 'tabloidization' and continued public intrigue. Both are based on the premise of the 'new man' – a truly postmodern term referring to an individual who is more sensitive, caring and in touch with his feminine side and/or someone concerned with male grooming (Beynon, 2002). In essence, 'new men' are defined in terms of a change in gender display while ignoring the continuity of structural positions of power and privilege (Hondagneu-Sotelo & Messner, 1994) and exist primarily at the level of media journalism (Edwards, 2006). As such, the term 'metrosexuality' is rather obsolete in contemporary accounts of masculinity theory, which emphasize a multiplicity of masculine identities and the changing nature of masculinity through history. In social constructionist perspectives of gender, the notion of cathexis has received little attention. Yet it is here that the conceptualizing of metrosexuality may begin and that its place within the gender order may be determined. With reference to the structure of cathexis, Connell draws heavily on the work of Freud (1953 [1905]). Freud's use of the term 'cathexis' referred to emotional energy – whether positive or negative – being attached to an object in the unconscious mind. Connell (1987) utilized Freud's psychoanalytic work, moving the discussion into the social arena to investigate sexual and emotional relations, attachments and commitments. As Connell (1994) contends, long before social constructionism became influential in discussions of gender, Freudian psychoanalysis had offered a picture of adult character as constructed through a long, conflict-ridden process within which the emotional attachment could not be entirely separated from the social.

Both men's and women's bodies can become 'cathected' in their own right (as can other inanimate objects and possessions, such as clothing, make-up, sports cars and even technology). It is perhaps here that we might locate Simpson's (1994, 1996) characterization of metrosexuality as a dimension of male identity, rather than as a brand of masculinity in itself; as a man's attachment to his body and to the image it presents. The attachment and image of metrosexuality reinforces the portrayal of heterosexual masculinities – strong, fit and aesthetically pleasing to the other sex – but the embodiment of the attachment involves routines more traditionally associated with femininity. The concept of metrosexuality, then, may be viewed as both a harmonized response to feminism and a rejection of it. The identity imperatives that associate, for example, Welsh rugby star Gavin Henson with the term 'metrosexual' are often a legitimation of patriarchy in themselves (see Harris & Clayton, 2007b), so that metrosexuality has become associated with white, middle-class men. As Berila & Choudhuri (2005) indicate, the embodiment of gay masculinities by heterosexual, middle-class men may suggest an increased tolerance to white gay masculinity, while simultaneously subordinating working-class and black and Asian gay masculinities. Similarly, Miller (2005) has noted how 'queerness' has become adopted by middle-class professional men, resignified as metrosexuality, and endorsed as a form of 'consultancy' for a conventional masculine life.

Men, masculinity and sport: survival of the prettiest?

> Henson is an icon unlike any ever to grace a Welsh rugby pitch. He gels his hair, shaves his legs and wears gold boots. Twenty years ago, when post-match celebrations meant drinking a skinful of beers and probably a bottle of aftershave, too, he would have been mocked. Now he is lionised – the first metrosexual rugby star.
>
> (*Observer*, 13 March 2005)

Judith Butler's (1990) concept of the heterosexual matrix refers to the 'grid of cultural intelligibility through which bodies, genders and desires are naturalized' (p.151). According to Butler (1990), identity is only intelligible as a gendered concept, where conformity to recognizable standards of stable sex (male or female) is expressed through stable gender (masculine or feminine). A significant part of the matrix is the body's natural desire for the other sex and its capacity for sensation, but moreover the construction of heterosexuality becomes a collective practice built upon an awareness of social patterns of gender. It is here, embroiled in masculinist discourse, that heterosexuality becomes an oppressive character as the cornerstone of male hegemony, subordinating gay masculinities (and femininities) as unorthodox, even unnatural, states of gender. As we have seen, sport has a strong association with the heterosexual matrix. It has been asserted, for example, that sport is the 'last bastion' of traditional male values and a traditional defence against the 'feminization' of society (Kimmel, 1987; Messner, 1987). Media sport has traditionally celebrated male physical prowess, 'lionized' its male participants and simultaneously eroticized and trivialized women athletes (Bernstein, 2002; Sabo & Jansen, 1992). The sports media has fabricated a clear hierarchy in sport through:

> the Herculean and pervasively nationalistic discourse applied to appropriate sporting bodies, adjacent to the narratives affixed to carefully selected symbols of athletic mediocrity, physicality and (hetero) sexuality.
>
> (Harris & Clayton, 2002a, p. 411)

In recent years female athletes, such as Anna Kournikova, have secured significantly more media attention than their more successful rivals, the focus of related reports being almost exclusively on sexuality and feminine identity (see also Vincent, 2004). While coverage of men's sport has tended to remain task-relevant and masculinized, women's sport, it seems, is more a case of 'survival of the prettiest' (Harris & Clayton, 2002b). Media sport, then, is implicated in the cultural sustenance of heteronormative gender identities. Yet the media, in all its forms, appears increasingly to be embracing the metrosexual athlete to such an extent that men's sport too is in danger of becoming a fight for the survival of the prettiest. Even the most resolute of masculinized sporting spaces have not escaped the onslaught of metrosexuality. Satirical columnist for the *Sun* newspaper Lorraine Kelly notes,

> Rugby players sure have changed. Instead of cauliflower ears and scars we have the buffed metrosexual look of Gavin Henson – the man who makes Charlotte Church[3] light up like a firework. Here he is on holiday looking splendidly like a model from Vogue. But if I were Charlotte would I want a man who clearly spends more time in front of the mirror than she does?
>
> (*Sun*, 23 July 2005)

Henson has been described as 'the David Beckham of Welsh rugby' (*Western Mail*, 16 December 2004) and 'the Beckham of Wales' (*Wales on Sunday*, 13 February 2005). Such comparisons are, perhaps, inevitable with his interest in fashion, changing hairstyles, and pop-star girlfriend, and, like Beckham, his appearance has become a focal point for the media, above and beyond his competencies as an athlete (Harris & Clayton, 2007b).

Henson has found a number of critics from within the machismo world of his sport. One of his predecessors in the centre position within the Wales national rugby team, John Devereux, noted,

> Gavin needs to decide whether he wants to be a rugby player or to pursue his other antics off the field. The way he's playing, I don't know whether his career could get any worse. The question I and other people are asking is: 'does he really want to be a rugby player?' At the moment, I'm not sure he does. Maybe he doesn't want to scar his pretty face.
>
> (*Daily Mail*, 20 September 2006)

Beckham, too, is no stranger to adverse commentary regarding his metrosexual identity. The German tabloid *Bild Zeitung* asked, 'Is Beckham turning into a woman?' allegedly declaring

> Football is an ultra-tough sport for men, but amidst the sweat and the shinpads, one superstar has suddenly discovered his feminine side. It is none other than England's national captain, David Beckham – or should that be MISS David Beckham? Her rather than him. His latest trick has been to paint his fingernails pink. 'She' slips on his wife Victoria's G-strings, wears dresses, £50,000 diamond rings, and clothes by Jean-Paul Gaultier and Gucci. Not to mention experimenting with his hair in front of the bathroom mirror every morning.
>
> (reported in the *Mirror*, 12 July 2002)

The proclaimed metrosexuality of male athletes, while seemingly newsworthy, is not always celebrated. English cricket's Darren Gough, since becoming recognized as a metrosexual in a traditionally masculine sport, has admitted to having to endure a lot of derision from team mates about his choice of attire and his appearance on the BBC dance show, *Celebrity Come Dancing*[4] (*Hello*, 12 January 2006). In addition, while appearing in the Channel 4 cookery programme *The F Word* on British television, Gough's sexuality was jokingly questioned by celebrity chef Gordon Ramsay (himself a former football player at Glasgow Rangers), as a result of Gough's pink polo shirt, choice of sport, and appearance on the celebrity dance show. That Gough's 'defence' of his (hetero)sexuality would be best articulated by his use of the term 'metrosexual' is an interesting one and demonstrates how the term is increasingly used in a range of different spheres. The term 'metrosexual' may be heard on a number of television shows and in many cases its use is simply seen as a justification/explanation for the adoption of what may be considered to be 'unmasculine' behaviours.

Throughout history, hegemonic discourses, such as those above, have been a familiar mark of male sporting practice. It is part of the same culture that has served to sanitize male sport (and other all-male milieux besides) through the exclusion, removal or concealment of 'suspect' masculinities. We might parallel the derision of the metrosexual athlete with the same oppressive character of heterosexuality which has compelled gay athletes to hide their sexuality altogether (Pronger, 1990) or to disclose their sexuality but fully engage with the heterosexist culture and performances of hegemonic masculinity (Anderson, 2002; Messner, 1992). In a culture where even straight men can encounter homophobia when their actions defy the hegemonic norms and values in play (see Clayton & Humberstone, 2006), the latter strategy for acceptance certainly appears apposite when looking at the treatment, by the media, and others, of metrosexuals. The perceived effeminacies of Gavin Henson, for example, are largely overlooked – sometimes celebrated – as long as his performances on the pitch are good and the team is winning (Harris & Clayton, 2007b). What is not to be ignored, of course, is that, unlike openly gay men, metrosexuals are rarely self-proclaimed but are established and promoted as such by the same mass media that then question their sexuality and their athletic prowess.

Far from being a case of 'survival of the prettiest', then, men's media sport still demands athletic competence and other familiar traits of masculinity. Being a 'pretty-boy' of sport may invite media exposure and ensuing celebrity and stardom, but an alleged metrosexual identity must also be offset by more 'traditional' portrayals of masculinity. That said, the metrosexual lifestyle and behaviours of media sport stars is not always seen as integral to their sporting identities but is often discussed as an entirely separate entity. For example, in the June 2002 issue of the men's magazine *GQ*, David Beckham could be seen to be wearing considerable facial make-up, torso dripping with baby oil, dressed in mainly white attire, open at the front. The *Mirror* (29 April 2002) headlined 'Camp David', selecting what seemed to be the most effeminate of all the photographs on offer to endorse the caption, featuring Beckham sporting a white silk scarf, an uncovered chest and nail varnish. The paper's centre pages took an altogether different tone, presenting the football star against the backdrop of the St Georges Cross, and employing a more explicitly heterosexual and fiercely nationalistic tenor. Metrosexuality may be viewed as antithetical to the project of patriarchy, but the ways in which it is embraced and popularized point to the reproduction of hegemonic forms of masculinity in sport. It remains worthy of media exposure perhaps simply because it is such a visible irony, and the persistent counterbalancing with heteronormative reporting of heroic masculinities serves to readdress and support the stability of masculine hegemony in men's sport (Harris & Clayton, 2007b). Similarly, Lafrance & Rail's (2001) assessment of Dennis Rodman's black-masculine subversity highlights how his effeminized identity can only be constructed within a framework of heteronormative formulations of gender and that his demeanour in fact reproduces aggressive, sexist modalities of masculinity. Rodman's alleged metrosexuality, therefore, in no way confuses perceptions of his masculine identity, having little implication for male hegemony as a whole.

Groomed and gorgeous: metrosexual identities and male narcissism

> Unlike their fathers, who didn't evolve beyond Brut 33, metrosexuals have tubs, scrubs and scents for every occasion, talk openly about wardrobe staples and embrace lycra.
>
> (*Scotsman*, 19 March 2004)

The metrosexual identities of Beckham and Henson are also reflected in the fact that both have, at various stages in their careers, secured endorsement contracts with Gillette. The increased incorporation of men into the traditionally female market of cosmetic and grooming products is an interesting development. As highlighted previously, this is also reflective of an increased sexualization and eroticization of the male body. The body has become a new identity project for men in late/high/post-modernity (Gill, Henwood & McLean, 2005). Advertisers have of course wrestled with the problem of selling newer grooming products to men. Using celebrity athletes alongside a reframing of discourse which promotes various products as more 'masculine' is a widely adopted strategy. The fact that athletes such as Beckham and Henson play what is, in their respective countries, *the* national sport, is also important to note. Few, if any, other figures are as representative of 'the nation' as are its leading athletes (Harris & Clayton, 2007a). The very nature of metrosexual identity is one where the sexual orientation of the individual may be rendered questionable/problematic, but for the most part a national sporting hero is beyond question/interrogation. Coupland

(2007, p. 57) has highlighted how 'this "male-ing" of a previously female market involves using suffixes which literally render products for men as lexically *marked* [emphasis in original]'. There are a range of mitigating discourses, often linked to sport, that advertisers use to 'offset potential attributes of unmanly narcissism' (Coupland, 2007, p. 57).

Conclusion: towards progression and changing masculine identities?

> There are a lot of things I have to do; shave my legs, put a bit of fake tan on, do my hair and have a shave. I do it all in the hotel but it seems to be catching on. Everybody shaves their legs now. I don't get hammered for it though. I think people are in awe of me. But once we cross the line it is all about the rugby, but if my hair does get messed up I put it back in place. They're pretty good products I use so it's okay.
>
> (Gavin Henson, quoted in Thornley, 2005)

The changing styles and subcultural routines of many high-profile athletes have stimulated a good deal of media interest in recent times. The metrosexual identities of certain athletes are largely media constructions reproducing, with emphasis, images of cathected bodies and the perceived effeminacies which are invoked. As discussed above, the idea that this imagery is in some way proof of the feminization of male sport is significantly flawed. Likewise, the idea that metrosexuality is a sign of progressive socio-cultural change is inconsistent with the behavioural patterns of purported metrosexual characters and the structuring of media reporting on sport and male sport stars. Amidst his many alleged transgressions, the metrosexual athlete reproduces dominant archetypes of masculinity, heteronormativity, and white, middle-class supremacy. The very existence of the metrosexual, by Simpson's (1994) original standards, is one of capitalist conventionality. When the metrosexual is also a sportsman, further manifestations of gendered power become apparent, linked to muscularity, national identity and the oppressive state of compulsory heterosexuality.

That identities are provisional, contingent and relatively unfixed is most visible in the (re)presentation of athletes and other 'celebrities' in the media. The mediated celebrity of Beckham and Henson provides interesting insights into the shifting and contested nature of identities (Cashmore & Parker, 2003; Harris & Clayton, 2007a, 2007b). For athletes, and male athletes in particular, their mediated identities change with alarming frequency. The pressure on players in the most popular team sports, as representatives of 'the nation', means that from game to game they can move from the position of hero to that of villain (see especially Harris & Clayton, 2007a; Whannel, 2001). Those who, in some ways, do not 'conform' to prescribed and established masculine norms find themselves easy targets for criticism. The same facets of an athlete's 'character' which may be celebrated at one moment may be criticized and condemned at another. As part of the Welsh team who in 2005 celebrated their country's first Grand Slam (defeating all opponents in the course of a Six Nations championship series) for more than twenty-five years, Henson's celebrity profiling and metrosexual identity was a central focus of many newspaper stories in Wales and even in other parts of Britain. Within a matter of months these same qualities were being focused upon and discussed as being the reasons behind the player's loss of form and perceived lack of focus.

Gendered identities have changed markedly in postmodern times. Perhaps, as Simpson (2004) has stated, 'in a makeover culture, metrosexuality is the ultimate makeover because what is being made over is masculinity itself'. Ultimately, metrosexuality depends on a certain anxiety about identity. As Coad (2005, p. 126) has noted, metrosexuality is not solely about moisturizers, manicures and matching colours but also 'problematizes our binary divisions based on gender'. In this chapter, we have been influenced by a Gramscian/Freudian perspective, as advocated by Connell (1987, 1995, 2005), in our understanding of media representations of metrosexuality in sport. Such an approach, while useful, is limited to thoroughly modern understandings of sport and identity, guided by the taken-for-granted presence of 'solid' identities – working-class/middle-class, black/white, masculine/feminine. Perhaps future research on sport and masculine identities might make central the 'liquid modernity' (Bauman, 2000), and the consequent anxiety about identity, which comes to define metrosexuality. Through this lens, metrosexual athletes may be seen not as the problematizers of divisions of gender but as men actively seeking the struggle for self and identity in an ambivalent society. The problem with such a perspective, as this chapter has argued, is that metrosexual identity in fact grounds itself in the 'solid' and only embodies ambivalence through some of its disconnected components. Undoubtedly, metrosexuality is an intricate concept concealed within a complex web of identity construction. As such, scholars need to leave behind the denotative truth that metrosexuality is a product of marketing and start to disentangle the identity imperatives that are obscured within it. Metrosexuality might just turn out to be the male identity of the future.

Notes

1. Salzman *et al.* are self-confessed 'trend-spotters' for the purposes of advising their clients on new markets. Their research, *The Future of Men* (2005), began as market research which surveyed 1058 men and women in the USA, asking about men's attitudes towards themselves as well as their current cosmetic and aesthetic spending habits.
2. Information cited in the *Sun* newspaper and not the original Sport England report by Tomlinson *et al.* (2005), which outlined the increasing rates of participation in 'lifestyle sports'.
3. Charlotte Church is a Welsh singer who first came to national prominence as a child opera star and was described as 'the voice of an angel'. Church's maturation and her transformation into a pop singer, and 'pin-up', became regular features within a range of media. Her choice of boyfriends and alleged drinking capacity became a focus for the tabloid newspapers who labelled her a 'wild child'. Church began dating Henson in 2005 and the couple had a baby together in 2007. In the summer of 2008 Church announced that the couple were expecting their second child.
4. A similar show in the USA is *Dancing with the Stars*.

References

Anderson, E. (2002) 'Openly gay athletes: Contesting hegemonic masculinity in a homophobic environment', *Gender and Society*, 16, 6, 860–877.

Andrews, D. & Jackson, S. (2001) (eds) *Sports Stars: The Cultural Politics of Sporting Celebrity*. London: Routledge.

Barrett, L. (1997) 'Black men in the mix: Badboys, heroes, sequins and Dennis Rodman', *Callaloo*, 20, 106–126.

Bauman, Z. (2000) *Liquid Modernity*. Cambridge: Polity.

Berila, B. & Choudhuri, D. (2005) 'Metrosexuality the middle class way: Exploring race, class and gender in Queer Eye for the Straight Guy', *Genders OnLine Journal*, 42. Retrieved 3 July 2006 from http://www.genders.org

Bernstein, A. (2002) 'Is it time for a victory lap? Changes in the media coverage of women's sport', *International Review for the Sociology of Sport*, 37, 415–428.

Beynon, J. (2002) *Masculinities and Culture*. Buckingham: Open University Press.

Butler, J. (1990) *Gender Trouble: Feminism and the Subversion of Identity*. London: Routledge.

Cashmore, E. (2004) *Beckham* (2nd edn). Cambridge: Polity.

Cashmore, E. & Parker, A. (2003) ' "One David Beckham ...?" Celebrity, masculinity and the soccerati', *Sociology of Sport Journal*, 20, 214–232.

Clayton, B. & Harris, J. (2004) 'Footballers' wives: The role of the soccer player's partner in the construction of idealised masculinity', *Soccer and Society*, 5, 3, 317–335.

Clayton, B. & Humberstone, B. (2006) 'Men's talk: A (pro)feminist analysis of university football players' discourse', *International Review for the Sociology of Sport*, 41, 3, 295–316.

Coad, D. (2005) 'Euro 2004 and football fashion', *Journal of Sport and Social Issues*, 29, 124–126.

Connell, R. (1987) *Gender and Power*. Cambridge: Polity.

Connell, R. (1994) 'Psychoanalysis on masculinity', in H. Brod & M. Kaufman (eds.) *Theorizing Masculinities*. London: Sage.

Connell, R. (1995) *Masculinities*. Cambridge: Polity.

Connell, R. (2005) *Masculinities* (2nd edn.) Cambridge: Polity.

Coupland, J. (2007) 'Gendered discourses on the problem of aging: Consumerized solutions', *Discourse & Communication*, 1, 37–61.

Edwards, T. (2006) *Cultures of Masculinity*. London: Routledge.

ESPN (2007a) 'Most likely to carry a European carry-all' (on-line). Available from http://espn.go.com/page2/s/gallery/metros.html (accessed on 19 Nov. 2007).

ESPN (2007b) 'Pedicures? Not these guys' (on-line). Available from http://espn.go.com/page2/s/gallery/nonmetros.html (accessed on 19 Nov. 2007).

Freud, S. (1953) [1905] *Three Essays on the Theory of Sexuality: Complete Psychological Works* (std edn, Vol. 7). London: Hogarth.

Gill, R., Henwood, K. & McLean, C. (2005) 'Body projects and the regulation of normative masculinity', *Body and Society*, 11, 37–62.

Harris, J. & Clayton, B. (2002a) 'Femininity, masculinity, physicality and the English tabloid press: The case of Anna Kournikova', *International Review for the Sociology of Sport*, 37, 397–414.

Harris, J. & Clayton, B. (2002b) 'Survival of the prettiest? (Re)presenting the female athlete'. Paper presented at the annual conference of the Leisure Studies Association, Preston, UK, July.

Harris, J. & Clayton, B. (2007a) 'David Beckham and the changing (re)presentations of English identity', *International Journal of Sport Management and Marketing*, 2, 208–221.

Harris, J. & Clayton, B. (2007b) 'The first metrosexual rugby star? Rugby Union, masculinity and celebrity in contemporary Wales', *Sociology of Sport Journal*, 24, 2, 145–164.

Hondagneu-Sotelo, P. & Messner, M. (1994) 'Gender displays and men's power: The "New Man" and the Mexican immigrant man', in H. Brod & M. Kaufman (eds) *Theorizing Masculinities*. London: Sage.

Kane, M. & Lenskyj, H. (1998) 'Media treatment of female athletes: Issues of gender and sexualities', in L. Wenner (ed.) *Media Sport*. London: Routledge.

Kimmel, M. (1987) *Changing Men: New Directions in Research on Men and Masculinities*. Newbury Park, CA: Sage.

Lafrance, M. & Rail, G. (2001) 'Excursions into otherness: Understanding Dennis Rodman and the limits of subversive agency', in D. Andrews & S. Jackson (eds) *Sport Stars: The Cultural Politics of Sporting Celebrity*. London: Routledge.

Messner, M. (1987) 'The life of a man's seasons: Male identity in the life-course of the jock', in M. Kimmel (ed.) *Changing Men: New Directions in Research on Men and Masculinity*. Beverly Hills, CA: Sage.

Messner, M. (1992) *Power at Play: Sports and the Problem of Masculinity*. Boston: Beacon Press.

Miller, T. (2005) 'A metrosexual eye on queer guy', *GLQ: A Journal of Lesbian and Gay Studies*, 11, 112–117.

Parker, A. (2001) 'Soccer, servitude and sub-cultural identity: Football traineeship and masculine construction', *Soccer and Society*, 2, 1, 59–80.

Parker, A. & Lyle, S. (2008) 'Sport, masculinity and consumption: Metrosexuality, "chav" culture and social class', in M. Atkinson & K. Young (eds) *Tribal Play: Sport Subcultures and Countercultures*. Oxford: Elsevier.

Pronger, B. (1990) 'Gay jocks: A phenomenology of gay men in athletics', in M. Messner & D. Sabo (eds) *Sport, Men and the Gender Order: Critical Feminist Perspectives*. Champaign, IL: Human Kinetics.

Sabo, D. & Jansen, S. (1992) 'Images of men in sport media: The social reproduction of gender', in S. Craig (ed.) *Men, Masculinity, and the Media*. London: Sage.

Salzman, M, Matathia, I. & O'Reilly, A. (2005) *The Future of Men*. London: Palgrave Macmillan.

Schacht, S. (1996) 'Misogyny on and off the pitch: The gendered world of male rugby players', *Gender and Society*, 10, 550–565.

Simpson, M. (1994) 'Here come the mirror men', *Independent*, 15 Nov.

Simpson, M. (1996) *It's a Queer World: Deviant Adventures in Pop Culture*. London: Vintage.

Simpson, M (2004) 'MetroDaddy speaks'. Retrieved 12 Apr. 2007 from www.marksimpson.com/pages/journalism/metrodaddyspeaks.html

Smart, B. (2005) *The Sport Star: Modern Sport and the Cultural Economy of Sporting Celebrity*. London: Sage.

Thornley, G. (2005) 'Making it up as he goes along', *The Irish Times*. Retrieved 29 Sept. 2005 from www.2005lions.net/nz2005_itin_005.shtml

Tomlinson, A., Ravenscroft, N., Wheaton, B. & Gilchrist, P. (2005) *Lifestyle Sports and National Sport Policy: An Agenda for Research*. Brighton: Sport England/Chelsea School Research Centre, University of Brighton.

Vincent, J. (2004) 'Game, sex and match: The construction of gender in British newspaper coverage of the 2000 Wimbledon championships', *Sociology of Sport Journal*, 21, 435–456.

Whannel, G. (2001) 'Punishment, redemption and celebration in the popular press: The case of David Beckham', in D. Andrews & S. Jackson (eds) *Sport Stars: The Cultural Politics of Sporting Celebrity*. London: Routledge.

Whannel, G. (2002) *Media Sport Stars: Masculinities and Moralities*. London: Routledge.

8
Sport, Celebrity and Identity: A Socio-legal Analysis

Andrew Parker

Sociological analyses of sport and the law are notoriously difficult to find and, some would argue, urgently needed. Conversely, the theme of sporting celebrity has attracted significant attention in recent times from both social scientists and legal practitioners alike. Evident amidst this literature is the sense that sports stars represent a key site through which social, cultural and economic change can be observed. Adopting a socio-legal perspective, this chapter assesses the extent to which current English law protects the rights of sporting celebrities amidst a rapidly changing social context. The central thesis is that while sports personalities can look to the law for protection in relation to their identities, the information upon which such legal decisions are based might be further enhanced by a consideration of wider social factors.

Sport, celebrity and social identity

As outlined in the introduction to this volume, broadly speaking the construction of social identity is about how we, as individuals (or indeed collectives), identify ourselves in the social world. It is about how we understand and interpret ourselves and those around us, how others do likewise and how, as a consequence, issues of difference and similarity arise. For Jenkins (2008), these on-going processes, involving internal and external definitions of the self, form the bedrock of identity construction (both individual and collective). Of course, social identity is also about how we construct ourselves in accordance with a range of broader social forces. Celebrity figures, for example, do not emerge in a social vacuum. On the contrary, they are products of the cultural, political and historical circumstances upon which their very existence depends. Technological advancements in recent years have spawned a growth and intensification of media resources, which has led to the wider popularization of sport as a cultural spectacle (Boyle & Haynes, 1999; Rowe, 2003; Whannel, 1992). Today sports coverage features large amidst the offerings of numerous television and communication networks as the sport–media relationship becomes ever more intimate and lucrative. Such interest necessarily brings with it fame and popular cultural appeal for a number of star performers. What this inevitably means is that the identities of particular celebrities become part of that sport–media equation.

Consequently, a relatively new theme has emerged both within the orbits of academic and legal debate: the identity of sporting celebrities themselves (Andrews & Jackson, 2001; Smart, 2005).[1] Of central interest for writers in the social sciences has been the extent to which modern-day professional sports stars might transcend their occupational locales to become wider public figures, national ambassadors and global commodities (Cashmore & Parker, 2003; Harris & Clayton, 2007).[2] Yet against this backdrop, there has been a tendency to neglect (or overlook) a broader range of issues, such as those concerning the legal status of sports personalities especially in relation to image rights. This chapter addresses the possible connections between sociological analyses of sporting celebrity and related discussion (and practice) in the legal domain. Viewed alongside each other, these distinct disciplinary areas raise a series of questions about how we might define, conceptualize and operationalize the notion of celebrityhood and, perhaps more importantly, how the identities of celebrity sports stars are both constructed and protected. In order to assess exactly what (if anything) these two discursive frameworks have to offer each other (at least within the context of English law), we must consider them separately in more detail. I begin with a brief discussion of sociological research on this topic.[3]

Sport, celebrity and sociology

At a collective level, sociologists have put forward a number of explanations as to why and how the cult of celebrity has emerged, the majority of which focus on the shifting social and cultural terrain of modern-day life. One of the most useful of these explanations is that of Rojek (2001), who identifies three main reasons for these shifts: (i) the democratization of society; (ii) the technological advancements of the mass-media age, and (iii) the demise of religion. Taken together, what these three factors appear to characterize is a change in the overall complexion of advanced industrial society in what some have called the postmodern age. For Rojek (2001), the demise of monarchical and religious influence, coupled with a ubiquitous saturation of media personalities, has lead to a new fluidity and redistribution of power in social life, broadly resulting in celebrities taking the place of previously dominant figures (see also Smart, 2005).

Like a host of other high-profile occupations, professional sport generates an institutional climate conducive to the construction of celebrity status. Sports performers become famous mostly as a result of their physical and cognitive abilities, their 'off-field' exploits and/or their charismatic demeanour. For a small number, fame transmutes into an altogether more intense form of recognition around which celebrities are born; according to Boorstin's (1961, p. 58) oft quoted phrase, they are simply 'well-known for their well-known-ness'. A plethora of writers have attempted to plot the logic of this transformative process, but the fact remains that celebrity is a highly contested concept that has eluded any real sense of academic definition to date.[4] Inherent in the mêlée of explanatory and analytical offerings on this subject is a conflation of terms and descriptors which are commonly rendered synonymous – 'stars', 'superstars' 'heroines', 'heroes', 'icons' – and yet which, in many ways, present their own specific differences and idiosyncrasies (Andrews & Jackson, 2001; Turner, 2004). Characterized by notions of fame, notoriety, charisma and exception, celebrityhood is a commodification of the human form; the epitome of economic fetishism, the process and product of representations and images promoted and exchanged via the complex nexus of modern-day media networks. Like global brands and fictional figures, sporting celebrities permeate every thread of the social fabric (Cashmore & Parker, 2003).

In essence, yet without any real sense of empirical accuracy, broader sociological discussions of celebrityhood confirm that the notion of the 'sports celebrity' remains relatively undefined. This is evident in analyses presented by social scientists concerning taxonomies of celebrity status where attention is often drawn to the various depths, levels and forms which celebrityhood can take. A number of views have been proffered on this subject around which issues of 'fame', 'celebrity' and 'iconicity' are contested.[5] In turn, writers have speculated on the on-going influence of celebrity status with regard to the extent to which such figures might transcend their local, regional and national contexts. What this work offers is an analysis of sporting celebrity in relation to the way in which different levels of fame and/or celebrityhood connect with notions of labour in relation to image creation and production and how celebrities themselves might be implicated in this process. At a commonsense level, such analyses may have something to offer the current English legal position on celebrity image rights and ownership. In attempting to assess whether or not this is the case, it is to a further exploration of the application of the law in this area that I now turn.

Sport, celebrity and the law

Like a number of sociologists, various legal commentators have viewed the cult of celebrity as something which has developed in more recent years largely as a consequence of broader social change and, in particular, the intensification of commercialism and consumer culture alongside the pervasive advancements of the mass media (Carty, 2004, 2007; Smith, 2004). In this sense, the rise of the celebrity has proved itself to be as much a legal phenomenon as a social one. At the heart of discussions surrounding celebrity and the law are a series of questions concerning individual identity, image and personal propriety and, perhaps most importantly, intellectual property rights (Boyd, 2002; Couchman & Korman, 1996; Farnsworth, 2001).

In contrast to corporeal or tangible property, the law of intellectual property deals with incorporeal or intangible entities, the rights attached to innovative creations of knowledge and information (Drahos, 1995, 1996). The problem of distinguishing between the intellectual creations of one person over another is labelled the 'idea/expression dichotomy'; a distinction which, Haynes (2005) argues, facilitates the separation of original ideas from their expressive use thereafter. This distinction dictates both the boundaries and legal mechanisms by which such rights are governed. At the philosophical core of intellectual property are the theories of economic exchange in relation to knowledge creation around which these legal mechanisms operate. Derived from the work of Locke, the labour theory of property proffers legal ownership as a reward for the personal creation of ideas.[6] This, in turn, generates the incentive for innovation to take place. Without these assumptions there would be no moral or legal infrastructure upon which the creation and exchange of such intangible goods could occur. Hence, intellectual property rights have come to be traded, policed and protected by a series of contemporary legal measures, all of which are drawn from long-established moral and philosophical ideals.

One specific aspect of the way in which intellectual property laws are used concerns the protection of individual image rights and, in particular, those of celebrity figures (Drahos & Braithwaite, 2002). Within this context, 'image rights', as a generic term, encompasses the commercial use of an individual's image/style, voice, likeness, name or signature – characteristics commonly classified as indicia. To this end, intellectual property law has been adapted by celebrities (and their representatives) to claim propriety rights over a personal image which they have created and established either by way of their labour (for example, as a music artist, sports personality, etc.) or simply by way of achieving fame or notoriety by some other means (Haynes, 2005).[7] Unlike in a number of other countries, the English courts have been reluctant to recognize a specific right of publicity that celebrities might use to protect their image from commercial exploitation and misappropriation, despite the merchandising and endorsement potential of such images and the increasing scope for exploitation amidst burgeoning global media markets (Carty, 2007; Lauterbach, 2005). Underpinning this reluctance, it seems, is a dismissal of the commodifiable nature of an individual's image. For Cornish (1999, p. 31) this stance is inherent. The English law, he explains,

> has steadfastly refused to adopt any embracing principle that a person has a right to his or her name, or, for that matter, to identifying characteristics, such as voice or image. An entitlement simply to demand that such characteristics without more amount to property in personality is highly regarded as a commodification too far.

If image rights represents the legal mechanism by which celebrity identity has come to be policed and protected, the legal issues upon which such protection is based are largely those concerning three main aspects of the law: (i) copyright; (ii) trademark licensing, and (iii) the common law tort of passing off (comprising the 'classical trinity' of misrepresentation, goodwill and damage). At the same time, case law deliberations over notions of fame and celebrity have considered the depth and value of celebrityhood, especially in relation to product merchandising, endorsement, sponsorship and branding, all of which are distinctive in their own right. Common also in legal circles are discussions surrounding the distinction between privacy rights and publicity rights.[8] Before going on to look at the potential of socio-legal analyses of celebrity image rights, it is worth considering the way in which these specific areas of law have been explored in relation to the broader celebrity sphere both overseas and in the UK.

Sport, celebrity and image rights

As is the case for other celebrity figures, debate surrounding the image rights of sports stars is based on the fundamental premise that an individual has propriety over particular facets of his or her own identity, an issue which, as we have seen, has its roots in the philosophy of intellectual property (Haynes, 2004, 2005).[9] In turn, the commercial value of the image rights of any sporting celebrity is determined by his or her ability to protect that right at law from unauthorized use or exploitation. There are a number of discrepancies in this respect with regard to a range of countries. Citizens in the USA, for example, are able to control how their image is used at a commercial level as a consequence of the historical establishment of the personality/privacy and (later) publicity rights which grew out of the advertising and marketing activities of the late nineteenth and early twentieth centuries and the accompanying cult of celebrity (Carty, 2004; Evans, 2005; Smith, 2004).

Emanating from the earlier (if somewhat ineffectual) establishment of a privacy or personality right (or tort of privacy), the common-law right of publicity (a property right in one's own image) was initially recognized in the 1953 US case between rival chewing gum manufacturers, *Haelean Laboratories* v *Topps Chewing Gum*,[10] where the plaintiffs had contracted with leading major-league baseball players for the exclusive right to use their images in connection with product sales. This case was important because it established that individuals could possess a property right in their own image and, furthermore, that it was possible for this to be appropriated by a third party. By 1977 the right of publicity had been recognized by the US Supreme Court and, as a consequence of both academic and legal debate, the overall remit of the action itself has seen further expansion, though the development of a privacy right has been less effective.

Similar propriety rights over the commercial marketing of an individual's image have been recognized by the Canadian courts following the establishment of the tort of appropriation of personality in *Krouse v Chrysler Canada Ltd*,[11] where a professional football player sued a motor car manufacturer for using a photograph of him in an advertisement without his consent, and later in *Athans v Canadian Adventure Camps Ltd*,[12] where a famous professional water-skier brought an action against a holiday company for the way in which it had appropriated a distinctive image of him in its advertising materials. In Australian law there is no equivalent right to personal propriety but ss.52 and 53 of the Trade Practices Act 1974 provide legislation against the misleading or deceptive use of sponsorship, approval or affiliation in the representation of goods and services. Moreover, the unauthorized use of personal images through the tort of passing off is protected in common law as a consequence of the decision in *Henderson v Radio Corpn*[13] where the plaintiff's case concerning the misappropriation of their photographic image as a form of product endorsement was upheld.[14]

Meanwhile in the European context, and in the absence of express publicity rights, a number of countries have more recently moved away from the rather limited focus on privacy, favouring instead an acceptance of the protection of an individual's image as an issue of propriety; this amidst increasing commercial pressures and the subsequent need to extend the scope of existing statutory provisions concerning privacy in a range of countries.[15] A case in point is that of the German professional footballer Oliver Khan[16] who, in 2004, successfully brought an action against the computer game manufacturer Electronic Arts under Articles 22 and 23 of the German Artistic Authors Rights Act for unlawful use of his name and 'portrait' in product advertisement. Within the UK similar issues have arisen but, in the absence of a distinct personality right, other legal mechanisms (i.e. defamation, breach of confidence, etc.) have come into play. The case of *Tolley v Fry*[17] provides an apt example of the way in which issues of defamation might arise within sports settings. Tolley was a well-known amateur golfer who was caricatured by the chocolate manufacturer Fry as endorsing one of their products. Tolley had not authorized the use of his likeness and brought an action against Fry for defamation on the basis that his reputation as an amateur could be damaged via the inference that he had been paid for the advertisement. In an era dominated by arguments surrounding the amateur/professional sporting divide, Tolley was successful in his legal fight on the grounds that the advertisement had compromised his amateur status. More recently in the UK the laws surrounding copyright, trademarking and (the tort of) passing off have been used to protect celebrity image rights, and it is to a closer examination of these that we now turn.

The UK Copyright, Designs and Patents Act (CDPA) 1988, s.1(1)(a-c) facilitates the protection of certain entities by confirming a propriety right in 'original literary, dramatic, musical or artistic works, sound recordings, films, broadcasts or cable programmes, and the typographical arrangement of published editions'. Yet, despite the fact that there may be copyright in a signature, in graphical representation, and in a photograph (though belonging to the photographer and not to the subject in question), the CDPA is limited with regard to the protection of individual image rights simply because there is no action available in relation to copyright of a face or name (Lewis & Taylor, 2003). For this reason, celebrities may alternatively look to trademark law for some form of legal protection.

The Trade Marks Act 1994, s.1(1) states that a trademark comprises 'any sign capable of being represented graphically which is capable of distinguishing goods or services of one undertaking from those of other undertakings. A trademark may, in particular, consist of words (including personal names), designs, letters, numerals or the shape of goods or their packaging'. Hence, while recognizable at a more general level, the indicia of a sports star must be distinct from that of others in order to be granted registration as a trademark; that is, it must represent a 'badge of origin' which is solely connected to the (authorized) identity of the individual in question. Famous figures (past and present) have met with mixed fortunes in their attempts to invoke protection via trademark law. The leading case here is that concerning the legal estate of Elvis Presley where the Court of Appeal held that the name 'Elvis' did not carry sufficient distinction for the late singer's commercial partners to claim sole ownership of it.[18] In UK sport, professional footballers David Beckham, Alan Shearer and Ryan Giggs have all been successful in registering their names as trademarks,[19] while others (i.e. Mark Hughes) have not. Others still, such as ex-England footballing stars Paul Gascoigne and David Seaman have acquired similarly favourable outcomes in their pursuit of distinctive nicknames; 'Gazza' and 'Safe Hands' respectively. In the broader sporting sphere, FIA Formula One World Championship racing drivers Jacques Villeneuve and Damon Hill have been equally successful in registering specific images of themselves (Harrington, 1999; Lewis & Taylor, 2003).

A further legal avenue by way of which celebrity figures might seek damages or protection for the exploitation or misappropriation of their image is that of the common-law tort of passing off; a law which prevents the presentation of a claimant's goods or services by another who seeks to make commercial gain from the goodwill (i.e. name or reputation) of the claimant's image or name without his or her authority. Despite the fact that passing off has come to offer a useful remedy for celebrities eager to maximize their (often short-lived) marketability, case-law examples involving sports personnel are somewhat rare. This is primarily because (in the UK at least) celebrity sports status is a relatively new phenomenon and, consequently, such individuals have only recently looked to this aspect of the law for protection. In this context, passing off has been used to challenge the illegitimate use of celebrity image, thereby safeguarding the various forms of business capital (i.e. goodwill and reputation) which might reside in an unregistered 'trademark'.

Historically, for such claims to succeed, it had to be established that the defendant was encroaching upon, or violating, the image (propriety) right(s) of the claimant by being engaged in a 'common field of activity', an approach most notably followed by Wynn-Parry J in what was, for some time, considered to be the leading case in the area, *McCulloch v Lewis A May Ltd.*[20] However, as a consequence of more recent events this situation has changed. A key juncture here was the 2002 case of *Irvine v Talksport*[21] in which the claimant, Formula One World Championship racing driver Eddie Irvine, brought an action against (the then named) Talk Radio for false endorsement. Talk Radio had included a manipulated photograph of Irvine in some of their promotional literature. In it he was pictured holding a radio set featuring their name. During the case the presiding judge (Laddie, J) suggested that established law in this field did not adequately reflect the changing nature of market practice and that the law of passing off should be seen to be responding to these changing social and economic circumstances. Drawing on the Australian case of *Henderson* v *Radio Corporation Pty Ltd,*[22] and the English case of *Harrods* v *Harrodian School Ltd,*[23] (both of which rejected the 'common field of activity' requirement), Laddie J stated:

> [T]he law of passing off now is of greater width than as applied by Wynn-Parry J in *McCulloch v May*. If someone acquires a valuable reputation or goodwill, the law of passing off will protect it from unlicensed use by other parties. Such use will frequently be damaging in the direct sense that it will involve selling inferior goods or services under the guise that they are from the claimant. But the action is not restricted to protecting against that sort of damage. The law will vindicate the claimant's exclusive right to the reputation or goodwill. It will not allow others to so use goodwill as to reduce, blur or diminish its exclusivity. It follows that it is not necessary to show that the claimant and the defendant share a common field of activity or that sales of products or services will be diminished either substantially or directly at least in the short term.

In stating this view, the judge was clearly proffering a change to existing legal practice where reputation and goodwill were threatened via false endorsement. Yet equally (if not more) important was Laddie J's ruling concerning the personal 'ownership' of such a reputation, concluding that: 'Mr Irvine has a property right in his goodwill which he can protect from unlicensed appropriation consisting of a false claim or suggestion of endorsement of a third party's goods or services'.[24] While Judge Laddie was also keen to note the limits of the *Irvine* ruling (drawing, for example, on the earlier events in *Elvis Presley Enterprises Inc.*)[25] the significance of the *Irvine* case for issues surrounding celebrity image rights should not be underestimated. Indeed, what this decision established was that if a celebrity was able to show that, at the time of false endorsement, his/her image carried a significant reputation (or level of goodwill), which was, in some way, undermined within a 'not insignificant' proportion of the market by a party proffering that his own goods were endorsed by the celebrity in question, then that celebrity would have a claim for passing off (Hennigan, 2003; Learmonth, 2002; Lewis & Taylor, 2003). Essentially, this decision fell short of establishing the kind of personality/publicity right available to those in other countries. Nevertheless, it marked a significant step forward in terms of the way in which celebrities might protect their commercial interests against illegitimate use. In the event, Irvine received £25,000 in damages (upheld on appeal), a sum which was estimated to be at least that which the defendants would have been required to pay for the legal endorsement of their product.[26]

Perhaps not surprisingly, it was not long before the *Irvine* precedent was taken up by other sports personalities. In 2002 ex-England cricketer Ian Botham was awarded damages against the brewing company Diageo (owners of the Guinness brand) who, in an advertising campaign for the beer, had used unauthorized images of Botham playing in the 1981 Ashes Test series against Australia. Claiming on grounds of false endorsement of the product, and that his reputation and goodwill had been exploited, Botham received an undisclosed settlement (thought to be a five-figure sum) and the advertising campaign was withdrawn (Carty, 2007; Haynes, 2004).

A third, and more recent, case was that of ex-British long-distance runner David Bedford who in 2003 brought a claim for false endorsement against the US-based telephone-directory service, The Number. Bedford alleged that The Number had violated his image rights by using a caricature of his persona as part of an advertising campaign for their UK 118 118 directory-enquiries service. The advertisement featured comedic role-play between two look-alike runners dressed and styled in a manner formerly associated with Bedford himself. Despite seemingly endorsing the campaign at its outset as a legitimate take on his previous personal demeanour, the growing appeal of the advertisements led Bedford to register a claim against the company. In January 2004 this was upheld by the

UK media regulator Ofcom on the grounds that the campaign breached the guidelines protecting the privacy and exploitation of the individual in Rule 6.5 of the Advertising Standards Code (ITC, 2002). While the case further reinforced the already-established momentum around the protection of celebrity image rights, Bedford, unlike Irvine and Botham, did not receive financial remuneration. According to Ofcom, the former runner had not incurred damages in terms of his reputation or financial situation and ruled that the advertising campaign could continue, given the amount of money already invested in it up to that point (Haynes, 2004, 2005; Ofcom, 2004; Vaver, 2006).

Clearly, the Bedford decision runs contrary to that of the previous two cases. Why, one might ask, was financial remuneration available to Irvine and Botham and not to Bedford? A possible explanation for this surrounds a consideration of the amount of damage to reputation and goodwill which each individual suffered given their celebrity status at the time of the false endorsement. Following the logic outlined by Judge Laddie in *Irvine*, it could be argued that because of the appeal of their respective sports, and the celebrity status (significance) which they had attained, both Irvine and Botham were likely to suffer more damage to reputation and goodwill than Bedford. Whether this kind of calculation was one upon which Ofcom made their final decision is unknown but it is certainly one that generated speculation from a number of onlookers (see Oliver, 2003; Pearce, 2004).

In sum, legal interpretations of celebrityhood primarily concern the appropriation and protection of individual identity. Taking into consideration aspects of status, reputation and career longevity, the English legal model appears to provide a relatively comprehensive protection mechanism in this respect. Despite the progress made in *Irvine*, the main criticism on offer here is the way in which the law has failed to keep pace with the broader commercial aspects of sports celebrity status. In this sense, overseas models concerning personal and propriety rights (especially those in the USA) would seem to hold a distinct advantage (Boyd, 2002; Farnsworth, 2001).

Discussion: towards a socio-legal analysis of sporting celebrity

What then do sociological and legal interpretations of celebrity status have in common and, perhaps more importantly, what can they offer each other in terms of the identities of sporting celebrities? Three main issues appear to stand out.

First, while clearly facilitating a degree of flexibility over their treatment of sports stars (as demonstrated in the differential rulings in the cases of Irvine, Botham and Bedford), it could be argued that legal definitions of celebrity status remain somewhat monolithic in nature. Indeed, what the cases of Irvine and Bedford reveal most poignantly is that while the social 'significance' (i.e. reputation and goodwill) of different celebrity figures is taken into account by the courts, such assessments appear to be made in a rather arbitrary way, based not on any form of rigorous assessment but on rather spurious assumptions surrounding the level of social and cultural appeal which an individual might possess at a particular point in time. If research concerning the various taxonomies of celebrity status were to be considered by the courts, this might facilitate a more precise evaluation of celebrity (commodified) value, especially within the context of claims for false endorsement and damages in the tort of passing off. Clearly the empirical assessment of such value would be difficult to ascertain. However, using the kind of taxonomic classifications discussed in more recent sociological accounts regarding the various depths, levels and forms of celebrityhood, it may be possible to make some useful distinctions between the nature of the legal claims of some against those of others. Clearly there is scope for a much more in-depth analysis to develop in relation to the cultural significance of celebrity sports performers. Additionally, there may also be benefits here within the orbits of employment contract negotiations, whereby some form of celebrity categorization might serve to inform further the legal processes involved between sports stars and their prospective employers.[27]

A second (and related) point concerns the concept of labour. A number of commentators (both legal and sociological) argue that crucial to any assessment of fame are considerations surrounding the labour process itself; how celebrities achieve their status and to what extent it is a product of their own creativity and innovation (see Beverley-Smith, 2002; Coombe, 1992; Haynes, 2005; Madow, 1993). Cashmore & Parker (2003), for example, have considered the way in which sporting labour might be legitimately viewed within the broader context of the capitalist labour process, adding to a previously well established sports/labour argument (see Brohm, 1978; Rigaeur, 1981). As well as reinforcing the potential of a classification or taxonomy of celebrity status, such analyses might be used to evaluate the degree to which celebrity status/image is authentically crafted in terms of the creative (innovative) skills and attributes of the individual concerned, hence allowing a more accurate assessment of image ownership to take place in line with the broader philosophical underpinnings of intellectual property rights. On this basis, not only might the courts be better informed as to the rights of certain celebrities, they might also be in a stronger position to discern the relative differences between the commodified value of particular individuals.

Finally, it is worth reaffirming that false endorsement, copyright and trademarking comprise only one side of a whole series of legal debates around celebrity image rights, another significant feature of which are issues of personal privacy. Central to such actions is the balance between the individual's right to privacy and the media's freedom of expression. As in claims of false endorsement and passing off, reputation and goodwill are often at stake where the right to privacy is raised. The case of *Tolley*[28] provides an early example of the way in which issues of defamation might arise within sports settings, and similar cases continue to emerge.[29] In turn, a series of wider privacy claims have been aided by the application of the European Convention for the Protection of Human Rights and Fundamental Freedoms (ECHR) and, more specifically, the UK Human Rights Act (HRA) 1998.[30] Once again, additional contextual commentary on the social and cultural significance of celebrity figures may provide supplementary information for the courts where claims for damages on grounds of personal privacy are considered.

Conclusion

Can sociological analyses aid the legal process in relation to notions of sporting identity? In this chapter I have argued that, while unable to provide an accurate assessment of the social significance of public figures, broader sociological commentary on the celebrity value of sports performers may offer legal discussion (and decision-making) a more holistic view of the social and economic value of such individuals on account of the broader contextual data which they contain and the classificatory frameworks which they adopt. In turn, I have argued that these accounts might be used by the courts to assess claims surrounding the notion of intellectual property, especially where issues of creativity, innovation and image rights arise. Is the emergence of a separate 'personality right' a likely proposition for the UK? If the present momentum towards the cult of celebrity is anything to go by, then it seems possible that such a right will eventually emerge. Just as the logic of capitalism necessitates further technological advancement, the development of consumer culture, and the prevalence of the visual image, so too the identities of celebrities continue to be formed in relation to the specific cultural and historical contexts in which they occur. The multifaceted identities of sports stars are forged before our very eyes. Yet a question mark remains over whether or not these identities are to be considered the property of those whose lifestyles, livelihoods and values they represent.

Notes

1. For further discussion on the sport/celebrity relationship, see Whannel (2002), Nalapat & Parker (2005) and Bolsman & Parker (2007). For more detailed insight into sporting celebrity and notoriety, see Cashmore (2004, 2005).
2. I use the term 'stars' here to denote sports performers who have become well known (and recognized) publicly as celebrity figures (see also Dyer, 1998).
3. For a broader overview of sport and the law, see Jarvie (2006).
4. Academic offerings on the concept of celebrity are nothing new. For more on this subject, see Debord (1968), Monaco (1978), Gamson (1994), Marshall (1997), Evans & Wilson (1999), Giles (2000) and Turner *et al.* (2000).
5. For specific discussion on taxonomies of celebrity, see Rojek (2001) and Turner (2004). For more on the icon/icnonicity dyad, see Kear & Steinberg (1999).
6. For further discussion on this connection to the work of Locke, see Carty (2004) and Haynes (2004, 2005). For a critique of the application of Locke's labour theory of property to intellectual and artistic creativity, see Bettig (1996).
7. For more in-depth commentary on the validity of propriety rights in personality and in relation to various forms of celebrity, see Coombe (1992), Madow (1993) and Beverley-Smith (2002).
8. See Gardiner *et al.* (2001), Lewis & Taylor (2003), Learmonth (2002), Hennigan (2003), Carty (2004, 2007) and Vahrenwald (1994, 2004). For discussion of image rights in relation to 'non-humans', see Tessensohn (2004).
9. I am especially indebted to the work of Richard Haynes (2004, 2005) on sport, media and intellectual property, and I draw on this throughout this chapter.
10. *Haelean Laboratories Inc. v. Topps Chewing Gum Inc.*, 202 F.2d 866 (2nd Cir.1953). The right of publicity established in this case is not a Federal right. Federal law in this area is appropriated under s.43(a) of the Lanham Trade Mark Act, 15 USCA 1125. See also Harrington (1999).
11. *Krouse v. Chrysler Canada Ltd* (1973) 40 DLR (3d) 15.
12. *Athans v. Canadian Adventure Camps Ltd* (1977) 17 OR (2d) 425, 435.
13. See *Henderson v. Radio Corpn* [1969] RPC 218 (approved by the full High Court of Australia in *Campomer Sociedad Ltda v. Nike International Ltd* (2000) 46 IPR 481). In *Henderson* the plaintiffs were well-known ballroom dancers and instructors who successfully opposed the non-authorised use of their photograph on the cover of a dance music record.
14. See also *Hogan v. Pacific Dunlop Ltd* (1989) 14 IPR 398, and *Hogan v. Koala Dundee Pty Ltd* (1988) 83 ALR 187 (Federal Court of Australia, Queensland District).
15. See Harrington (2002) and Carty (2004, 2007).

16. *Khan v. Electronic Arts Gmbh* Ent. L.R. (2004) 15(5), N41. For further discussion of image rights issues within the German context, see Lauterbach (2005). See also Hennigan (2003).
17. *Tolley v. Fry* [1931] AC 333.
18. *Elvis Presley Enterprises Inc. v. Sid Shaw Elvisly Yours* [1999] RPC 567, CA. See also Wall (2003).
19. See also *Arnold Palmer v. Schonhorn Enterprises Inc* [1967] 232 A.2d 458. See also Davies (2004) for recent developments in UK trademark law.
20. *McCulloch v. Lewis A May Ltd*, [1947] 2 All ER 845, Ch D.
21. *Edmund Irvine Tidewell Ltd v. Talksport* Ltd [2002] 2 All ER 414.
22. *Henderson v Radio Corpn* [1969] RPC 218.
23. *Harrods v. Harrodian School Ltd* [1996] RPC 697, CA. Here the plaintiffs, Harrods, argued that their name had been used deliberately in order that the defendants might benefit from the goodwill generated by the Harrods label and that, as a result, the reputation associated with that business name would be damaged.
24. *Edmund Irvine Tidewell Ltd v. Talksport* Ltd [2002] 2 All ER 414 at 436.
25. *Elvis Presley Enterprises Inc. v. Sid Shaw Elvisly Yours* [1999] RPC 567, CA.
26. For a detailed critique of the judgement of Laddie J in *Irvine*, see Scanlan (2003).
27. For further discussion on these processes, see Lewis & Taylor (2003), Haynes (2004), Milligan (2004) and Dulin (2005).
28. *Tolley v. Fry* [1931] AC 333.
29. See *Lance Armstrong v. Times Newspapers Ltd, David Walsh, Alan English* [2005] EWHC 2816. See also Rutherford (2005) and Gibb (2006).
30. Two specific sections of the HRA 1998 are important here: Section 8(1) The right to privacy, and Article 1 of Protocol 1 The right to peaceful enjoyment of property. See, for example, *Campbell v. MGN Ltd* [2004] UKHL 22; *Douglas v. Hello! Ltd* [2001] 2 All ER 289.

References

Andrews, D. & Jackson, S. (2001) (eds) *Sports Stars: The Cultural Politics of Sporting Celebrity*. London: Routledge.
Bettig, R. (1996) *Copyrighting Culture: The Political Economy of Intellectual Property*. Westview: Oxford.
Beverley-Smith, H. (2002) *The Commercial Appropriation of Personality*. Cambridge: Cambridge University Press.
Bolsmann, C. & Parker, A. (2007) 'Soccer, South Africa and celebrity status: Mark Fish, popular culture and the post-apartheid state', *Soccer and Society*, 8 (1), 109–124.
Boorstin, D. (1961) *The Image: A Guide to Pseudo-Events in America*. New York: Atheneum.
Boyd, S. (2002) 'Does English law recognise the concept of an image or personality right?', *Entertainment Law Review*, 13 (1), 1–7.
Boyle, R. & Haynes, R. (1999) *Power Play: Sport, the Media and Popular Culture*. London: Longman.
Brohm, J-M. (1978) *Sport: A Prison of Measured Time*. London: Pluto.

Carty, H. (2004) 'Advertising, publicity rights and English law', *Intellectual Property Quarterly*, 3, 209–258.

Carty, H (2007) 'The common law and the quest for the IP effect', *Intellectual Property Quarterly*, 3, 237–266.

Cashmore, E. (2004) *Beckham* (2nd edn). Cambridge: Polity.

Cashmore, E. (2005) *Tyson. Nurture of the Beast*. Cambridge: Polity.

Cashmore, E. & Parker, A. (2003) ' "One David Beckham ...?" Celebrity, masculinity and the soccerati', *Sociology of Sport Journal*, 20 (3), 214–232.

Coombe, R. (1992) 'The celebrity image and cultural identity: Publicity rights and the subaltern politics of gender', *Discourse: Berkeley Journal for Theoretical Studies in Media and Culture*, 59 (61), 59–88.

Coombe, R. (1998) *The Cultural Life of Intellectual Properties: Authorship, Appropriation and the Law*. London: Duke University Press.

Cornish, W. (1999) *Intellectual Property* (4th edn). London: Sweet and Maxwell.

Couchman, N. (2002a) 'Public Image Limited', *Guardian*, 1 May, available at <http://media.guardian.co.uk/print/0,3858,4404634-105237,00.html>

Couchman, N. (2002b) 'Constituent parts of image rights', *Guardian*, 1 May, available at <http://media.guardian.co.uk/marketingandpr/story/0„707773,00. html>

Couchman, N. (2002c) 'The computer game case', *Guardian*, 1 May, available at http://media.guardian.co.uk/marketingandpr/story/0„707777,00.html

Couchman, N. & Korman, A (1996) 'The cult of the personality', *Sports Law Administration and Practice*, July/Aug., 9

Davies, G. (2004) 'The cult of celebrity and trade marks: The next instalment', 1:2 *SCRIPTed* 230: www.law.ed.ac.uk/ahrc/script-ed/docs/agents.asp>

Debord, G. (1968) *Society of the Spectacle*. Detroit: Black and Red.

Drahos, P. (1995) 'Information feudalism in the information society', *The Information Society*, 11, 209–222.

Drahos, P. (1996) *A Philosophy of Intellectual Property*. Aldershot: Dartmouth Publishing.

Drahos, P. & Braithwaite, J. (2002) *Information Feudalism: Who Owns the Knowledge Economy?* London: Earthscan.

Dulin, D. (2005) 'All in a name as Trundle takes lead from Beckham to secure image rights', *The Times*, 27 Oct., p. 98.

Dyer, R. (1998) *Stars*. London: British Film Institute Publishing.

Evans, J. (2005) 'Celebrity, media and history', in J. Evans & D. Hesmondhalgh (eds) *Understanding Media: Inside Celebrity*. Buckingham: Open University Press.

Evans, A. & Wilson, G. (1999) *Fame: The Psychology of Stardom*. London: Vision.

Farnsworth, D. (2001) 'Does English law lack personality?', *International Sports Law Review*, 3, Aug., 210–218.

Gamson, J. (1994) *Claims to Fame: Celebrity in Contemporary America*. Berkeley, CA: University of California Press.

Gardiner, S., James, M., O'Leary, J., Welch, R., Blackshaw, I., Boyes, S. & Caiger, A. (2001) *Sports Law* (2nd edn). London: Cavendish Publishing.

Gibb, F. (2006) 'England star sues over reports on "bisexual" players', *The Times*, 3 Mar., p. 21.

Giles, D. (2000) *Illusions of Immortality: A Psychology of Fame and Celebrity*. London: Macmillan.

Harrington, D. (1999) 'Unauthorised use of sports stars' image in the UK and internationally – a level playing field?, Part 1', *Sport Character and Licensing*, 16, 18–19.

Harrington, D. (2002) 'Image rights – Overview of protection in key markets', *Sports Law Administration and Practice*, 9 (2), 11–15.

Harris, J. & Clayton, B. (2007)'The first metrosexual rugby star: Rugby Union, masculinity and celebrity in contemporary Wales', *Sociology of Sport Journal*, 24 (2), 145–164.

Haynes, R. (2004) 'The fame game: The peculiarities of sports image rights in the United Kingdom', *Trends In Communication*, 12 (2), 101–116.

Haynes, R. (2005) *Media Rights and Intellectual Property*. Edinburgh: Edinburgh University Press.

Hennigan, J. (2003) 'Altered image rights', *Entertainment Law Review*, 14 (7), 161–163.

ITC (2002) *The ITC Advertising Standards Code*. Available at www.ofcom.org. uk/static/archive/itc/itc_publications/codes_guidance/advertising_standards_ practice2/index.asp.html>

Jarvie, G. (2006) *Sport, Culture and Society: An Introduction*. London: Routledge.

Jenkins, R. (2008) *Social Identity* (3rd edn). London: Routledge.

Kear, A. & Steinberg, D. L. (1999) (eds) *Mourning Diana: Nation, Culture and the Performance of Grief*. London: Routledge.

Lauterbach, T. (2005) 'US-style "personality" right in the UK – *en route* from Strasbourg?', 20th BILETA Conference, Over-commoditised; Over-centralised; Over-observed: The New Digital Legal World?, Apr. Queen's University of Belfast.

Learmonth, A. (2002) 'Eddie, are you okay?: Product endorsement and passing off', *Intellectual Property Quarterly*, 3, 306–313.

Lewis, A. & Taylor, J. (2003) *Sport: Law and Practice*. London: Butterworths Lexis Nexis.

Madow, M. (1993) 'Private ownership of public image: Popular culture and publicity rights', *California Law Review*, (81) 125. Available at <http://cyber.law.harvard.edu/property00/respect/madow.html>

Marshall, P. (1997) *Celebrity and Power: fame in contemporary culture*. Minneapolis, MN: University of Minnesota Press.

Milligan, A. (2004) *Brand it like Beckham: The Story of how Brand Beckham was Built*. London: Cyan Books.

Monaco, J. (1978) *Celebrity: The Media as Image Makers*. New York: Delta.

Nalapat, A. & Parker, A. (2005) 'Sport, celebrity and popular culture: Sachin Tendulkar, cricket and Indian nationalisms', *International Review for the Sociology of Sport*, 40 (4), 433–446.

Ofcom (2004) 'Outcome of appeal by The Number (UK) Ltd regarding complaint by David Bedford', 27 Jan. Available at <http://www.ofcom.org.uk/bulletins. adv_com/content_board/?a=87101>

Oliver, M. (2003) 'Former athlete to sue over directory ads', *Guardian*, 6 Oct. Available at www.guardian.co.uk/uk_news/story/0,,1056607,00.html>

Pearce, M. (2004) 'An advert or the real thing?, *Media Guardian*, 9 Feb.. Available at <http://media.guardian.co.uk/mediaguardian/story/0,,1143717,00.html?>

Rigaeur, B. (1981) *Sport and Work*. New York: Columbia University Press.

Rojek, C. (2001) *Celebrity*. London: Reaktion.

Rowe, D. (2003). *Sport, Culture and the Media*. Buckingham: Open University Press.

Rutherford, M. (2005) 'Private lives in the public eye – Do our libel laws work?', *The Times*, 22 Nov., p. 5.

Scanlan, G. (2003) 'Personality, endorsement and everything: The modern law of passing off and the myth of the personality right', *European Intellectual Property Review*, 25 (12), 563–569.

Smart, B. (2005) *The Sport Star: Modern Sport and the Cultural Economy of Sporting Celebrity*. London: Sage.

Smith, S. (2004) 'The changing face of image protection in sport', *International Sports Law Review*, 2 (May), 37–43.

Tessensohn, J. (2004) 'Supreme Court of Japan reins in publicity rights for horses', *Entertainment Law Review*, 15 (8), N70-71.

Turner, G. (2004) *Understanding Celebrity*. London: Sage.

Turner, G., Bonner, F. & Marshall, P. (2000) *Fame Games: The Production of Celebrity in Australia*. Melbourne: Cambridge University Press.

Vahrenwald, A. (1994) 'Photographs and privacy in Germany', *Entertainment Law Review*, 5 (6), 205–222.

Vahrenwald, A. (2004) 'Germany: Personality rights – computer game "FIFA Soccer Championship 2004"', *Entertainment Law Review*, 15 (5), N41.

Vaver, D. (2006) 'Advertising using an individual's image: A comparative note', *Law Quarterly Review*, 122, July, 362–369.

Wall, D. (2003) 'Policing Elvis: Legal action and the shaping of post-mortem celebrity culture as contested space', *Entertainment Law*, 2 (3), 35–69.

Whannel, G. (1992) *Fields in Vision: Television, Sport and Cultural Transformation*. London: Routledge.

Whannel, G. (2002) *Media Sports Stars: Masculinities and Moralities*. London: Routledge.

Afterword: Sport and Social Identities Reconsidered

John Harris and Andrew Parker

We began this book by suggesting that the term 'social identity' is one which has largely eluded conceptual definition but which has appeared more frequently within academic discourse in recent years, often serving as a convenient 'catch-all' to encompass a broad range of issues and ideas. Our intention has not been to present a definitive treatise on what social identity means or how it is performed; rather, it has been our aim to shed light upon the ways in which sport might be seen to facilitate processes of identification and how individuals and groups might frame their attachments and affiliations to particular sports settings. In turn, we have sought to demonstrate the way in which social identities are not only constructed, shaped and maintained in and through sport, but how specific identities are challenged, contested and reworked across particular sporting terrains. In pursuit of these aims we have addressed a number of questions in relation to identity formation: How and why does sport contribute to the construction of social identities? What kinds of identity-making processes do sports facilitate? How are individual and collective identities negotiated and produced in and through sport? As we have seen, previous writers in this area have been especially keen to map out the historical and cultural contexts within which identities are formed and, in so doing, have highlighted also the necessity of considering power relations and social divisions in any such analysis. To this end, much of the work presented within the preceding pages has explored the shifting and contested nature of identity construction within particular sports settings. In this concluding chapter we draw together some of the key issues and ideas that have been raised by our contributors, focusing specifically on three general themes: (i) the characteristics of identity formation, (ii) sporting identities and power relations, and (iii) social identities and the future.

Sport and the characteristics of social identity

We noted in our introductory remarks that the study of social identity has traditionally been characterized by a number of key themes: similarity and difference, belonging and recognition, attachment and affiliation, and inequality and social justice. A further characteristic of such discussion is the shifting, fluid and unstable nature of identities. What then, we might ask, have our individual contributors had to say about these issues?

As we have seen, identity formation is a social process involving interaction, communication and negotiation. It is underpinned by notions of who we are, who we are not, and how and why we identify ourselves in relation to others. Sport certainly provides an environment where identities can be established. Yet the relationship between sport and social identity is not without its problems. Grant Jarvie has emphasized this point in his chapter on the transformative potential of sport. As part of a broader plea for a reconceptualization of identity politics in the interests of wider social change, Jarvie reminds us of one crucial issue: the more that individuals and groups assert their identities in and through sport, the greater the risk of fragmentation for the sporting world as a whole. For Jarvie, the challenge for sport is not simply to engender and facilitate a 'healthy cultural identities' (through the mobilization of a balanced politics of recognition and redistribution) but also to maintain and reinforce notions of commonality and community.

There is certainly a sense of the fragmentary potential of identity politics in the work of our other contributors. Perhaps one of the clearest examples of this appears in the work of P. David Howe, in which he has highlighted the extent to which issues of similarity and difference shape the contours of the identities of Paralympic athletes, not simply in relation to broader social norms but also within the Paralympic community itself. Identity for these individuals is about the classification of their abilities in line with established mechanisms of control and regulation; a process which locates them within the organizational structure of their sport and allows the similarities and differences between athletes to become evident. For Howe, such mechanisms create a hierarchy of bodies which may serve to impact negatively on the broader identities of certain individuals. At the same time, the sporting events in which these athletes take part also carry particular cultural values and meanings, which inevitably impact upon their own sense of self and how others perceive them. Ultimately, then, the regulatory systems in place act as both an exclusive and an inclusive force, working positively for some and negatively for others.

Likewise, notions of similarity, difference and affiliation are central to the work of Harris on women collegiate football players. Here we have evidence of the construction of identities both within and against the established cultural values and meanings concerning the male footballing fraternity in England. Using the male game as some kind of behavioural benchmark, these women demonstrate a degree of collusion (and, it might be argued, similarity) with the hegemonic masculine norms prevalent in this particular sports setting. Yet at the same time there is also clear evidence in this account of the way in which these women set themselves apart from such values and meanings by adopting and developing different styles of play (in terms of both physical and relational enactment) and by rejecting culturally prevalent ideas and assumptions concerning the sexuality of female sports participants. As Harris notes, what all of this demonstrates is how difference and sameness are implicated in the marking of gendered boundaries and how, even in relatively non-political ways, sporting affiliations and attachments have the potential to reconfigure highly restrictive cultural norms. Harris's work also raises a series of questions about the organizational governance of football in England, and the extent to which the game's governing bodies might be seen to promote and exacerbate its heavily gendered complexion.

Sporting identities and relations of power

This brings us to our second point: the connection between sporting identities and relations of power. One of the issues raised by all of our contributors is that of the role of organizations and institutions in defining social identities, and the relationships of power which are so often imbued within such processes. Indeed, a key factor in the creation and maintenance of sporting identities, and a central facet of the literature surrounding the 'politics of identity' *per se*, are the struggles which individuals and groups face within and against organizations and institutions in their quest for acknowledgement and recognition. A central feature of all of the preceding chapters is the role of institutional power in identity formation.

The power of institutions and organizations to determine and define sporting identities is clearly evident in Nancy Theberge's chapter, which has looked at the factors and conditions which serve to shape the professional identities of health care practitioners in Canadian sports medicine. What emerges from this research is the potential for individuals to redefine institutionally circumscribed identities by the way in which they are expected to operate (and interrelate) in their various medical roles. Despite the pressures and expectations of modern-day, mass-spectator sport and the distinct traditions of medical practice in Canada, Theberge argues that while the professional identity of sport medicine practitioners is important with regard to their working relations, professional roles and relationships also vary across the different settings in which sport medicine is practised. Moreover, these data show that a sense of collectivity and collaboration may override historically constructed notions of professional identity when the common goal is the facilitation of the needs of elite sports performers.

Such findings signify the influential nature of social norms and values on the construction of identities in sporting spheres but, as we noted at the outset of this book, there is perhaps nothing more powerful in this respect than the nation state. Over the years, numerous commentators have elucidated the role of sport in state dominance and in the creation and reinforcement of value systems. In some cases, sport has been used as part of a series of broader social measures, the underlying purpose of which has been to create division, discrimination and injustice. One of the best-known examples of this is the apartheid years in South Africa. Recognized as much for the sporting boycotts and campaigns which it spawned as it is for the social and economic legacy which it left behind, apartheid provided ample evidence of the way in which sport can be abused by nation states resulting in the isolation of individuals from participating in a range of both competitive and non-competitive sporting forms and at a variety of levels. The history of South African sport during the apartheid years has been well rehearsed by academics and journalists alike (e.g. Booth, 1998; Bose, 1994; Guelke, 1986, 1993; Jarvie, 1985; Lapchick, 1975), but less common are in-depth accounts of the personal struggles of sports men and women during this period. Theresa Walton has countered this trend in her analysis of the life of the black athlete Sydney Maree, whose sporting identity was fashioned and refined amidst the racial prejudices of his homeland (South Africa) and the nationalistic expectations of the country to which he subsequently relocated, the USA. Utilizing a range of sources, Walton's contribution highlights how (like other social institutions) sport can be utilized by the state as a means by which ideological values and assumptions might be promoted and reinforced. In turn, Walton's chapter outlines the shifting and dynamic nature of identity construction and, in particular, how identities are subject to reprioritization and change over time. Shore (1993) has suggested that we can view an individual's identity as comprising a collection of concentric rings where each one marks a separate identity and, moreover, that at different stages of the life course a particular identity becomes prominent. Viewed in this way, social identities become the 'anchor' of self-definition at particular points in time. The life of Sydney Maree, as depicted by Theresa Walton, illustrates in a number of ways how notions of time, space and place can dictate the shifting and dynamic nature of identity formation and how processes of reprioritization might take effect.

Of course, one of the most influential institutions of our time is the mass media, and, in their chapter on the interface between formalized religion, sport and schooling, Samaya Farooq and Andrew Parker have outlined the extent to which media discourse has the potential to impact the lives of those who are often far removed from its overarching gaze.Writing in response to more recent calls for a better understanding of Asian (and particularly Muslim) masculinities (Ahmed, 2003; Esposito, 2002; Shah, 2006), Farooq and Parker set out to contribute to the increasing body of literature on marginalized and stigmatized identities, citing schools as a key player in the identity-making process. In contrast to other areas of academic study, it would be fair to say that the sociology of sport has an established track record in research surrounding Asian males (see Burdsey, 2007; Dimeo & Mills, 2001; Ismond, 2003). Common within this literature is the belief that sport is viewed as a relatively insignificant aspect of Asian culture when compared to broader lifestyle activities such as earning power, family commitments, social mobility and academic achievement (Fleming, 1994; Maguire & Collins, 1998). More specifically, Islam's position on sport has been largely overlooked and there is certainly little research on the connections between Islamic independent schools and physical education. By directly addressing these issues, Farooq and Parker uncover some of the tensions and contradictions resulting from negative media depictions of Muslim males. In turn, they describe the various ways in which their own respondents utilized sports settings to construct and negotiate their identities in response to such media discourse. What this work demonstrates is that as the crucible in which many young male (and female) identities are forged, schools represent both a challenge and an opportunity in terms of the role of sport in identity formation and its relationship to broader social forces.

Further consideration of the power of the media in shaping identities is provided by Ben Clayton and John Harris in their analysis of sports-media reportage, which examines some of the ways in which sporting identities are constructed in and through the media, seemingly without any in-depth consideration of who sports performers actually are or what they represent. Taking as their main theme of enquiry issues of masculinity and sexuality and, in particular, the interplay between popular cultural narratives of masculinity and the changing nature of sporting masculine identities, Clayton and Harris provide yet more evidence of how the sport/media relationship has intensified in recent years, especially in relation to those sporting figures whose popular cultural exposure has bestowed upon them a sense of celebrity. Examining media representations of athletes described as 'metrosexual sport stars', this chapter has uncovered the way in which superstar status and masculine identity come together. Utilizing the theoretical offerings of Connell (1987, 2005) and, in particular, the notion of 'cathexis', Clayton and Harris provide yet more evidence of two specific examples of contemporary sporting masculinity – David Beckham and Gavin Henson – and explore how male identities might be moulded amidst print-media portrayals of the metrosexual lifestyle. The central issue here is not simply the extent to which the sport/media nexus manifests itself in an everyday sense but, more importantly, the power which the media holds in terms of the creation and maintenance of particular sporting identities, which may, or may not, constitute accurate representations of the individuals in question.

Relatedly, it is to issues of power and control in relation to both the English legal system and the mass media that Andrew Parker turns in his analysis of social identity within the context of celebrity image rights. Focusing specifically on the social aspects of identity construction; i.e. the way in which identification takes place in accordance with broader social, cultural, political and historical circumstances, Parker's assessment of the extent to which current English law protects the rights of sporting celebrities highlights once again the power of social institutions (in this case the English legal system and the UK print media) to determine how the contours of individual identities are shaped. What becomes clear from Parker's work is that there exists a distinct difference between the kind of legal protection offered to celebrity figures in the USA and that offered to those in the UK. Parker's central thesis is that while sports personalities can (and do) look to the English courts for protection in relation to their identities, the information upon which such legal decisions are made might be further enhanced by a consideration of a broader set of factors concerning their wider social significance. In the hope of stimulating further sociological research into sport and the law, Parker's argument ultimately provides evidence of the ways in which celebrity identities are shaped and formed at the social level and how their multifaceted nature can bring as many problems as it can pleasures.

Sport, social identities and the future

We can see throughout these discussions that sporting identities do not simply emerge out of thin air, but that they are constructed in and against broader social influences, assumptions and ideas. Woodward (2007, p. 15) notes that 'identity always involves some negotiation between the self as agent in the discursive position in which the self is positioned'. Hall (1996, p. 4) concurs with this view, suggesting that it is '[p]recisely because identities are constructed within, not outside, discourse, we need to understand them as produced in specific historical and institutional sites within specific discursive formations and practices by specific enunciative strategies'.

All of which brings us to our final point. Perhaps one of the historical weaknesses of research in the sociology of sport is that its 'situatedness' has not always been acknowledged. Our research findings, and indeed our social identities, can only begin to make sense when understood within a particular cultural context. Drawing upon the work of Mills (1959), Harris (2006), for example, has argued that scholars within the subdiscipline should more readily consider the specifics of time and place when discussing construction identity. That is to say, it is important that research on sport and social identities is clearly located within its social, geographical and historical context. The research presented within this collection offers different examples of identity formation and in different places, ranging from participatory/collegiate sporting environments through to the highest levels of competitive sport, such as the Paralympic and Olympic Games. Insight has been offered into how sporting contexts are influenced by (for example) dominant gendered and racialized ideologies, although, there is, of course, no one theoretical or conceptual position applicable across all social settings.

It is also important to know more about the theoretical and personal locatedness of the scholars whose words and interpretations frame just how identities are formed, for although within such work we have tended to borrow a philosophy from the natural sciences (based on an objective methodology), sociologically informed research on sport and social identities is largely a subjective, reflexive science. There is certainly a need for more research involving reflexive accounts of identities which critically examines the ways in which writers make sense of the actions of those being studied. There is already some insightful work in this area (e.g. Obel, 2004; Tsang, 2000) but more is needed in a wider range of contexts.

In the sociology of sport, as in most other academic disciplines, we operate in a world increasingly characterized by a proliferation of concepts and ideas. We are conscious that much sociological writing is often considered to be laden with impenetrable jargon and perceived by beginning scholars to be somewhat inaccessible. In this collection we have attempted to strike a balance between the presentation of empirical research findings and theoretical discussion. To touch upon just one of the themes visible in some of the chapters presented here, a postmodern perspective highlights that identities are provisional, contingent and relatively unfixed. Postmodernism, as we understand it, mounts a challenge to the 'grand narratives' of traditional social theory and facilitates a focus on the specifics of time and place in understanding how identities are formed and understood. Of course, such an approach is by no means new; almost half a century ago C. Wright Mills (1959) outlined the problematic nature of grand theory. To understand and/or appreciate such a position does not mean that one has to adopt a 'postmodernist' label, for the changing structures of our social worlds can be described in many ways. A combination of micro and macro analysis recognizes the historical and theoretical background of subjects but also looks specifically at a particular time and place as a means of developing a contextually based understanding of identity formation. Poststructuralist thinkers also highlight the shifting dynamic of social identities and appear to offer much in terms of allowing us to consider more carefully the limitations of established dualisms and the complex interrelationships between traditional binaries.

Following this line of thought, social identities, it seems, are increasingly viewed as taking shape along some kind of journey. In this sense, 'routes' are believed to be replacing 'roots' as an integral part of our identities. As highlighted on numerous occasions within this text, social identities refer not only to who we are but also to who we want to be or, to put it another way, identity should be seen to belong as much to the future as it does to the past (Hall, 1990). The challenge now is further to develop work which critically examines the relationship between sport and social identities, for there are any number of different identities to be considered and problematized. There is, for example, little, if any, in-depth discussion of youth sport, sport for the elderly, or the relationship between sport and public health within this collection. Those topics which do appear are intended as snapshots of the ways in which social identities are formed and how sociological investigations of identity formation might be carried out. Collectively they offer a range of insights into sport across cultures and at varying participatory levels. The rapidly

changing and shifting landscapes of sport offer fertile ground for exploring social identities and, as we have outlined, the shifting and contested
nature of social identities means that there will always be more stories
to be told.

As we stated at the outset of this book, our aim here has not been
simply to reflect on the ways in which sports participation and practice
might challenge the discriminatory and politically exclusive features of
broader social life but also to add to the growing body of research which
seeks to document the ways in which these challenges take place. Of
course, it is only through a continuation of such challenges that sport
can remain a key site for the creation, definition and maintenance of
social identities.

References

Ahmed, A. (2003) *Islam under Siege: Living Dangerously in a Post-Honor World*.
Cambridge: Polity.
Booth, D. (1998) *The Race Game: Sport and Politics in South Africa*. London:
Frank Cass.
Bose, M. (1994) *Sporting Colours: Sport and Politics in South Africa*. London: Robson.
Burdsey, D. (2007) *British Asians and Football: Culture, Identity, Exclusion*. London:
Routledge.
Connell, R. (1987) *Gender and Power*. Cambridge: Polity.
Connell, R. (2005) *Masculinities* (2nd edn). Cambridge: Polity.
Dimeo, P. & Mills, J. (eds) (2001) *Soccer in South Asia: Empire, Nation, Diaspora*.
London: Frank Cass.
Esposito, J. (2002) *Unholy War: Terror in the Name of Islam*. Oxford: Oxford
University Press.
Fleming, S. (1994) *Home and Away: Sport and South Asian Male Youth*. Aldershot:
Avebury.
Guelke, A. (1986) 'The politicization of South African Sport', in L. Allison (ed.)
The Politics of Sport. Manchester: Manchester University Press.
Guelke, A. (1993) 'Sport and the end of apartheid', in L. Allison (ed.), *The Changing
Politics of Sport*. Manchester: Manchester University Press.
Hall, S. (1990) 'Cultural identity and diaspora', in J. Rutherford (ed.) *Identity,
Community Culture, Difference*. London: Lawrence and Wishart.
Hall, S. (1996) 'Introduction: Who needs 'identity'?', in S. Hall & P du Gay (eds)
Questions of Cultural Identity. London: Sage.
Harris, J. (2006) 'The science of research in sport and tourism: Some reflections
on the promise of the sociological imagination', *Journal of Sport and Tourism*,
11(2), 153–172.
Ismond, P. (2003) *Black and Asian Athletes in British Sport and Society. A Sporting
Chance?* Basingstoke: Palgrave.
Jarvie, G. (1985) *Class, Race and Sport in South Africa's Political Economy*. London:
Routledge & Kegan Paul.

Lapchick, R. (1975) *The Politics of Race and International Sport: The Case of South Africa*. Westport, CT: Greenwood Press.

Maguire, B. & Collins, D. (1998) 'Sport, ethnicity and racism: The experience of Asian heritage boys', *Sport Education and Society*, 3, 1, 79–81.

Mills, C. W. (1959) *The Sociological Imagination*. Oxford: Oxford University Press.

Obel, C. (2004) 'Researching rugby in New Zealand: Reflections on writing the self and the research problem', *Sociology of Sport Journal*, 21(4), 418–434.

Shah, S. (2006) 'Leading multiethnic schools: A new understanding of Muslim youth identity', *Educational Management Administration and Leadership*, 34, 2, 215–237.

Shore, C. (1993) 'Ethnicity as revolutionary strategy: Communist identity construction in Italy', in S. Macdonald (ed.) *Inside European Identities*. Oxford: Berg.

Tsang, T. (2000) 'Let me tell you a story', *Sociology of Sport Journal*, 17(1), 44–59.

Woodward, K. (2007) *Boxing, Masculinity and Identity*. London: Routledge.

Index